FOR OUR OWN
Safety

Examining the Safety of

High-Risk Interventions for

Children and Young People

Edited by

Michael A. Nunno,

David M. Day,

& Lloyd B. Bullard

CHILD WELFARE LEAGUE OF AMERICA, INC.
Headquarters: 2345 Crystal Drive, Suite 250, Arlington, VA 22202-4801
E-mail: books@cwla.org

CURRENT PRINTING (last digit)
10 9 8 7 6 5 4 3 2

Edited by Jennifer M. Price
Cover and text design by Jennifer R. Geanakos

Printed in the United States of America
ISBN #978-1-58760-000-5

Library of Congress Cataloging-in-Publication Data
For our own safety: examining the safety of high-risk interventions for children and young people / edited by Michael A. Nunno, David M. Day, and Lloyd B. Bullard.
    p. cm.
  Includes index.
  Papers originally presented at an international symposium entitled,
Examining the Safety of High-Risk Interventions for Children and Young
People held at Cornell University, Ithaca, New York on June 1-4, 2005.
  ISBN 978-1-58760-000-5 (pbk.)
  1. Children—Institutional care. 2. Youth—Institutional care. 3. Restraint of patients.
  4. Child welfare. I. Nunno, Michael A. II. Day, David M., 1957- III. Bullard, Lloyd.
  IV. Child Welfare League of America. V. Title.

HV965.F67 2007
362.74—dc22   2007013098

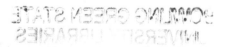

Contents

Foreword

Violence, Restraints, and International Standards

THERE IS A CONVINCING BODY OF RESEARCH DATA showing that children in residential care and/or treatment—and that can be the case for various reasons—are subject to violence, including torture and cruel, inhuman and degrading treatment.

This is confirmed in the recent UN Study on violence against children presented to the UN General Assembly in October 2006. This Study—covering all forms of violence[1] calls for a prohibition by law of all forms of violence against children in all settings including corporal punishment. In addition States should invest in systematic education and training of all professionals working with or for children to prevent, detect and respond to violence against children.

Codes of conduct and clear standards of practice, incorporating the prohibition and rejection of all forms of violence, should be formulated and implemented. These and other recommendations are supported by a resolution of the General Assembly in which States are urged to take various actions to prevent, reduce and eliminate violence against children[2].

---

1. United Nations Study on Violence against Children Report submitted by Paulo Sergio Pinheiro, Independent Expert appointed by the Secretary General UN Doc. A/61/299). This study was recommended by the UN Committee on the Rights of the Child (see Recommendations adopted after the Days of General Discussions on Violence against Children in 2000 and 2001.

The Study distinguishes the following settings in which violence against children occurs: the home and family, schools and educational settings, care and justice institutions, places of work and the community. It contains overarching and setting specific recommendations.

2. Resolution 61/146 on the Rights of the Child adopted by the General Assembly of the UN on 19 December 2006 at the 81st plenary meeting of its Sixty-First Session (UN Doc. A/RES/61/246; 23 January 2007).

But in the midst of all this almost no attention was paid to the use of force (or: violence if you want) in efforts to control or contain aggressive or violent behaviour of children in residential care.[3] The focus is much more on the prevention of physical and mental punishment of children in residential care and on measures to introduce non-violent forms of disciplining and control.[4] But this emphasis gives sometimes rise to confusion and the suggestion that the prohibition of corporal punishment means that professionals working in institutions are not allowed to use any kind of force to address aggressive behaviour of children.

This was a reason for the UN Committee on the Rights of the Child to explicitly recognize—in its General Comment on Corporal Punishment[5] that those working with children in institutions may be confronted by dangerous behaviour which justifies the use of reasonable restraint to control it and observes:

> "Here too there is a clear distinction between the use of force motivated by the need to protect the child or others and the use of force to punish. The principle of the minimum necessary use of force for the shortest necessary period of time must always apply. Detailed guidance and training is also required, both to minimize the necessity to use restraint and to ensure that any methods used are safe and proportionate to the situation and do not involve the deliberate infliction of pain as a focus of control."

In General Comment No 10 on Children's Rights in Juvenile Justice[6] the Committee elaborates on the use of force of restraint for children deprived of their liberty, including pre-trial detention and post-trial incarceration as follows:

> "Restraint or force can be used when the child poses an imminent threat of injury to him or herself or others, and

---

3 In the World Report on Violence against children —which accompanied the report submitted to the General Assembly—chapter 5 is devoted to Violence against children in care and justice institutions. In that chapter some attention is given to "Violence on the guise of treatment" describing some forms of electroshock and use of drugs to control children's behaviour. This World Report can be consulted and downloaded on http://www.violencestudy.org .

4. See e.g. Stuart N. Hart (ed.) with Joan Durrant, Peter Newell and F. Clark Power: Eliminating Corporal Punishment. The way forward to constructive child discipline (UNESCO 2005).

5. General Comment No 8 on The right of the child to protection from corporal punishment and other cruel or degrading forms of punishment (Articles 19, 28(2) and 37 inter alia); CRC/C/GC/8 May 2006.

6. General comment No. 10 on Children's Rights in Juvenile Justice, adopted by the CRC Committee in February 2007 (U.N. Doc, CRC/C/GC/10).

only when all other means of control have been exhausted. The use of restraint or force, including physical, mechanical and medical restraints, should be under close and direct control of a medical and/or psychological professional. It must never be used as a means of punishment. Staff of the facility should receive training on the applicable standards and members of the staff who use restraint or force in violation of the rules and standards should be punished appropriately?"

In the light of these observations and recommendations of the UN Committee on the Rights of the Child providing some international standards for the use of restraint or force I very welcome this book *For Our Own Safety: Examining the Safety of High Risk Interventions for Children and Young People*.

It provides excellent information on the various theoretical and practical aspects of the complexity of the use of restraints and force in order to control or contain aggressive or violent behaviour of children and young people in residential institutions. More in particular it shows how we can ensure safety and manage risk and reduce the need to use restraints through organizational changes.

It also informs us about the need to use legal and other remedies in case of violation of the rules and standards for the use of restraints or force. In that regard I like to underscore that every child in residential juvenile or other institutions should have the right to make complaints, without censorship as to the substance, to the central administration, the judicial authority or other proper independent authority and to be informed of the response to the complaint without delay.

I very much hope—and in that I concur with the conclusion of the editors — that our efforts as described in this book will ultimately contribute to the eradication of the conditions under which physical constraints are used. It is my opinion that the adoption of a public health model to reduce violence and restraints in children's residential care facilities as suggested by Paterson, Leadbetter, Miller, and Crichton (chapter 7) can best be realized by a full respect for and implementation of the rights of the child as enshrined in the Convention of the Rights of the Child. Let me in this regard quote one of the principles of rules that need to be observed and that the UN Committee on the Rights of the Child presents in its General Comment No 10 (par. 28c on treatment and conditions in cases of depuration of liberty) "Children should be provided with a physical environment and accommodations which are in keeping with rehabilitative aims of residential placement, and due regard must be given to the needs of the child for privacy, sensory stimuli, opportunities for association with peers, and participation in sports, physical exercise, the arts and leisure-time activities". These and other principles and rules e.g. in terms of provision of education, adequate health care and contact with the family and the wider community can contribute to the eradication of the use of physical constraints and/or force in residential care facilities.

Everybody interested in contributing to this eradication should read this book and implement the lessons it presents.

—Jaap E. Doek
CHAIRPERSON OF THE UN COMMITTEE
ON THE RIGHTS OF THE CHILD (2001-2007)

Introduction

On June 1–4, 2005, an international symposium entitled, *Examining the Safety of High-Risk Interventions for Children and Young People*, took place at Cornell University, Ithaca, New York. Cornell's Family Life Development Center in conjunction with Stirling University, Stirling, Scotland and the Child Welfare League of America (CWLA) cosponsored the symposium. More than 90 researchers, policymakers, attorneys, advocates, and intervention system providers from the United States, Canada, England, Wales, Scotland, Australia, and Ireland participated. The professions represented included social work, law, medicine, psychology, and education. Presentations covered topics such as the legal, ethical, and historical uses of physical restraints and seclusion; safety, psychological and emotional impact; and guidelines for development and use, as well as clinical and organizational strategies likely to reduce use in children's treatment facilities.

This book was born out of the papers and the presentations of this symposium that are available online at www.rccp.cornell.edu/symposium.htm. All the contributors and the book editors participated in the symposium. Rather than reiterate and strictly reproduce the presentations and the papers from the symposium, the authors of the various chapters had the luxury of incorporating into their text much of the discussion, learning, and new research discussed at the symposium. To our awareness this book is the only volume that is devoted entirely to the subject of, and risks associated with, restraint and seclusion. The book is organized into six sections—young people and physical restraints, theoretical and historical issues, ensuring safety and managing risk, reducing restraints through organizational change, legal issues, and conclusions.

The reader should apply broad operational definitions of both restraints and seclusions. Consider the following definitions. *Restraints* are defined as any manual method or physical or mechanical device, material, or equipment attached or adjacent to the patient's body that he* cannot easily remove that restricts freedom of movement or normal access to one's body (United States General Accounting Office, 1999). *Seclusion* is defined as the involuntary confinement of a patient alone in a room or an area from which the patient is physically prevented from leaving (Council on Accreditation of Services for Families and Children, 2003). The reader should also consider that restraints and seclusions are complex and foreseeable. Given the nature of our juvenile corrections, psychiatric, and child welfare institutions and the nature of the population they serve, it is foreseeable that the fabric or culture of the institution may be prone to aggression and violence.

To acknowledge their complexity and foreseeability, restraints and seclusions should be seen as a process with antecedents, precursors, unique interpersonal dynamics, consequences, and meaning beyond the limited scope of a one-time event. This complex process should extend beyond the individual child to include the staff, other children, the families, the treatment organization, and the community. Recognizing that these events are complex also demands that prevention, de-escalation and monitoring strategies are driven and guided by organizational leadership, all levels of staff, as well as the youth and their families (Bullard, Fulmore, & Johnson, 2003).

This book is written for anyone interested in learning from the expertise and experience of a broad spectrum of North American and British academics, scholars, agency directors, clinicians, quality assurance personnel, and crisis management systems experts. While the book's point of view is varied, as a whole it is biased towards the emerging international consensus to reduce restraints and seclusion to only those matters that involve immediate safety (British Institute for Learning Disorders, 2001; Child Welfare League of America, 2002; National Executive Training Institute, 2003; United Nations General Assembly, 1989). The editors selected the chapters because they represent a full range and diversity of the issues presented at the Cornell symposium, and, likewise, represent the best that we know at this point of time. The volume begins with children and young people's voices. These voices provide perspective to the discussion and tell us that the consequences and resolution of the intervention has to do with the qualities of the adult-child relationship and the qualities of the organization's

---

* For the ease of explanation and to avoid sexist language, we alternate between the personal pronouns, he and she, throughout the book.

culture. We hope that the contents challenge the reader to move the field to fewer, safer, and more appropriate uses of restraints and seclusion.

A Short Conversation About the Field's Evidence

Many of the contributing authors have pointed out that the applications and uses of restraints and seclusion are not as evidence-based as they need to be, especially given the emotional and developmental vulnerability of the child population in residential facilities, and the physical risks associated with restraint and seclusion use (Nunno, Holden, & Tollar, 2006). It is appropriate here to acknowledge some of the reasons for the shortcomings of the evidence base since acknowledging these shortcomings can alert the reader to the parts of the field that need immediate attention. Although as editors we hesitate to say definitively that there is no therapeutic value to restraints or seclusions, the reader will hear arguments throughout these chapters that there is scant evidence for even limited clinical benefit.

The Limitations of Study Designs

A limitation of the field's evidence is the same limitation that exists in the general child mental health and child welfare field: weak study designs and methodologies that hamper the ability to generalize. For example, there are no research studies in the restraint literature that use true experimental designs with random assignment to address the impact of restraints, used during aggressive or violent episodes while in treatment, on a child's psychological, social, emotional development, on clinical outcomes, or on the therapeutic alliance between the child and the adult. The lack of experimental designs extends to studies that examine the impact aggression, violence, and restraints have on staff morale, the possibility for primary and secondary trauma to staff, or the organizational environments in which staff work. Few quantitative studies even use control or comparison groups as reference points for determining change. Even existing qualitative studies are rarely large enough or rigorous enough in their methodology to achieve anything but anecdotal information, and very few studies or evaluations combine qualitative and quantitative designs that have the potential to balance each methodology's limitations to give a multidimensional richness and depth to our learning (see Kazdin, 2006, for a recent discussion of these methodological issues in the social sciences).

The qualitative and quantitative study designs in this book represent some progress in that they add complexity to our knowledge base. Well-designed studies that measure the impact of restraint-reduction programs are crucial, as section 4 of this volume points out. Data-driven approaches are essential to strategies that discover, energize, and monitor successful efforts, but only if the data produced are reliable, accurate, and timely.

The Interchangeability of Age and Population Specific Literature

Much of the restraint literature cited as evidence for programs and initiatives within the field are both age-specific and population-specific. The vast majority of the restraint and seclusion literature refers to geriatric, adult psychiatric, or adult corrections populations, and not to children or young people. This adult and elderly literature is used interchangeably within the child literature and often without warning to the reader. This haphazard interchangeability is a problem because the adult and geriatric populations do not have the same, and necessary, considerations for child safety and child development. The field has long recognized that for children in residential care, any practice or procedure that is not based on their unique safety and developmental needs may be considered abusive (Thomas, 1990). Although it would be foolish to ignore other related literature and research, the reader would do well to measure the applicability and validity of the adult and geriatric literature against the safety issues, programs, and the developmental needs of children in care.

How We View Aggression and Violence

Another limitation of the restraint literature is that the literature tends to see aggression and violence as one unidimensional phenomenon, and it often does not differentiate aggression from violence nor does it differentiate among the subtypes of aggression or see aggression on a continuum. For example, the field rarely makes a distinction between *reactive* aggression that is a sign of impulsivity, frustration, and immaturity; and *proactive* aggression or violence that is revengeful and planned. By not distinguishing between the two the field limits the effectiveness of our organizational initiatives to curb aggression and violence, creating obstacles and perpetuating misunderstanding, and limits strategies and treatment options that organizations and professionals need to address the complexity of aggression and violence in treatment organizations.

Perhaps the most important consequence to the lack of an operational definition and the lack of differentiation of subtypes of aggression is that with few exceptions, notably in the corrections and law enforcement field, the literature does not balance the safety and risk of the aggressive and violent behaviors professionals and practitioners are trying to contain against the levels of intervention risk or the potential consequences (Desmedt, 1995). In other words the literature does not address the question "Does this intervention have more risk than the aggressive or violent behavior we are trying to control or contain?" This book contributes answers to this important question.

Lack of Models

The literature cited in the following chapters also indicates that the descriptions of the restraint phenomena are varied and mixed. It is often uncertain whether we are addressing the phenomena of workplace violence with planned assaults by mentally ill children, or the phenomena of staff initiated or triggered violence or aggression, or even safety interventions that teach developmentally appropriate methods of coping. There are few, if any, models that address how or why restraints occur in children's treatment facilities beyond the interactional model portrayed by, for example, Jones & Timbers, (2002). This lack of multiple models (or one unifying model) has hampered the development and the consensus on the intervening variables or mediators that impact the restraint event. Without a clear articulation of these intervening variables we have a more difficult time determining the characteristics of an aggressive or violent event and we reduce our understanding of the types and degrees of interventions necessary to prevent aggression and violence in treatment facilities. Ultimately, we reduce our effectiveness to prevent or reduce restraints and seclusions. Therefore, the introduction of the public health model to prevent or reduce aggression, violence, and restraints (chapter 7, this volume) is a significant contribution to the field.

The Dynamics of Restraint Episodes and Organizational Responses

This book contains examples of the power and determination of leaders who motivate and challenge their staff to overcome and change established practices that are not in the best interests of their client population. This book documents, with original research and observations, circumstances in which restraints and seclusions are troubling. Examples of these troubling practices include the disproportionate use of restraints with younger children and the reliance on the use of restraints with children who are restrained multiple times even when their use appears to be ineffective in modifying the child's maladaptive behavior. Further, Suess (chapter 12, this volume) points out that leaders need to discover the discrepancies between their own organization's "official" beliefs and attitudes regarding seclusion and restraints and how and why restraints and seclusion are actually used in practice. It is evident that decreasing these inappropriate restraint episodes in children's treatment facilities depend on knowing the aggregate and individual treatment needs of the child population that facilities serve, and providing strong systems of care with programs that build enduring and positive staff and child relationships. These enduring and positive relationships between adults and children have the potential to reduce aggression and mitigate its consequences when it does occur. The agencies that have been successful in reducing restraints all have strong systems of care that have the best interests of children as their core mission and strong, values-driven leadership that monitor interactions and incidents to ensure compliance to core values and positive adult-child relationships.

Qualities of Values-Driven Leadership and the Motivation to Change

Leadership has been cited as an essential component of national and international efforts to reduce aggression and violence (Bullard et al., 2003). However, the literature does not document the characteristics of effective leadership in this effort. A number of chapters in this volume fill this void and afford strong examples of leaders who are optimistic and committed, who communicate clearly and consistently, who establish new paradigms, especially among clinical staff, and who share leadership and responsibility throughout the organization. The leaders responsible for the organizations discussed in these chapters understand that learning does not necessarily occur with tragedy but stems from self-reflection and self-examination. These leaders also understand that training does have an impact on the reduction of aggressive and violent incidents but only if training is part of an overall reduction plan, the organization over-trains staff with immediate and corrective feedback, and training is reinforced by on-the-job supervision.

This book supplies examples of a leader's vital role in organizational restraint-reduction activities that are initiated from sources external to the agency. External sources, such as governmental regulatory and licensing agencies or professional accreditation councils, can mandate restraint-reduction efforts through edict, law, or regulation. Penalties for noncompliance can often accompany these mandates, and staff reaction can be resentful and angry. Restraint-reduction efforts also can emerge from more benign external sources. For example, multiple chapters cite invited individuals who are considered experts or "visionaries" and who motivate an organization to develop aggression-free or restraint-free treatment environments for children. Although some staff initially are skeptical, these efforts are generally viewed positively and often with great enthusiasm. The leader's role in the first case is to overcome the natural organizational anger and resistance when pressure for change comes from external sources; in the second case the leader's role is to marshal staff enthusiasm into sustainable strategies. In either case effective leaders exemplified in this book used these opportunities to employ sound psychological and organizational theories to shift the treatment and environmental paradigms of their organization to serve safer and harm-free environments.

Goal of This Volume

The primary goal of this volume is to contribute to the discussion on the appropriate use of high-risk interventions, and, therefore, to improve the general quality of young people's and children's correction, residential, and psychiatric treatment. The book is intended for use by those who want to address the impact of aggression and violence in residential care settings within the context of evidence-based practice and the national and international impetus to reduce the use of restraints and seclusions. The editors trust that the reader will be able to convert her information needs related to practice and policy into answerable questions and track down or uncover the best evidence with which to address them. The reader can then undertake a critical appraisal of this best evidence, as well as its validity, impact and usefulness, and apply the results to his own practice and policy decisions. The reader can find ways to improve upon these practice and policy decisions based on the information and evidence presented.

—*Michael A. Nunno*
David M. Day
Lloyd B.Bullard

References

British Institute for Learning Disorders. (2001). *BILD code of practice for trainers in the use of physical interventions*. London: Author.

Bullard, L., Fulmore, D., & Johnson, K. (2003). *Reducing the use of restraints and seclusion: Promising practices and successful strategies*. Washington, DC: Child Welfare League of America.

Child Welfare League of America. (2002). *CWLA best practice guideline: Behavior management*. Washington, DC: CWLA.

Council on Accreditation of Services for Families and Children. (2003). *Standards for agency management and service delivery*. New York: Council on Accreditation of Services for Families and Children, Inc.

Desmedt, J. C. (1995). The physical intervention paradigm for enforcement and corrections. Available online at www.protectivesafetysystems.com/uofm.htm. Fairfax, VA: Protective Safety Systems.

Jones, R. J., & Timbers, G. D. (2002). An analysis of the restraint event and its behavioral effects on clients and staff. *Reclaiming Children and Youth, 11*(1).

Kazdin, A. E. (2006). Arbitrary metrics. *American Psychologist, 61*(1), 42–49.

National Executive Training Institute. (2003). *Training curriculum for the reduction of seclusion and restraint* (3rd ed.). Alexandria, VA: National Technical Assistance Center, National Association of State Mental Health Program Directors.

Nunno, M., Holden, M., & Tollar, A. (2006). Learning from tragedy: A survey of child and adolescent restraint fatalities. *Child Abuse & Neglect: The International Journal, 30*(12), 1333–1342.

Thomas, G. (1990). Institutional child abuse: The making and prevention of an un-problem. *Journal of Child and Youth Care, 4*, 1–22.

United Nations General Assembly. (1989 November 20). *Adoption of a convention on the rights of the child.* New York: Author.

U.S. General Accounting Office. (1999). *Mental Health: Improper restraint or seclusion places people at risk, GAO/HEHS-99-176.* Washington, DC: Author.

PART I

YOUNG PEOPLE AND PHYSICAL RESTRAINTS

CHAPTER 1

Young People's Experiences of Physical Restraint in Residential Care

Subtlety and Complexity in Policy and Practice

Laura Steckley and
Andrew Kendrick

Introduction

Over a number of years, children and young people have expressed concern about the use of physical restraint in residential child care in the United Kingdom. For the most part, this evidence has emerged in the context of the abuse of children and young people (Hart & Howell, 2004). The National Association of Young People in Care (NAYPIC), in a study of 50 complaints to the association during a three-month period, found that 40 of the young people complained of forcible restraint that they felt was unnecessary (Moss, Sharpe, & Fay, 1990; see also Safe & Sound, 1995; Who Cares? Scotland, nd). Unwarranted and excessive use of force in physically restraining youth was identified in the inquiries into abuse in Leicestershire and North Wales (Kirkwood, 1993; Waterhouse, 2000).

Very little research, however, has focused on physical restraint in residential child care. The perspectives of children and young people have rarely been sought (Day, 2000), and indeed, the views of service users across all ages and client groups are largely unknown (Chien, Chan, Lam, & Kam, 2005; Gallop, McCay, Guha, & Khan, 1999; Hawkins, Allen, & Jenkins, 2005; Ray, Myers, & Rappaport, 1996; Wynn, 2004). Mohr, Mahon, and Noone (1998) described in an *Archives of Psychiatric Nursing* article the traumatization of 19 previously hospitalized children, based on their experiences and memories. They identify three forms of traumatization: vicarious trauma, alienation from staff, and direct trauma. Another analysis of 81 debriefing incidents relating to both seclusion and restraint in an inpatient youth service showed 65% of the patients felt safe during the seclusion or restraint and 70% felt that their dignity and privacy had been respected (Petti, Mohr, Somers, & Sims, 2001).

Lindow (2000, p.2), in the context of work for the National Task Force on Violence Against Care Staff, highlighted that "the voices of the service users concerned do not sound out from the research" and that their views could point to answers to preventing or managing violent and aggressive situations (see also Day, 2000).

The issues and difficulties concerning physically restraining children and young people have led to ongoing demands for government guidance. A number of enquiries has recommended that the government issue full guidance for staff on matters of control, restraint, and physical contact with children in residential care. Some debate whether such full guidance has been achieved and highlight the lack of clarity and inconsistencies in the United Kingdom around these issues:

> There are some basic principles which are common to all
> settings: physical restraint as a 'last resort'; the use of mini-
> mum force and for the shortest possible duration; restraint
> must not be used as a punishment. Otherwise, there is little
> commonality (Hart & Howell, 2004, p.4).

Leadbetter (1996) argues that the failure to produce practical guidance and training is likely to drive the practice underground and to reinforce the high levels of stress experienced by those residential staff who regularly deal with challenging and difficult behavior.

The lack of clarity is compounded by the legal complexity that surrounds this area of practice. It involves general criminal law relating to assault, culpable and reckless conduct, and self-defense. It also involves health and safety legislation relating to staff members' welfare against foreseeable risks and the need for training to ensure a safe working environment (Hart & Howell, 2004). Educational legislation is also relevant in this area, as are the regulations relating to care services, looked-after children, residential establishments, refuges for children, and secure accommodation (Davidson, McCullough, Steckley, & Warren, 2005). In Scotland, national standards relating to services for children also refer to physical restraint and address written policy and procedures, training and support of staff, recording of the use of restraint, and support for young people after an episode of restraint. The standards state that restraint should only be used when there is likely to be harm or damage and that staff are trained to anticipate and calm down possibly dangerous situations (Scottish Executive, 2002, p. 20).

Overarching this legislation and regulation, the Human Rights Act 1998 establishes important protections from abuse by state organizations and employees. Article 3 prohibits "torture or inhuman or degrading treatment or punishment." Hart and Howell (2004, p.11), in reviewing case law in the United Kingdom, conclude that, "particular consideration thus needs to be given as to whether a method of restraint thought not to breach the rights of an adult may still breach those of a child."

The U. N. Convention on the Rights of the Child, which came into force on September 2, 1990, is also important and relevant to the issue of restraint (U.N. General Assembly, 1989). The U.N. Committee on the Rights of the Child report (2002) expresses concern at the numbers of children who had sustained injuries as a result of restraints and measures of control applied in prison and at the frequent use of physical restraint in residential institutions and in custody. It called for a review of the use of restraints and solitary confinement to ensure compliance with the Convention, in particular articles 25 and 37.

Although this review has not taken place, the Scottish Executive approached the Scottish Institute of Residential Child Care to produce, in consultation with key stakeholders in Scotland, a guide on the use of physical restraint for residential child care workers and managers (Davidson et al., 2005). It emphasizes the need for practitioners to have the right skills, knowledge, and attitudes so as to be prepared for those occasions when restraint is absolutely necessary and to reduce the need to restrain a young person in the first place. This guidance was developed in parallel to the research presented in this chapter.

The Study in Context

Though part of the United Kingdom, Scotland has a devolved parliament and government responsible for, among other things, education, health, local government, social work, housing, and justice. There are 32 directly elected local authorities in Scotland that provide local services and are responsible for looking after children and young people in need of care or protection or who have committed offenses. The Children's Hearings system decides whether children should be looked after and in care. Consisting of three lay volunteers, the Hearing Panel considers cases of children referred on grounds of offenses, child protection, or nonattendance at school. One option of the Hearings is to place children in residential care.

Children and young people may be looked after in a range of residential establishments in Scotland; the main types are children's homes, residential schools, and secure accommodation establishments. Children's homes are small establishments, with an average of six beds, which do not provide education on site; they tend to be run by local authorities. Residential schools are larger establishments that also provide education and tend to be run by private (for-profit) or voluntary (not-for-profit) organizations. Secure accommodation services are locked facilities run by both local authorities and voluntary organizations. Children and young people are placed in residential care for a number of reasons, with the primary ones being offending and behavior problems; abuse and neglect; and family support. The majority are adolescents, although a significant proportion is less than 12 years old (Kendrick, 1995; Milligan, Hunter, & Kendrick, 2006).

Data for March 31, 2005, show that local authorities looked after 12,185 children; the majority of these were being looked after at home with their family. Children looked after in residential accommodation accounted for 14% (1,539)—716 in local authority homes; 57 in voluntary sector homes; 618 in residential schools; 82 in secure accommodation; and 66 in other residential accommodation (Scottish Executive, 2005).

Physical restraint is defined as "an intervention in which staff hold a child to restrict his or her movement and should only be used to prevent harm" (Davidson et al., 2005, p.vii). In the United Kingdom, mechanical and chemical restraints are only rarely used in residential services for children. The focus of this study is on physical restraint by staff. We will present the results of a study that explored the experiences and views of 37 children and young people and 41 staff in a range of residential establishments in Scotland. Save the Children funded the study.

The study's main aim is to give voice to those most directly affected by the use of physical restraint in residential child care in order to further inform the development of policy and practice. This chapter focuses on the views and experiences of the children and young people and highlights that their perspectives are subtle and complex; they discuss positive as well as negative aspects of physical restraint. This complexity needs to be recognized and taken into account in policy and practice, and, through input to the development of the Scottish guidance, this process has already started.

Method

The study adopted a qualitative methodology to explore the views and experiences of children, young people, and staff in a range of residential establishments in Scotland. Semistructured interviews were carried out with 37 children and young people between the ages of 10 and 17, of which 26 were male and 11 were female. The research involved 20 establishments, evenly divided between those run by local authorities and those run by private or voluntary organizations. The establishments included children's homes, residential schools, and secure accommodation services. In addition to interviewing children and youth, 41 staff in the establishments were interviewed (see Steckley & Kendrick, 2005, for discussion of staff views). The interviews took place between February 2004 and May 2005.

The interview schedule for children and young people covered a broad range of topics, including: views about the acceptability of restraint, experiences of being restrained, experiences of witnessing other young people being restrained, understanding of staff guidelines related to restraining young people, views about times when staff got it wrong, and the impact of being restrained on relationships with those staff who did the restraining. The interviews also used a series of four vignettes—short scenarios representing a situation involving potential harm with three levels of escalation and potentially involving physical restraint. They were constructed around some common types of situations in residential child care. The four situations were: threats leading to the throwing of food and property destruction; threats by youth to abscond leading to an attempt to abscond; perceived unfairness leading to verbal abuse, spitting, and a physical attack on a staff member; and a conflict between young people leading to a serious physical altercation.

Such vignettes offer a range of potential benefits in qualitative research (Barter & Renold, 2000). They can provide space and flexibility for participants to construct the scenario according to their own experience and, as a result, afford them greater control. Discussing scenarios can often be experienced as less threatening than being asked direct questions, which can be of particular benefit when covering a sensitive subject. They provide a more varied interview format that can make participation more interesting, and their use alongside semistructured questions can increase the likelihood of capturing beliefs, meanings, judgments, and actions more deeply and comprehensively. The use of vignettes also involves a standardization process within the interview that permits more reliable and comparable generalization, and could be useful for cross-national comparisons.

Some of the young people seemed to relish the chance to discuss what they thought staff should do in the various situations. Others jumped directly into recounting their own experiences of escalation or being restrained, and did not engage in a more hypothetical discussion of what they thought should happen. A small number of young people appeared uncomfortable with the vignettes and it seemed that they felt they needed to come up with the right answer (despite assurances to the contrary). When the young person did not engage with the vignettes, the vignettes were abandoned. Overall, however,

they served well the purposes of allowing the young people to explore the use
of physical restraint in different circumstances and situations.

All interviews were transcribed, and coding and analysis of the material
utilized qualitative research software. Five main themes, detailed below, were
identified within this process and form the framework for this chapter.

Ethical Issues

Due to the sensitive nature of the research, significant attention was focused
on issues of informed consent, confidentiality, and practices in the event that
allegations of abuse might occur during the course of interviews (Alderson,
1995; Lee, 1993). The study was subject to the procedures for ethical
approval of the University of Strathclyde. Information in a child-friendly format was made available to young people and time was spent prior to the interview to clarify or answer any questions. Each young person at the start of the
interview signed a consent form. Where appropriate, parental consent was
also obtained, although this was a challenging obstacle because the research
was sometimes not necessarily a priority for busy residential staff, nor for parents of the children and young people.

It was made clear to children and young people that they could choose
not to answer any questions or discontinue the interview at any point. At several points throughout each interview, the researcher would check in with the
young person as to how they felt and whether they were happy to continue.
None of the young people showed outward signs of distress during or
immediately after the interviews, though discussions with unit staff took place
covering the potential for delayed or displaced feelings resulting from the
interviews so that staff were prepared to monitor and offer extra support if
necessary. In a very small number of cases, young people spoke about incidents related to physical restraints that could be interpreted as involving poor
practice. With the knowledge of the young person, these were discussed with
the head of the establishment so that appropriate action could be taken. In
order to ensure the confidentiality and anonymity of the children and young
people who took part in the research, names have been changed and minor
details may have been altered. When children and young people have referred
to staff, those names have been changed as well.

Themes and Issues

Much of the debate surrounding the physical restraint of children has taken
place in the context of abuse and that youth views have been predominantly
negative. The subsequent analysis of the interviews with children and young

people show that, in fact, the issues are much more subtle and complex. We address the views of children and young people according to the following five main themes:

- in general, a belief in the necessity of physically restraining children and young people in certain situations,
- the reasons for physical restraint,
- experiences and emotions related to physical restraint,
- concerns about how physical restraint is done, and
- relationships and physical restraint.

A Belief in the Necessity of Physically Restraining Children and Young People in Certain Situations

Either in discussion of the vignettes or in response to a direct question, almost all the children and young people stated that, on some occasions, a physical restraint should occur. Similar to results identified by the Children's Rights Director in England who consulted with six groups of children and young people in residential care, children and young people in this study recognize that physical restraint can be necessary to prevent injury and ensure the safety of others (Morgan, 2005).

Brian: Well, if it's to protect themselves and other boys, yeah,
    I do think so.

Dennis: It would depend. I think it might be good if it's going to
    keep them safe...If there was a safety issue.

Sharon: If they're hitting people...Putting them self at risk...
    Or other people...And that's about it.

Helen: Aye, I think restraints should be done; they've helped me,
    but I don't think they should be done in every single circumstance.

While young people were also clear that not all escalating behavior warrants being physically restrained, property destruction was also considered, in itself, as an acceptable reason for physical restraint by most young people. In fact, young people tended to have a more liberal view than staff of property destruction as an acceptable reason for physical restraint (Steckley & Kendrick, 2005).

Jason: Well you shouldn't get restrained just for saying, 'Aye, fuck off, I don't like
    this shit, this school'. Okay. But if it comes to the point where you're smash-
    ing things and wrecking your room and that, you should be restrained, okay.
    Because there's, you've got to live in it, you know what I mean?

Despite this general view of physical restraint being necessary in certain situations, there was also evidence of ambivalence amongst those interviewed. Hayden (1997) also identifies ambivalence in the views of four young people interviewed about physical restraint in children's residential care in England. While youth clearly stated that a young person should be restrained in a particular situation, a small minority later contradicted themselves. For example, one young person who, in discussion of a vignette related to an attack on staff, had stated that physical restraint should occur but later stated that it should never happen.

Callum: No...Just they're rubbish anyway...Shouldn't have them.

Interviewer: Shouldn't have them at all? Even when somebody's a danger?

Callum: No, they should be put into a secure unit...Well big, a risk, a big risk to themselves.

Interviewer: Should young people be restrained in secure units then?

Callum: Yes...Well if they're a danger, no, they shouldn't because if they're a danger to themselves they should just be put in their room...Staff, it's different, because they're here to help you.

Another young person, within one statement, shifted his opinion as he thought of a life-threatening situation that would necessitate restraint.

Lee: I think restraint, no. Something else, yes...I think that if someone was endangering someone's well being, someone's life, then yes, you have the right to remain violent.

A couple of the young people, although recognizing the need for physical restraint in some situations, also suggested alternatives to restraint when young people are escalated to the point of becoming a danger.

Jason: ...when you're angry or if you're, you just even swing for something, you even kick something, you're just gonna get put down on the ground.

Interviewer: And what do you think about that? Is that maybe what should happen or it shouldn't?

Jason: No, it shouldn't happen, just getting put on the floor. You should, there should be somewhere that you could go, yeah, in places like that and just take your anger out on something.

Interviewer: Like what?

Jason: A big soft room of something...so you can take your anger out.

Perhaps all of these instances of ambivalence and contradiction reflect a longing for a better way of managing potential and actual harm, though most of the youth acknowledged a lack of easy answers.

> *Wendy:* I think it's difficult, like, restraint…I think they are trying to find out another way of handling it instead of restraints. But I mean, I don't know if there would be another way. It's unfortunate that it has to get to such an extent.

The Reasons for Physical Restraint

We have seen that when discussing the reasons why a young person should be restrained, almost all young people made connections to risk and safety, or to property destruction. Almost all young people, however, also described being physically restrained or witnessing a physical restraint on at least one occasion when they did not perceive a safety risk.

> *Jason:* Aye, sometimes like that, they're at me and I didn't even do anything. 'What you restraining me for'?
>
> *Interviewer:* Was there ever a time, Michael, that you got restrained when really you weren't a danger to anybody?
>
> *Michael:* Aye.
>
> *Interviewer:* Yeah? What do you think that was about?
>
> *Michael:* I don't know. I wasn't happy about it anyway.
>
> Interviewer: Does that happen very often?
>
> *Michael:* …it doesn't happen a lot, but it can.

Young people, then, distinguished between those situations in which they felt they needed to be physically restrained, and those in which they felt they did not but were restrained anyway.

> *John:* I was just wondering why they were doing it, why they were doing this, when there was not need for it…Because I was sent to my room, and then they confronted me, when I asked politely several times to let me get back to my room.

This recalls examples in the Grimshaw and Berridge (1994, p. 94) study of residential schools where physical restraint was used "where the circumstances included children's attempts to move out of a supervised area or to refuse compliance with the routine." Morgan (2005) also describes youth who felt they had been restrained when they should not have been.

Just over a quarter of young people were able to compare the difference between being physically restrained in their current residential placement, and either another residential establishment, a foster home, or their own home.

John, who described the previous incident, also gave his perceptions about physical restraint in another placement and these contrasted markedly.

> *John:* I know that when I get restrained I always need it in here...because mainly it's for my own safety that they are doing it and all they want to do is see that the staff I get on with, and make sure that I don't hurt myself and that I don't hurt other people.

In addition to concerns over inadequate reasons for being physically restrained, young people were also aware of notions of last resort (though they may not have used that specific phrase).

> *Tim:* Sometimes we get really like unsafe, and I don't think you should go to the hold and that...Sometimes they hold you too quick.

This young person was able to recognize the need for intervention without it necessarily going to a restraint. Other young people, however, spoke more positively about staff members' attempts to intervene less intrusively.

> *Steve:* If there's other ways around it then they can try and stop me getting restrained, but if there's not then...
>
> *Interviewer:* Then that's what happens?
>
> *Steve:* Yeah.

While they did not appear aware of specific techniques or tactics staff used to help them calm down, close to a quarter seemed aware of and valued staff's efforts to find other ways to help them through an escalated situation.

> *Helen:* The staff tries their hardest not to restrain people. The staff hates restraining people. They don't like doing it, but the staff will only restrain you when it's in desperate need to be restrained. The first thing they do is try and calm you down. If that's not going to work, call the police or if they don't phone the police and you don't calm down, they might restrain you.

Participants stressed the overall importance of staff talking to young people to try and help them through highly escalated situations, although in the second quote the young person singled out a specific staff member in comparison to others in the establishment.

> *Peter:* In here they'll talk things through rather than restrain you.
>
> *Brian:* Aye, they're too quick...they don't really talk to you a lot...
>
> *Interviewer:* ... they don't try other things at that point, like talking to you, helping you?
>
> *Brian:* Well only sometimes. I know Linda's good for talking to you. Yeah. She's really good for that, talking and calming you down.

Experiences and Emotions Related to Physical Restraint

A broad array of experiences was reflected in the responses of the study participants. A small minority stated they had no memory of or feelings about incidents of being restrained. This may possibly be due to a desire to avoid thinking or talking about painful feelings, though interestingly, two young people asked to skip the related question. A more concerning possibility might be that some young people have "shut down," either cognitively or emotionally, as a result of being traumatized or retraumatized by being restrained. There is no way to be certain about the reason for these types of responses, but it does seem apparent that many of these particular youth have not been able to work through and make sense of their experiences.

Not surprisingly, given previous literature and evidence, of the young people who had been restrained and discussed feelings surrounding being restrained, all described at least some of their experiences negatively.

Lee: I felt shocked, disappointed, humiliated in front of my peers. Disgusted, abused. But most of all I felt, how did I feel? Most of all I felt violated.

The strength of emotions expressed by this particular participant sets it apart from the rest and may be due, in part, to the fact that two staff members were disciplined as a result of this restraint. Other young people expressed their negative experiences in more general terms.

Jason: I don't like restraints, well I don't like them, no, just me cos I see 'em and it's not nice to be put down.

Allen: It's shit.

A variety of negative emotions related to the experience of being restrained were identified, including: sadness, frustration, embarrassment, regret, hate or aggression towards staff, and hate or aggression towards self. A small minority described feeling like they were going "mental" or otherwise described feelings of losing emotional control.

Michael: Well there's a couple of weeks ago and...I really felt like losing the rag. ...

Interviewer: What was happening leading up to you getting a restraint?

Michael: Just some stuff at home.

Interviewer: ...What was going through your head, do you remember?

Michael: No. No.

Interviewer: How about how were you feeling?...what sort of feelings?

Michael: Psycho-ish…But it was very, very dangerous what happened.

Interestingly, very few youth mentioned fear and those that did either had never been restrained themselves or expressed fear in relation to seeing another young person get restrained.

The overriding and most readily identified emotion was anger, and almost three-quarters of the young people expressed anger for an assortment of reasons. Some were angry with staff, especially if they felt a restraint was initiated too quickly, implemented for inadequate reasons, or carried out too roughly. Some were angry with staff or fellow peers in the lead up to the restraint; others found being held against their will to be the source of extreme anger and some felt angry with themselves.

Sharon: I just, I don't know, I feel really angry and stuff, and hurt.

Interviewer: Hurt that they're restraining you?

Sharon: Not hurt as in they're hurting us, just hurt because of the problems and you're angry and stuff…You feel upset that you couldn't like, go to someone at the time. You didn't feel at that time that you could go to somebody and talk about it.

A small minority of young people spoke about restraint being used almost as a release valve to vent anger.

Jason: There's some boys in here…there's boys that speak to each other and like say, 'Aye, I feel like I like getting restrained to take my anger out away.'

Interviewer: Some boys say they like getting restrained to get their anger out?

Jason: Aye, aye, some boys feel that's the way to take their anger away from them.

One young woman spoke movingly about the cathartic experience of being physically restrained.

Helen: I think I just needed a cuddle…That's just my way of dealing with anger…most of my restraints have been my fault, and it's through drinking…

Interviewer: You said early on in the interview that you felt like you got restrained, sometimes, to be able to cry.

Helen: Aye.

Interviewer: Do you think sometimes you get restrained to let your anger out?

Helen: Aye, that's what gets me angry, and I cry…When I'm restrained still, I try and fidget about…the staff will sit there as long as until I calm down…I'm that much angry with all these people around me and I

> can't get any control, and then I start getting angry and then, my eyes
> all fill up and then I cry, and once I've cried, then I'm alright again,
> and then I get up and maybe the staff will talk to me...and I feel
> better again.

These quotes do, however, raise the concern that young people may become entrenched in a destructive dependency on physical restraint as a coping mechanism for their emotions, and this was reflected in staff interviews (Steckley & Kendrick, 2005). Another possibility is that physical restraint is experienced by young people as part of a greater process that helps them to internalize their own coping mechanisms for uncontainable emotions, and interestingly, Helen did say that she had now developed alternative ways of managing her feelings and had not been restrained for over a year.

Witnessing other young people being restrained also generated a range of emotions and feelings. Just under half expressed frustration, upset or anger at seeing a peer restrained, with anger being the predominant emotion cited. About the same number either claimed to have no feelings or stated they were happy because they thought the restraint was "right" to do. It is unclear whether an absence of feeling is merely a defense against deeper feelings on the issue or desensitization to the exposure to the distress of other young people.

> *Interviewer:* Do you remember how that felt to see somebody else
>   get restrained?...
>
> *Craig:* I was alright with it, I just got on with my work.
>
> *Interviewer:* How did it feel to hear somebody else being restrained?
>
> *Jason:* I just laughed at it cos he laughs at me when I get restrained so
>   I just laughed at him.

Conversely, some young people may have experienced a feeling of safety, which was potentially the case when two young people described seeing the school bully get restrained during an episode of significant aggression.

Under a quarter of young people, however, did seem attuned to the feelings of their fellow resident and connected this empathy with their own negative feelings.

> *Wendy:* When the staff really did get him down and calm and he was on
>   the floor, then he would cry and it would be a painful cry, you know?
>   Not an anger cry like, he wouldn't be shoutin' and swearin' at the staff
>   any more by this point...like really just upsettin' to watch, it was really
>   upsettin' to watch.

This young person did go on to clarify that she would mostly hear rather than see this boy, as staff had removed the rest of the group on these occasions. The vividness of the description, however, bears testament to the intensity some feel from hearing their peers' pain.

Concerns About How Physical Restraint Is Done

Another dominant concern that was raised by a significant number of young people centered on how roughly they were restrained. This research directly echoes previous concerns of children and young people about the use of physical restraint (Morgan, 2005; Moss et al., 1990; Paterson, Watson, & Whiteford, 2003; Safe & Sound, 1995; Snow & Finlay, 1998; Who Cares? Scotland, nd). Over half of the young people described restraints as being physically painful, and a small minority told of coming away with abrasions or bruises.

> *Matt:* But half the time when they restrain you they just purely hurt you...well I get hurt most of the time. I had a mark, a carpet burn, right, and it's starting to go, like, hurting on my shoulder...like marks on my chest.

Almost all of these young people indicated that their injuries were an unintentional product of the violence of the incident and that staff were doing the best that they could in difficult situations.

> *Interviewer:* You mentioned a restraint where your nose got burst [a bloody nose]. Do you think that was on purpose?
>
> *Peter:* No, my granny, she had died and I just flipped when they phoned me and told me. So I was going to jump out the flat window and George grabbed me and I punched him. And he just grabbed me and flung me on the ground.
>
> *Interviewer:* So it wasn't on purpose to hurt you?
>
> *Peter:* No.

Others, however, were more ambivalent about staff being too rough.

> *Sharon:* Because some of them are too rough and like the one down...in that house where I was smashing stuff up and that...it felt like he wasn't trying to keep me safe. He was just angry because I'd smashed his stuff up...And what I called him. And like that felt really uncomfortable and he hurt me.

As we explored this incident further, the young person did convey that she did not think the staff member had hurt her intentionally. She also showed remarkable insight into his triggers and how they likely interfered with his ability to keep her safety and well-being paramount in such a heated situation.

Of much greater concern were those incidents where young people, albeit a small minority, considered that staff hurt them intentionally.

Jason: And he squeezed it more...and squeezed it, then let go, so he did.

Interviewer: And when he squeezed it, what did you take that to mean?

Jason: He was just being a prick basically...some staff, some staff are right assholes...They just pure squeeze tight and everything, and you are, like, 'Ahhh, ahhh, leave me alone!'

One young person stated he believed staff used excessive force instrumentally on young people in order to "teach them a lesson." Interestingly, another youth used the degree of force during a restraint as a barometer for how much he could trust the member of staff. This issue of the relationship between young people and staff in the context of physical restraint provides the last, and possibly most important, theme of the research.

Relationships and Physical Restraint

"Restraint happens in the context of a relationship," and a key area of interest in this study is how the relationships between children and staff are affected by the experience of physical restraint (Fisher, 2003, p.73). The existence of strong, positive relationships with staff certainly seemed to affect about a quarter of young people's experience of restraint.

Sharon: Mine were all pretty comfortable because I felt comfortable with those people...

Interviewer: How would you make a person understand what you meant by using the word comfortable?

Sharon: Like, you don't feel unsafe and some dirty person's going to hold me to try and do something to me and stuff. You feel comfortable with it. It's, I don't know. It's not like trying to hurt you or that, they're trying to keep you safe.

Helen: Eddy's always been there, but me and Eddy have bonded all well, that's what I'm saying. I call him, he's my dad, you know what I mean, but he seemed to have always been there when I was restrained or, anytime I'm angry, I've left the building, he always seems to be there.

Jason: Billy's my best staff in this house school...I was angry one day and I kicked that telly there, and...Billy restrained me and I just thought, 'Whoa, here's Billy restraining me, I want to calm down,' you know, I

didn't want him to be restraining me so I just stopped. I just eased off
and then they let me up.

Interviewer: Why didn't you want him to restrain you?

Jason: Because of, I built a good relationship with him.

Young people in the *Who Cares? Scotland* consultation also talked about
feeling safe if a restraint was done correctly (Paterson et al., 2003, p. 35).

The experience of being physically restrained could also have an ongoing
effect on the relationships between young people and staff. Not in all cases,
though, and over half of young people stated that it had no long-term effect.

Interviewer: You know when you've been restrained and then afterward, not
just the few minutes afterward, but overall afterward, have you noticed
whether it affects your relationship with those staff?

Jason: No, it doesn't. They just, the staff, staff don't…staff hate it as much
as we hate it.

Just under a third felt that being physically restrained had negative
impacts; half of these young people believed them to be in the short term and
the other half described more long term effects.

Henry: You won't be happy with them at first but it wouldn't bother me all
the time.

Interviewer: So maybe short term you'd feel a bit unhappier with them, but
long term?

Henry: It doesn't bother me.

Interviewer: Did you have good relationships with any of the staff there?

Kevin: Yeah, yeah.

Interviewer: How about the ones that restrained you? How were your relationships with them?

Kevin: It was fine up until that day.

Interviewer: And then after that, how was it, how did it affect the relationship?

Kevin: I hated them.

Interviewer: Yep, always after that you hated them?

Kevin: Aye, and I wish I'd never met them.

Whatever occurred (or did not occur that should have) within the context
of this restraint, it marked a turning point for the worse in the relationship
between the young person and staff.

Conversely, a surprising number of young people, almost a third, spoke
of the experience of being physically restrained as having a positive impact on

their relationships with staff. It became clear, with further probing, that the restraint itself was not responsible for the improvement. Rather, it was how the entire situation was managed, of which the restraint was only a part, that influenced how the young person felt about the staff member.

Interviewer: What about the other side of the coin? Has it ever made you feel like the relationship's a bit better, in some way, after a staff member has held on to you?

Brian: Sometimes, because it makes, like, they're protecting me, man. They feel like you're, you feel like they're protecting you, so you feel got up with your confidence with them...

Interviewer: So you feel more confidence with them? Maybe trust?

Brian: Like, because I've only ever been held with the likes of Collin, my key worker. That made me feel a wee bit better in my relationship with him.

Sharon: And like when that guy, Jimmy, came in there, he was like holding me in a like, you know it was like a fatherly way or something, making sure I was safe and that.

Interviewer: And that feels?

Sharon: Like he's caring for me.

The complexities, however, of how young people may view the interplay between relationships with staff and the role of physical restraint is encapsulated in the following quote.

Peter: Yes. I didn't like Mr. Brown that much until he restrained me.

Interviewer: Is there a trust factor involved in all that too?

Peter: Yes, if somebody restrains you and you trust them again, you are alright. But if somebody restrains you and you don't like them, you are not going to trust them. But if they restrain you and they do it alright, you trust them again, like me and Mr. Brown, we're alright.

Discussion

Containment is often referred to as a primary task in residential child care (Ward, 1995; Simpson, 1995; Woodhead, 1999; Sprince, 2002). In some cases, the use of the word simply refers to a literal sense of physical care and limits on behavior. It is the extreme end of this interpretation, the physical containment of potentially harmful behavior, that has generally been applied to physical restraint (Day, 2000).

The term "containment" also refers to a way of understanding the more complex process of staff receiving the projected, unbearable emotions of children and young people and through the vehicle of the relationship, helping them learn to manage those feelings. This involves staff providing warmth, perspective, and boundaries in order to provide an environment in which a young person can begin to feel secure and accepted. Deacon rightly points out the difficulty, in practice, of holding "in mind the relationship between external, physical containment and internal, therapeutic containment" (2004, p. 88).

When one looks at those young people who spoke of positive experiences of physical restraint, as well as their descriptions of their relationships with staff who restrained them, it may be possible or even likely that they have experienced a therapeutic integration of physical and relational containment over time. This may be particularly true of those young people who described their use of restraint for cathartic purposes. Within this context, being physically held as a last resort when there was legitimate risk of harm and in a professional, caring manner was likely a significant part of the overall therapeutic experience of containment. It must be emphasized that, as Ward (1995) points out, containment is not an isolated event but rather a complex, multilayered process involving various networks of relationships within a care establishment. Thus, for young people to positively make sense of their experiences of restraint, they must have positive experiences of care and relationships as an overarching context for those restraints. Conversely, deficits in the other aspects of containing care or an overall lack of integration between physical and relational containment may be a factor for those young people who become entrenched in a destructive dependency on physical restraint.

Last, the meaning youth ascribe to the experience of restraint emerges from their values, beliefs, and previous experiences (Garfat, 2004), and also from their relationships and interactions with other young people and staff (Chien et al., 2005; Hawkins et al., 2005). The processes through which these meanings are constructed are of clear significance and this is reflected in all of the five themes addressed and analyzed by the study. While almost all of the young people agreed that there is sometimes a need for physical restraint, almost all were also unhappy with either the reasons for some of their restraints or the way in which some of the restraints were conducted (or both). It is impossible to imagine that this would not impact what sense is made of the event. The experience of physical pain during a restraint, especially combined with the preceding concerns, can only serve to reduce any possibility that the restraint is experienced or understood as helpful or positive.

The strength of relationships between the young person and staff involved colors not only the meaning made of the experience itself, but also the perception of the reasons for and the way in which the restraint is carried out. All of these factors contribute to whether a young person experiences a restraint as a situation in which staff abuse their power merely to control (or worse, retaliate), or as a caring act aimed at maintaining safety.

Attending to processes through which young people make sense of their experiences of physical restraint, then, involves developing and maintaining the overall culture of the establishment, supporting and equipping staff to develop and maintain therapeutic relationships with young people, and consistently and rigorously debriefing staff and young people after each restraint has occurred (see Davidson et al., 2005, for specifics related to these).

Conclusion

The views and experiences of youth reflect the complex and multifaceted nature of physical restraint in residential child care. Within this complexity, children and young people make varying sense of these experiences. In comparing the perspectives of children and young people and staff, there seem to be important commonalities between staff and young people related to what physical restraint means (Steckley & Kendrick, 2005).

We have shown that children and young people do not reject the use of physical restraints out of hand. They recognize that in certain situations a restraint is the most appropriate intervention to ensure the safety of the young person. They do, however, question in a telling way poor practice in the use of restraint. Our research therefore confirms the concerns reported by respondents in previous consultations with children and young people. For example, the entire 37 study participants in the present investigation felt that, in certain situations, staff had been too ready to intervene physically, had physically restrained young people when it was not justified, or, in extreme cases, had inflicted unnecessary pain in restraints.

Providing new insight, the children and young people in our study stressed the importance of relationships. This related not only to the context in which young people experience restraint but also to the process by which children and young people construct for themselves the longer-term meanings and implications. The quality of relationships has a marked impact on the experience of children and young people, and trust appears to be an essential factor in determining whether that experience is positive or negative. This finding has not been highlighted in the previous literature.

Congruence between staff members' affect, action, and communication of "care" and "last resort" throughout an intervention involving restraint is vital. The meaning and use of physical restraint must be communicated clearly and continually explored through open dialogue. An understanding and integration of physical and relational containing care, and the place of restraint within it, might go some way toward eliminating unnecessary restraints and ensuring that those that do occur are done in a professional, caring manner. This, then, emphasizes the importance of the role of staff teams and management, and the overarching culture within residential establishments. The culture of an establishment must also promote safe and productive ways to challenge poor practice in others, and to reflect on one's own practice when it falls short of the ideal. It is also likely that this type of culture would engender confidence amongst young people to raise concerns and know that they would be seriously addressed.

We would argue that taking on board the perspectives of children and young people is crucial in this contentious and sensitive area of practice in residential child care. As we have stated, this process has begun through input to the development of the Scottish guidance for residential child care practitioners and managers about physically restraining children and young people (Davidson et al., 2005). Further research and policy development is necessary, but to have a positive impact on the lives of children and young people in care, its design and development must take into account the subtlety and complexity of youth experiences.

References

Alderson, P. (1995). *Listening to children: Children, ethics and social research.* Ilford: Barnardos.

Barter, C., & Renold, E. (2000). 'I wanna tell you a story': Exploring the application of vignettes in qualitative research with children and young people. *International Journal of Social Research Methodology, 3*(4), 307–323.

Chien, W-T., Chan, C. W. H., Lam, L-W., & Kam, C-W. (2005). Psychiatric inpatients' perceptions of positive and negative aspects of physical restraint. *Patient Education and Counseling, 59*, 80–86.

Davidson, J., McCullough, Steckley, L., & Warren, T. (2005). *Holding safely: A guide for residential child care practitioners and managers about physically restraining children and young people.* Glasgow: Scottish Institute for Residential Child Care.

Day, D. M. (2000). *A review of the literature on restraints and seclusion with children and youth: Toward the development of a perspective in practice.* Report to the Intersectoral/Interministerial Steering Committee on Behaviour Management Interventions for Children and Youth in Residential and Hospital Settings, Toronto, Ontario.

Deacon, J. (2004). Testing boundaries: The social context of physical and relational containment in a maximum secure psychiatric hospital. *Journal of Social Work Practice 18*(1), 81–97.

Fisher, J. A. (2003). Curtailing the use of restraint in psychiatric settings. *Journal of Humanistic Psychology, 43*(2), 69–95.

Gallop, R., McCay, E., Guha, M., & Khan, P. (1999). The experience of hospitalization and restraint of women who have a history of childhood sexual abuse. *Health Care for Women International, 20*(4), 401–416.

Garfat, T. (2004). Meaning making and intervention in child and youth care practice. *Scottish Journal of Residential Child Care 3*(1), 9–16.

Grimshaw, R., & Berridge, D. (1994). *Educating disruptive children: Placement and progress in residential special schools for pupils with emotional and behavioural difficulties.* London: National Children's Bureau.

Hart, D., & Howell, S. (2004). *Report on the use of physical intervention across children's services.* London: National Children's Bureau.

Hawkins, S., Allen, D., & Jenkins, R. (2005). The use of physical interventions with people with intellectual disabilities and challenging behaviour—the experiences of service users and staff members. *Journal of Applied Research in Intellectual Disabilities, 18,* 19–34.

Hayden, C. (1997). Physical restraint in children's residential care. *Social Services Research and Information Unit Report No. 37.* Portsmouth: University of Plymouth.

Human Rights Act 1998. Chapter 42. Edinburgh: Stationery Office.

Kendrick, A. (1995). *Residential care in the integration of child care services.* Edinburgh: Scottish Office.

Kirkwood, A. (1993). *The Leicestershire Inquiry 1992.* Leicester: Leicestershire County Council.

Leadbetter, D. (1996). Technical aspects of physical restraint. In M. Linday (Ed.), *Physical restraint: Practice, legal, medical & technical considerations* (pp. 33–48). Glasgow: Centre for Residential Child Care.

Lee, R. (1993). *Doing research on sensitive topics.* London: Sage.

Lindow, V. (2000). Commentary on papers for the research seminar on 20th September from a service user perspective. Obtained from the National Task Force on Violence Against Social Care Staff.

Milligan, I., Hunter, L., & Kendrick, A. (2006). *Current trends in the use of residential child care in Scotland.* Glasgow: Scottish Institute for Residential Child Care.

Mohr, W. K., Mahon, M. M., & Noone, M. J. (1998). A restraint on restraints: The need to reconsider the use of restrictive interventions. *Archives of Psychiatric Nursing, 12*(2), 95–106.

Morgan, R. (2005). *Children's views on restraint: The views of children and young people in residential homes and residential special schools.* Available online at www.rights4me.org.uk/pdfs/restraint_report.pdf. England: Commission for Social Care Inspection.

Moss, M., Sharpe, S., & Fay, C. (1990). *Abuse in the care system: A pilot study by the National Association of Young People in Care.* London: National Association of Young People in Care (NAYPIC).

Paterson, S., Watson, D., & Whiteford, J. (2003). *Let's face it! Care 2003: Young people tell us how it is.* Glasgow: Who Cares? Scotland.

Petti, T. A., Mohr, W. K., Somers, J. W., & Sims, L. (2001). Perceptions of seclusion and restraint by patients and staff in an intermediate-term care facility. *Journal of Child and Adolescent Psychiatric Nursing 14*(3), 115–127.

Ray, N. K., Myers, K. J., & Rappaport, M. E. (1996). Patient perspectives on restraint and seclusion experiences: A survey of former patients of New York state psychiatric facilities. *Psychiatric Rehabilitation Journal, 20*(1), 11–18.

Safe & Sound. (1995). *So who are we meant to trust now? Responding to abuse in care: The experiences of young people.* London: NSPCC.

Scottish Executive. (2002). *National care standards: Care homes for children and young people.* Edinburgh: The Stationery Office.

Scottish Executive. (2005). *Children's social work statistics 2004–05.* Edinburgh: Scottish Executive National Statistics Publications.

Simpson, J. (1995, November/December). Containment versus dignity. *Scottish Child.* 22.

Snow, K., & Finlay, J. (1998). *Voices from within: Youth speak out.* Toronto, Ontario: Office of the Child and Family Service Advocacy.

Sprince, J. (2002). Developing containment: Psychoanalytic consultancy to a therapeutic community for traumatized children. *Journal of Child Psychotherapy, 28*(2), 147–161.

Steckley, L., & Kendrick, A. (2005, June 29–July 3). Physical restraint in residential child care: The experiences of young people and residential workers. *Childhoods 2005: Children and Youth in Emerging and Transforming Societies.* University of Oslo, Norway.

U.N. Committee on the Rights of the Child (2002). *Consideration of reports submitted by states parties under Article 44 of the Convention. Concluding observations of the Committee on the Rights of the Child: United Kingdom of Great Britain and Northern Ireland.* Geneva: United Nations.

U.N. General Assembly. (1989, November 20). *Adoption of a convention of the rights of the child.* New York: Author.

Ward, A. (1995). The impact of parental suicide on children and staff in residential care: A case study in the function of containment. *Journal of Social Work Practice, 9*(1), 23–32.

Waterhouse, R. (2000). *Lost in care: Report of the tribunal of inquiry into the abuse of children in care in the former County Council areas of Gwynedd and Clwyd since 1974.* London: Stationery Office.

Who Cares? Scotland (no date). *Feeling safe? report: The views of young people.* Glasgow: Who Cares? Scotland.

Woodhead, J. (1999). Containing Care. In A. Hardwick & J. Woodhead (Eds.), *Loving, hating and survival: A handbook for all who work with troubled children and young people* (pp. 2–21). Aldershot: Ashgate Arena.

Wynn, R. (2004). Psychiatric inpatients' experiences of restraint. *Journal of Forensic Psychiatry & Psychology, 15*(1), 124–144.

PART II

THEORETICAL AND HISTORICAL ISSUES

Literature on the Therapeutic Effectiveness of Physical Restraints with Children and Youth

David M. Day

Historical Background

The use of restraints in psychiatric inpatient treatment has a long and controversial history. As Masters (Chapter 3, this volume) noted, in 1794, Philippe Pinel and his assistant, Jean Baptiste Pussin, of Bicetre Hospital near Paris, ushered in a new period of enlightenment in psychiatric treatment when he called for, among other things, the safe and humane use of restrictive devices as a means of preventing mental patients from harming themselves. This stood in contrast to the cruel and barbaric treatment of madmen and madwomen in the institutions of the day who might have been confined in chains and isolated in dungeons for long periods of time, even many years (Angold, 1989).

John Conolly, at Hanwell County Asylum in Middlesex, England, who, in 1839, instituted a policy of non-use of mechanical restraints taking the position of limiting the use of restraints even further (Angold, 1989). Fifteen years later, in 1854, a Lunacy Commission was established in England to monitor and regulate the use of restraints in asylums, viewing the practice "as a non-therapeutic approach to psychological distress" (American Academy of Child and Adolescent Psychiatry, 2002, p. 8S). In the asylums of the United States, however, the psychiatric profession took the opposite view, endorsing the use of restraints as therapeutic (American Academy of Child and Adolescent Psychiatry, 2002). In the years since, the practice has continued unabated in both the United Kingdom and the United States (Visalli, McNasser, Johnstone, & Lazzaro, 1997) while the issue lay dormant like a sleeping giant only to be awoken by a series of investigative articles that appeared in the *Hartford*

Courant in October 1998 (Weiss, Altimari, Blint, & Megan, 1998). The exposé brought to public attention the commonplace use of restraints and the number of deaths that resulted from its practice, particularly of children.

The use of restraints with children and youth also has been the subject of considerable controversy, debate, and discussion, although over a much briefer history. Redl and Wineman (1952) advocated the use of physical restraints as one of their "techniques for the antiseptic manipulation of surface behavior" (p. 153). Reflecting the enormous influence of Freud's psychodynamic theory, they stated that children with severe ego disturbances "will invariably be given to violent fits of rage, accompanied by a total lack of control" (p. 209). These outbursts may be contained by the use of physical restraints, for "ego-support," accompanied by talking to the child in a comforting and soothing manner until the child's "ego is back in commission" (p. 212). A similar rationalization for the use of restraints is seen in the writings of Trieschman, Whittaker, and Brendtro (1969) who state that "[t]he wild child struggling in your arms does not have enough ego to control his own body, much less enough ego to attend to any subtle comments on your part about his past, his parents, or his problems" (p. 179).

More recently, in several textbooks, on childhood psychopathology (DiLorenzo, 1988) and residential care for children (Swanson & Richard, 1988), physical restraints were described as a common way to manage violent and aggressive behavior and psychotic clients. DiLorenzo remarked further that physical restraints might be used as a means of behavior modification, though he noted that there is little research in this regard. This comment is of interest because it reflects the theoretical dominance of the behavioral movement, alongside the psychoanalytic approach, that carried the field of clinical child and adolescent psychology for so many years. Strident debates took place in the academic literature among theorists of different orientations, at the expense of conducting carefully designed, systematic, empirical studies on the underlying causes of childhood disorders and their treatment. This ultimately slowed the progress of clinical work with young people throughout much of the 20th Century (Dumas & Nilson, 2003). Indeed, progress into the development of guidelines for the safe and appropriate use of restraints has similarly been hampered by the absence of rigorous, well-conceived research to inform practice, in favor of methodologically flawed studies and a plethora of "expert" opinions that, in some cases, are based on inappropriate, unsubstantiated, or outdated theoretical models (Day, 2002)

Current Debate

A great deal has been written about the use of seclusion and physical restraints, collectively referred to as intrusive or restrictive measures, with children and youth. In a review of the literature covering the period from 1965 to 2001, Day (2002) found 111 articles on the topic, published in psychiatric, nursing, and childcare journals. He characterized the literature as addressing a broad range of issues and as highly diverse in the range of opinions expressed on the practice as well as in the reported rates of use, reasons for use, and methods of use. He concluded that this diversity represents both a strength and a weakness of the literature. It is a strength because the broad range of perspectives encourages a dialogue and sharing of ideas. Positions taken on all sides invite further comments, disagreements, and discussion and serve to facilitate developments, challenge old assumptions, and promote the need for empirical investigation and evaluation. It is a weakness because of the lack of consensus on many aspects of the issue, leading to a lack of clarity about the practice.

One of the more contentious issues in the literature concerns the therapeutic use of physical restraints with children and youth. On the one side of the issue are those who claim that physical restraints have clear therapeutic benefits for young people (Barlow, 1989; Bath, 1994; Myeroff, Mertlich, & Gross, 1999; Rich, 1997; Sourander, Aurela, & Piha, 1996; Ziegler, 2001). On the other side are those who contend that restraints are harmful, have potentially fatal outcomes, and should be used with extreme caution, if at all (Delaney, 2001; American Academy of Child and Adolescent Psychiatry, 2002; Mohr, Mahon, & Noone, 1998; Mohr, Petti, & Mohr, 2003; Singh, Singh, Davis, Latham, & Ayers, 1999; Walsh & Randall, 1995). Indeed, writers on both sides of the issue express their views with equal passion and conviction. For example, Barlow (1989) asserted that physical restraints are an "effective, humane, method for handling aggressive, out-of-control often abused children" (p. 10) while Delaney (2001) maintained "[p]hysical restraint is a dangerous, sometimes deadly practice, with no therapeutic benefit" (p. 129). As Day (2002) noted, the debate about the safe and appropriate use of restraints rages on, in part, at least, because the assumptions underlying their use have not been critically examined, including the theoretical underpinnings of their clinical utility.

While this issue was examined by Day, the intent of this chapter is to extend the discussion and clarify some of the extant currents underlying the debate through an updated literature review. The issues to be examined here include the use of terms and their definition, the reasons underlying the use of physical restraints, and the evidence for the therapeutic utility of restraints. In particular, four questions are addressed:

1. What terms are used in the literature to refer to physical restraints?

2. How are they defined and distinguished?

3. What are the reasons for their use, including the therapeutic effects?

4. Are the intended therapeutic effects achieved?

Each of these questions is complex, multilayered, and fraught with difficulties, which can lead to considerable ambiguity, confusion, and the perpetuation of controversy. It is suggested that this complexity may also account for the wide variability in the practice of restrictive measures and the diversity of opinions that characterize much of the literature.

Methodology

Several steps were taken to retrieve articles for this literature review. A search was conducted of a number of electronic databases, including PsycINFO, MEDLINE, ERIC, Social Services Abstract, Sociology Abstracts, and Criminal Justice Abstracts. Keywords included *physical restraints, holding therapy, therapeutic holding, children, youth,* and *adolescents.* Reference lists were reviewed for additional sources and unpublished reports were requested, where available.

While the previous review (Day, 2002) included materials on both seclusion and restraints (including physical, mechanical, and chemical restraints), this chapter is concerned only with physical restraints. Articles that dealt with restraint use with adults also were excluded, although some of these sources were used for background material. Third, this review was not concerned with the use of restraints with children who have developmental delays, brain injuries, or autism. Although an important topic in its own right, this chapter was concerned with the use of restraints with children and youth who are average to high functioning and display social-emotional behavioral problems (e.g., attention deficit-hyperactivity disorder, conduct disorder). The reason for this exclusion criterion was that the underlying rationale for the use of restraints with lower functioning children (e.g., to stop self-injurious behavior) might not apply across the board to other populations of children living in settings where they might experience restraints (e.g., inpatient psychiatric units, facilities for juvenile offenders). Disentangling this issue was difficult, however, because children from a range of diagnostic categories (e.g., conduct disorder, psychotic, autistic) were included in studies described in some articles (e.g., Miller, Walker, & Friedman, 1989; Sourander, Ellilä, Välimäki, & Piha, 2002). Last, only articles published in the English-language journals were included. This criterion excluded nine articles on the use of therapeutic holding, largely with autistic children, found in German-language publications (for a brief review of these articles see Mercer, 2001).

The search yielded a total of 135 articles and reports. Materials spanned a period of 37 years, from 1969 to 2006. A total of 65 articles were literature reviews, position papers, or articles about restraints, 61 were empirical studies, and 9 were letters to the editor. The empirical studies examined a wide range of issues including predictors and correlates of restraint use (i.e., child, staff, and setting variables), staff attitudes about the practice, and the effects of various organizational initiatives to reduce its use.

Terms Used and Their Definitions

What Is a Physical Restraint?

There is no standard definition of a physical restraint (Jerome, 1998; LeBel, Stomberg, Duckworth, Kerzner, Goldstein, Weeks et al., 2004). Much depends on the particular technique or term that is used and the reason for its use. At the same time, within the general rubric of *restraint*, physical restraints are commonly distinguished from mechanical restraints (e.g., the use of leather or cloth straps, cuffs or belts for the wrist, ankle, waist, chest, or knee, Posey vests, or body jackets) and chemical restraints (e.g., sedative antihistaminics and neuroleptics, such as thioridazene, chlorpromazine, and haloperidol, administered on a p.r.n. basis and without patient consent) (Jerome, 1998; American Academy of Child and Adolescent Psychiatry, 2002). In spite of the variation in definition, physical restraints are conventionally defined as:

- holding a child or young person to stop him/her from being aggressive or violent. (Bell, 1997, p. 40)
- any physical method of restricting an individual's freedom of movement, physical activity, or normal access to his or her body. (Ryan & Peterson, 2004, p. 154)
- 'an external control or supportive technique' (Drisko, 1976, p. 469) that involves the use of physical force by one or more staff to restrict the movement of a child, using a variety of holding techniques, with 'the least amount of force necessary' (Mullen, 2000, p. 92). (Day, 2002, p. 266)

Terms Used to Refer to Physical Restraints

A wide variety of terms have been used to refer to physical restraints including, manual, ambulatory, interpersonal, passive, supine, prone, and therapeutic restraints, basket holds, wrist-holds, therapeutic holds, and "take downs." At times these terms have been used interchangeably and in other instances they have been clearly distinguished from one another. Sometimes the terms are distinguished on the basis of the particular technique to which they refer (e.g., a wrist-hold) (Sugar, 1994). Sometimes the terms are indistinguishable, except for the expected goal of the restraint (e.g., emergency use for containment or pro-grammatic use to facilitate coping). Sometimes distinctions are made on concep-tual grounds or on the basis of the length of time the child is held (e.g., less than or more than 10 to 15 minutes). In some articles, the terms are not defined at all.

When a Restraint Is Not a Restraint

The variability in the use of terms and their definition poses a problem in com-paring studies in that, in some articles, certain types of restraints are consid-ered, while other types are not. For example, in a recent investigation, basket holds and restraints that lasted for less than 15 minutes were not counted as "restraints" (Donovan, Plant, Peller, Siegel, & Martin, 2003). While this is in keeping with the Joint Commission on the Accreditation of Healthcare Organizations (JCAHO, 2001) definition, it is not consistent with other stud-ies and other jurisdictions (Greene, Ablon, & Martin, 2006), such as that of the province of Ontario, Canada, which defines a physical restraint as "using a holding technique to restrict the resident's ability to move freely" (*Child and Family Services Act*, 1990), irrespective of how long the individual was held.

As stated above, the lack of consistency in the definition of terms poses a significant challenge in accumulating findings, comparing its use across stud-ies, and gleaning a perspective on the practice, based on the evidence report-ed in the literature. As well, some have suggested that there is a need to define related terms such as "out-of-control," "danger to himself or herself and/or others," and "aggressivity" (Garrison, 1984; Raychaba, 1992). To be sure, the issue of standardized definitions needs to be given careful consideration in future research if the field is to develop a fully informed perspective on the safe and appropriate use of restraints with children and youth.

Distinguishing Physical Restraints from Therapeutic Holds

A further problem exists when terms (e.g., physical restraints) are *conflated* with certain intended goals or outcomes (e.g., have therapeutic effects). In other words, *saying* a restraint is therapeutic does not *make it* so. This is seen, for example, in the phrase "therapeutic use of physical restraint" (Drisko, 1981, p. 318) and the statements "physical restraints can be very therapeutic" (Hunter, 1989, p. 143) and "physical restraint...should be used sparingly and in a therapeutic manner" (Rich, 1997, p. 1). Moreover, some definitions of therapeutic holding appear to be indistinguishable from a physical restraint. That is, there appears to be noth-ing inherently therapeutic about the practice in the following definitions.

- Therapeutic holding is the physical restraint of an aggressive child by at least two nursing personnel, as soon as safely feasi-ble after an aggressive act. (Barlow, 1989, p. 10)

- Therapeutic holding was defined as one or more staff holding a child in a supportive posture for a period of 10 minutes or less while preventing the child from injuring himself or herself. (Berrios & Jacobowitz, 1998, p. 8)

- The use of therapeutic holding...refers to a treatment technique in which members of staff physically restrain a violent patient. (Sourander et al., 2002, p. 163)

- Therapeutic holding is a method in which one or more adults physically hold children in order to contain unsafe behaviors. (Lundy & McGuffin, 2005, p. 135)

These definitions only add confusion to the issue of using restraints for therapeutic purposes because they fail to identify the particular therapeutic component of the restraint or holding procedure.

Moving towards greater conceptual clarification, and more clearly differentiating a therapeutic hold from a "nontherapeutic" physical restraint, the definition of therapeutic holding by the American Academy of Pediatrics Committee on Pediatric Emergency Medicine (1997) at least includes an intended outcome, conveying a purported therapeutic effect—though, again, without articulating a clear statement of either what makes the technique therapeutic, that is, the "active ingredient," or the theoretical justification for the intended outcome.

- Therapeutic holding is the physical restraint of a child by at least two people to assist the child who has lost control of behavior to regain control of strong emotions. (p. 497)

Finally, moving even further toward conceptual clarification on the therapeutic use of restraints, beyond the surface and superficial construction of the concept at the definitional level, some articles provide detailed descriptions of holding therapy and its variants (e.g., attachment therapy), including the particular techniques that are used, intended outcomes, and theoretical justification (Bath, 1994; Drisko, 1981; Myeroff et al., 1999; Rich, 1997; Ziegler, 2001). This information will be considered in the next two sections.

Reason for Use: Safety and Containment or Therapeutic Change

The reasons underlying the use of restraints with children and youth reflect the current assumptions and theoretical perspectives regarding their practical and clinical utility in institutional (e.g., inpatient psychiatric units, juvenile detention and custody centers) and other residential care (e.g., group homes) facilities. Within current paradigms of residential treatment, the use of restraints has been widely endorsed as an important means of behavioral management, among a range of techniques available to staff (Swanson & Richard, 1988).

In general, their utility has been justified from several perspectives, in essence, in keeping with either the *prevention* of harm (safety and containment) or the *promotion* of learning or personal growth and development and the acquisition of new and adaptive behaviors (therapeutic change). With regard to the former, restraints are used primarily as a preventative measure to respond to a child or youth who is deemed to be "out of control," "at-risk of harm to self, others, or property," or in "imminent danger" (however these terms are defined). Common behaviors calling for the use of restraints include agitation, violence, and aggression. With regard to the latter, restraints are used to help children develop effective self-control skills through the use of external control mechanisms. According to Jerome (1998, p. 267), for example, "[t]herapeutic holding is a way of conveying that an adult is able to provide control for a child who is out of control and thus indicates caring and nurturing." Berrios and Jacobowitz (1998) state that "therapeutic holding serves as a 'ritual of inclusion' that engenders security, and reassures the children that their behaviors can be contained by adults, turning a frightening experience into a comforting one" (p. 18). Moreover, somewhat controversially, a number of authors discuss the use of confrontive, forced, proactive, or "planned holding therapies" (Bath, 1994, p. 43), and of a child "in need of physical restraint" (Rich, 1997, p. 3).

The underlying rationale for the latter position poses a bit of a slippery slope and should be based on sound theoretical principles of developmental psychopathology and clinical child psychology. The former position has been more widely cited as a justification for the use of restraints and requires fewer assumptions about their utility and effectiveness. So what is the theoretic basis for the use of restraints for therapeutic purposes?

Theories Underlying the Therapeutic Use of Restraints

The therapeutic change process has primarily been described from two theoretical positions: attachment theory, based on the work of Bowlby (1973), Cline (1979), and Zaslow (Zaslow & Breger, 1979; Zaslow & Menta, 1975), and psychodynamic theory, based on the work of ego psychologist Donald Winnicott (1960, 1965).

From an attachment perspective, holding is thought to promote a positive client-caregiver relationship through the process of bonding, which fosters effective problem-solving and coping skills and enables the child to learn to develop trust within relationships (Stirling & McHugh, 1998). It is believed that children with certain disorders, including autism, reactive attachment disorders (RAD), conduct disorder, borderline personality disorders, and sociopathy, but also adoptive and foster children, failed in infancy to develop a secure attachment with a parent or primary caregiver (Bath, 1994). This can lead the child to become defensive, rigid, and mistrustful; develop maladaptive self-control and coping skills; display destructive, violent, and aggressive behavior; and experience difficulty with interpersonal contact.

The techniques employed in holding therapy vary depending on whose particular approach is used. These approaches include Zaslow's rage reduction method (Zaslow & Breger, 1969) and the Z-process (Zaslow & Menta, 1975), Cline's rage reduction therapy (Cline, 1979), and Welch's method (1983). In general, the techniques involve holding the child, typically across the lap, by one or more therapist or the parent, in order to restrict the movement of the child's limbs, establishing and maintaining eye contact, and talking to the child in a calm and soothing manner (Mercer, 2001, 2002). Many approaches involve more coercive techniques including provoking the child, such as with verbal taunts and threats (Chaffin, Hanson, Saunders, Nicols et al., 2006; Mercer, 2002), and, in order to ensure that eye contact is maintained, pushing "the skin above the child's eyelid upward in order to open the eyes" (Zaslow & Breger, 1969, p. 272). All these methods use planned, forced, or proactive restraints in order to break through the child's defense systems.

The therapy is said to proceed through two or three stages. For example, Sourander et al. (1996) described a two-phase process of holding, consisting of a *resistance* phase, which is characterized by confrontation by staff and rejection by the child, and a *resolution* phase, which is characterized by an 'intense closeness' between carer and child" (p. 375). The "active ingredients" of holding therapy are thought to be the holding, which provides the child with a safe and secure feeling and the "the cathartic expression of pent-up rage" (Bath, 1994, p. 44), which enables the child to form a healthy attachment with the parent or caregiver (Myeroff et al., 1999).

From a psychodynamic perspective, therapeutic holdings are thought to have a cathartic effect for the child and lead to the expression of difficult feelings, allowing the child to become "psychologically more real and available" (Ziegler, 2004, p. 3) and learn more adaptive ways of coping with strong emotions. According to Rich (1997), holding therapy is effective with children who display acting-out behavior that results from the expression of unconscious wishes or impulses due to immature ego defenses. Early in life, a child may develop a defensive orientation, a sort of fixation, as a way of coping with the environment, but which, over time, becomes no longer adaptive.

The therapeutic milieu creates these *alloplastic* defenses (Hartmann, 1939), in which the source of blame for all problems is externalized, may be contained by a "holding environment" (Winnicott, 1965). According to Winnicott, the mother (as the child's main caregiver) naturally creates a holding environment through her sensitive, responsive, and empathic interactions with her child. This environment allows the infant to be "contained" and "experienced" while expressing painful feelings, which leads to the development of a healthy sense of separateness from the mother (individuation) and of self-integration. Winnicott views holding as an essential element of maternal care and as important for infant development.

According to Rich (1997), the symbolic meaning of a holding environment is transformed into the literal, presymbolic act of physically holding the child "in need of physical restraint" (p. 3). This interpretation is not inconsistent with Winnicott (1965) who states that "[h]olding includes...the physical holding of the infant, which is a form of loving" (p. 49). Moreover, Winnicott remarked that, in working with certain types of clients, the therapist might occasionally need to physically hold the person in order to convey that the client's deepest anxieties are understood and acknowledged. However, he also observed that, ultimately, "it will be understanding and empathy" (p. 240), conveyed verbally, that will be necessary for effective therapy.

Although the literature provides few details about the particular techniques that are used in holding therapy from a psychodynamic perspective, Rich (1997) notes that, like the attachment-based approaches, holding therapy is planned and proactive and consists of three stages: a holding phase, a verbal phase, and a resolution phase. During the holding phase, the child is told in a reassuring manner that the restraint is to assist him or her to gain self-control and that no discussion of the child's concerns will take place while he or she is resisting. During the verbal phase, the child begins to verbally process salient issues, during which time the therapist needs to stay attuned to the child's "observing ego" (p. 8) to ensure that the child is open to processing issues and is not becoming defensive. The resolution phase provides for an opportunity for the child to address any unresolved issues. This latter process may take up to several days to achieve.

Evidence for the Therapeutic Effectiveness of Physical Restraints

What is the evidence for the therapeutic use of physical restraints? Currently, there is scant evidence to support the therapeutic utility. Only a handful of studies are available that speak to the issue and each is hampered by methodological problems. Moreover, in considering the evidence in support of the claims for the therapeutic effects of physical restraints, we should keep in mind Kazdin's (2000) point that "[t]reatment ought to be connected with what we know about the factors related to onset, maintenance, termination, and recurrence of the problem" (p. 831). In other words, the evidence should be examined in relation to current conceptualizations of developmental psychopathology and clinical child psychology.

Also as noted by Kazdin (Kazdin & Nock, 2003), advances in the safe and effective use of clinical interventions with children are achieved when assumptions underlying their use and the causal mechanisms of the change process are critically examined. In these regards, claims of therapeutic benefits need to be supported by empirical evidence of (a) long-term, clinically meaningful change, that is, the hypothesized effects, for example, formation of new attachments, enhanced problem-solving, coping skills, and so forth; and (b) the specific change mechanisms or processes through which therapeutic change took place, that is, the "active ingredients," in order to identify *how* and *why* the intervention worked. For example, if disrupted attachment is associated with the onset or maintenance of a disorder, how and why does holding therapy lead to the formation of new attachments? What is the causal mechanism of this change process? In other words, how does this treatment achieve change and what are the "active ingredients?" Last, what is the evidence that attachment is changed as a result of undergoing holding therapy?

With respect to the empirical evidence, some studies have relied on the use of unverifiable, and hence questionable, anecdotal evidence and case reports (e.g., Berrios & Jacobowitz, 1998; Rich, 1997; Sugar, 1994; Zaslow & Breger, 1969). For example, in a study of restraint use over a three-month period in a pediatric psychiatric inpatient unit, Berrios and Jacobowitz (1998) reported that "anecdotal observations by the staff were that therapeutic holding facilitates positive learning experiences with the psychiatrically disordered children, particularly those who have experienced physical abuse" (p. 18). As well, drawing upon attachment theory and based on a sample of nine children who had been restrained in an inpatient psychiatric unit, Sourander et al. (1996) found a significant improvement in the "relationship between the child and the nurse" (p. 378) in 70% of the holding occasions. However, no operational definition of the nature of the child-nurse relationship was provided, making it difficult to say exactly what changes in the nature of the relationship transpired.

Last, without providing any supportive evidence, Lowenstein (1998) observed that, of the 28 children who had been restrained at his facility, their reactions were initially anger and humiliation, followed by acceptance and eventually gratitude. He went on to note "[t]his should, in the long term, provide the child and future adult with the capacity eventually to develop self-control under stressful situations" (p. 52). Indeed, despite the common refrain that restraint use leads to greater self-control (e.g., Ziegler, 2001), no study has been conducted to determine whether the use of restraints results in a significant change or improvement in coping abilities in children.

A number of studies have used more quantitative approaches in their data collection. Miller, et al. (1989) compared the amount of time a youth spent in restraints and seclusion, as a measure of the procedure's effectiveness to calm an individual. They reported that the use of restraints was superior to the use of seclusion in that the individuals were able to regain behavioral control more quickly while being held by staff (21.2 minutes, on average, with a range of 1 to 90 minutes) than the 4 to 16 hours that is often reported in the literature as being required for the use of seclusion. No evidence was provided, however, for any long-term changes in the sample as a result of the procedure. Shechory (2005) reported that, in comparison to children in residential care who received either no restraints or between one and five restraints, children who underwent six or more restraints evinced a significant reduction in suicidal, but not aggressive, behavior, over a one-year period, in spite of the fact that aggression was the target behavior for a restraint. However, this observed reduction may reflect *regression to the mean*, given that the latter group was higher on suicidal behavior at the outset of the study, compared to the other two groups, and that both the no restraint group and the no more than five restraint group showed an increase on this variable from Time 1 to Time 2.

Last, using a two-group, pretest-posttest quasi-experimental design, Myeroff et al. (1999) reported a significant effect for the use of therapeutic holdings, compared to a no-treatment control group. The dependent variables were the Aggression and Delinquency scales of the Child Behavior Checklist (CBCL) (Achenbach & Edelbrock, 1983), a widely used parent-report measure of child behavior problems. The sample size was 23 children and their parents (12 in the treatment group and 11 in the comparison group).

As others have pointed out (e.g., Mercer, 2002), there are myriad problems with the Myeroff et al. (1999) study, both conceptually and methodologically, not the least of which is the inability to address the possible threats to the *internal validity* of the study. Internal validity concerns the ability to demonstrate that the observed changes were the result of only the manipulation of the independent variable and not due to other unmeasured or uncontrolled confounding variables (Cook & Campbell, 1979). Many factors could have accounted for the observed effects, such as parent motivation to see change among parents in the treatment group or simply attending the treatment center, which the comparison group did not do, two factors that were not controlled for in the study. Furthermore, the researchers did not attempt to assess whether there were any changes in the child's attachment, which would seem to be a "gold standard" criterion for evaluating the effectiveness of this treatment. As well, the fact that the study was carried out at the Attachment Center at Evergreen, Colorado, where this holding therapy was developed, suggests a lack of independence of the treatment evaluation.

In addition, the small sample size compromises the *external validity* of the study, that is, the ability to generalize the findings to other populations (Cook & Campbell, 1979). Indeed, the use of this quasi-experimental design severely limits any conclusions that may be drawn from the investigation, calling for a *very* cautious interpretation of the results, something the authors did not do, for example, when they remarked that "[t]he hypothesis that holding therapy will reduce aggressive behavior in the special needs adopted population was supported" (p. 311). Such a conclusion is not warranted from the findings. At best, this study might be described as "pseudo-science;" at worst, bad science.

In keeping with this notion, a further problem with the whole line of inquiry is that the theoretical positions used to justify the therapeutic use of restraints— outdated psychodynamic and attachment models—do not lend themselves well to empirical scrutiny and so cannot be demonstrated to be false. This principle of "falsifiability" is an essential element of a good theory (Popper, 1959). Therefore, the continued use of these "folk" theories as the conceptual basis for the therapeutic use of physical restraints will undermine the efforts to demonstrate their effectiveness from a scientific perspective. Indeed, while it is all well and good to speculate about the role of ego control or insecure attachment on the development of aggression, these concepts have not translated well into a practice of clinical psychotherapy with children and youth, particularly the use of holding as "therapy." If the field of child and adolescent therapy is to continue to progress, advances must be informed by scientific evidence and current conceptualizations of developmental psychopathology. Likewise, the practice of restraints must be guided by what is known about its use based on the accumulation of evidence and by further investigations to uncover and address what is not known. Currently, there is a great deal that is not known.

In summary, there is no empirical evidence to support the therapeutic use of physical restraints. As well, the theories upon which the therapeutic use of restraints is based remain unsubstantiated. The few studies that have examined the issue have failed to provide evidence for any long-term change or to demonstrate that the observed changes were the result of the hypothesized causal mechanism of the change process and not due to some other factor, an essential element of rigorous research.

Moreover, in a series of articles that appeared in a recent issue of the journal *Attachment and Human Development*, attachment researchers have clearly distanced themselves from the practice of holding therapy. According to Dozier (2003, p. 253), "holding therapy does not emanate in any logical way from attachment theory or from attachment research" and O'Connor and Zeanah stated that

> although holding therapy is thought to enhance the child's capacity to attach to others, it is not clear how and indeed if this happens...There is as yet no systematic evidence that holding therapy is effective and so enthusiastic adoption of this treatment model is unsupported. (2003, p. 236, 238)

Directions for Further Research

There is a limited scientific base for the use of physical restraints with children and youth in spite of the large number of articles and reports that have been written on the topic. At the same time, a review of this literature indicates that the extant research has evolved considerably over time. The first generation of studies was largely descriptive and sought to identify the factors associated with the practice, essentially addressing the question: Who is doing what to whom, when, where, and for what reasons? The second generation of studies, emerging in the early 1990s, examined the effectiveness of various organizational initiatives to reduce the use of restraint and seclusion. It is suggested that the next generation of studies build on both these important issues but adds a corollary to the "who, what, where" question of "with what effect?"

Although some research has attempted to address this complex issue (e.g., Steckley & Kendrick, chapter 1, this volume), further studies are needed that use multiple samples; valid, reliable, and replicable methods of observation and measurement; and a range of research designs, including qualitative and quantitative methods. This work should be guided by the development of theoretical models that delineate the processes through which physical restraints impact children's psychological growth and development. Jones and Timbers (2002), for example, describe a behavioral model in which restraints lead to an increase in the very behaviors staff wish to diminish. The guiding question of this research could be whether and under what conditions physical restraint use helps or harms. Outcome variables could focus on the development of various self-systems, such as a child's sense of safety, trust, control and mastery over one's environment, self-concept, and affective and behavioral self-regulation, as well as symptoms of trauma and psychopathology (e.g., aggression, depression, and anxiety). Moderating and mediating variables that influence these outcomes could include age, gender, attachment style, and history of abuse.

As long as the use of restraints with children and youth continues, and it shows no signs of waning, in spite of the reported deaths associated with the practice (Nunno, et al., in press), it is essential that the impact on children and youth be carefully scrutinized using high quality, rigorous research designs. The plethora of opinions needs to be carefully tested, particularly with regard to the alleged effects on coping, problem solving, self-control, aggression, and noncompliance.

It is suggested that research incorporate a rights-based approach, in keeping with the United Nations Convention on the Rights of the Child (U.N. General Assembly, 1989). Empirical questions that could be examined from this perspective include, how are parents and children involved in decisions about restraints? How is the use of restraints explained at the time of admission? Is there an option for "consent refusal" (Selekman & Snyder, 1997)? A rights-based approach would ensure that the research, and hence the practice, is child-centered and accountable to the young clients. Second, the third generation of research could view restraints as part of a *process,* with its distal and proximal antecedents and its immediate, short-term, and long-term consequences, rather than simply as an *event.* Last, it is suggested that the research take a developmental, eco-behavioral approach in understanding restraints use (Goren, Singh, & Best, 1993; Mohr & Anderson, 2001; Singh et al., 1999). This approach would widen the lens to consider a range of influences on restraint use, including child, staff, and other variables. It is only through the long-term accumulation of research findings that the practice of physical restraints with children and youth could be made safer and more responsive to the needs of children and youth; or its use could be eliminated altogether.

References

Achenbach, T. M., & Edelbrock, C. (1983). *Manual for the child behavior checklist and revised behavior profile.* Burlington, VT: University Associates in Psychiatry.

American Academy of Child and Adolescent Psychiatry. (2002). Practice parameter for the prevention and management of aggressive behavior in child and adolescent psychiatric institutions, with special reference to seclusion and restraint. *Journal of the American Academy of Child and Adolescent Psychiatry, 41,* 4S–25S.

American Academy of Pediatrics Committee on Pediatric Emergency Medicine. (1997). The use of physical restraint interventions for children and adolescents in the acute care setting. *Pediatrics, 99,* 497–498.

Angold, A. (1989). Seclusion. *British Journal of Psychiatry, 154,* 437–444.

Barlow, D. J. (1989). Therapeutic holding: Effective intervention with the aggressive child. *Journal of Psychosocial Nursing, 27*, 10–14.

Bath, H. (1994). The physical restraint of children: Is it therapeutic? *American Journal of Orthopsychiatry, 64*, 40–49.

Bell, L. (1997). The physical restraint of young people. *Child and Family Social Work, 1*, 37–47.

Berrios, C. D., & Jacobowitz, W. H. (1998). Therapeutic holding: Outcomes of a pilot study. *Journal of Psychosocial Nursing, 36*, 14–18.

Bowlby, J. (1973). *Attachment and loss: Vol 2. Separation, anxiety, and anger.* New York: Basic Book.

Chaffin, M., Hanson, R., Saunders, B. E., Nicols, T., Barnett, D., Zeanah, C., Berliner, L., Egeland, B., Newman, E., Lyon, T., LeTourneau, E., & Miller-Perrin, C. (2006). Report of the APSAC Task Force on attachment therapy, reactive attachment disorder, and attachment problems. *Child Maltreatment, 11*, 76–89.

Child and Family Services Acts, R.S.O. 1990, c. C.11.

Cline, F. W. (1979). *What shall we do with this kid? Understanding and treating the disturbed child.* Evergreen, CO: Evergreen Consultants.

Cook, T. D., & Campbell, D. T. (1979). *Quasi-experimentation: Design and analysis issues for field settings.* Boston, MA: Houghton Mifflin.

Day, D. M. (2002). Examining the therapeutic utility of restraints and seclusion with children and youth: The role of theory and research in practice. *American Journal of Orthospychiatry, 72*, 266–278.

Delaney, K. R. (2001). Developing a restraint-reduction program for child/adolescent inpatient treatment. *Journal of Child and Adolescent Psychiatric Nursing, 14*, 128–140.

DiLorenzo, T. M. (1988). Operant and classical conditioning. In J. L. Matson (Ed.), *Handbook of treatment approaches in childhood psychopathology* (pp. 65–78). New York: Plenum.

Donovan, A., Plant, R., Peller, A., Siegel, L., & Martin, A. (2003). Two-year trends in the use of seclusion and restraint among psychiatrically hospitalized youths. *Psychiatric Services, 54*, 987–993.

Dozier, M. (2003). Attachment-based treatment for vulnerable children. *Attachment and Human Development, 5*, 253–257.

Drisko, J. W. (1976). Memo to institution staff: Physical involvement with children—a therapeutic intervention. *Child Welfare, 54*, 469–477.

Drisko, J. W. (1981). Therapeutic use of physical restraint. *Child Care Quarterly, 10*, 318–328.

Dumas, J. E., & Nilson, W. J. (2003). *Abnormal child and adolescent psychology.* New York: Allyn & Bacon.

Garrison, W. T. (1984). Inpatient psychiatric treatment of the difficult child. *Children and Youth Services Review, 6*, 353–365.

Goren, S., Singh, N. N., & Best, A. M. (1993). The aggression-coercion cycle: Use of seclusion and restraint in a child psychiatric hospital. *Journal of Child and Family Studies, 2*, 61–73.

Greene, R. W., Ablon, J. S., & Martin, A. (2006). Use of collaborative problem-solving to reduce seclusion and restraint in child and adolescent inpatient units. *Psychiatric Services, 57*, 610–612.

Hartmann, H. (1939). *Ego psychology and the problem of adaptation.* New York: International University Press.

Hunter, D. S. (1989). The use of physical restraint in managing out-of-control behavior in youth: A frontline perspective. *Child and Youth Care Quarterly, 18*, 141–154.

Jerome, L. W. (1998). Seclusion and restraint. In R. M. Anderson, T. L. Needels, & H. V. Hall (Eds.). *Avoiding ethical misconduct in psychology speciality areas* (pp. 258–275). Springfield, IL: Charles C. Thomas.

Joint Commission on the Accreditation of Healthcare Organizations. (2001). *Restraint and seclusion standards for behavioral health.* Oakbrook Terrace, IL: JCAHO.

Jones, R. J., & Timbers, G. D. (2002). An analysis of the restraint event and its behavioral effects on clients and staff. *Reclaiming Children and Youth, 11,* 37–41.

Kazdin, A. E. (2000). Developing a research agenda for child and adolescent psychotherapy. *Archives of General Psychiatry, 57,* 829–835.

Kazdin, A. E., & Nock, M. K. (2003). Delineating the mechanisms of change in child and adolescent therapy: Methodological issues and research recommendations. *Journal of Child Psychology and Psychiatry, 44,* 1116–1129.

LeBel, J., Stomberg, N., Duckworth, K., Kerzner, J., Goldstein, R., Weeks, M., Harper, G., LaFlair, L., & Studders, M. (2004). Child and adolescent inpatient restraint reduction: A state initiative to promote strength-based care. *Journal of the American Academy of Child and Adolescent Psychiatry, 43,* 37–45.

Lowenstein, L. (1998). The physical restraining of children. *Education Today, 48,* 47–54.

Lundy, H., & McGuffin, P. (2005). Using dance/movement therapy to augment the effectiveness of therapeutic holding with children. *Journal of Child and Adolescent Psychiatric Nursing, 18,* 135–145.

Mercer, J. (2001). Attachment therapy using deliberate restraint: An object lesson on the identification of unvalidated treatment. *Journal of Child and Adolescent Psychiatric Nursing, 14,* 105–114.

Mercer, J. (2002). Attachment therapy: A treatment without empirical support. *The Scientific Review of Mental Health Practice, 1,* 105–112.

Miller, D., Walker, M. C., & Friedman, D. (1989). Use of a holding technique to control the violent behavior of seriously disturbed adolescents. *Hospital and Community Psychiatry, 40,* 520–524.

Mohr, W. K., & Anderson, J. A. (2001). Faulty assumptions associated with the use of restraints with children. *Journal of Child and Adolescent Psychiatric Nursing, 14,* 141–151.

Mohr, W. K., Mahon, M. M., & Noone, M. J. (1998). A restraint on restraints: The need to reconsider the use of restrictive interventions. *Archives of Psychiatric Nursing, 12,* 95–106.

Mohr, W. K., Petti, T. A., & Mohr, B. D. (2003). Adverse effects associated with physical restraint. *Canadian Journal of Psychiatry, 48,* 330–337.

Mullen, J. K. (2000). The physical restraint controversy. *Reclaiming Children and Youth, 9,* 92–94, 124.

Myeroff, R., Mertlich, G., & Gross, J. (1999). Comparative effectiveness of holding therapy with aggressive children. *Child Psychiatry and Human Development, 29,* 303–313.

Nunno, M. A., Holden, M. J., & Tollar, A. (2006). Learning from tragedy: A survey of child and adolescent restraint fatalities. *Child Abuse and Neglect, 30*(12), 1333–1342.

O'Connor, T. G., & Zeanah, C. H. (2003). Attachment disorders: Assessment strategies and treatment approaches. *Attachment and Human Development, 5,* 223–244.

Popper, K. R. (1959). *The logic of scientific discovery.* New York: Basic Books.

Raychaba, B. (1992). Commentary—"Out of control": A youth perspective on secure treatments and physical restraint. *Journal of Child and Youth Care, 7,* 83–87.

Redl, F., & Wineman, D. (1952). *Controls from within: Techniques for the treatment of the aggressive child.* New York: Free Press.

Rich, C. R. (1997). The use of physical restraint in residential treatment: An ego psychology perspective. *Residential Treatment for Children and Youth, 14,* 1–12.

Ryan, J. B., & Peterson, R. L. (2004). Physical restraint in school. *Behavioral Disorders, 29*, 154–168.

Selekman, J., & Snyder, B. (1997). Institutional policies on the use of physical restraints on children. *Pediatric Nursing, 23*, 531–537.

Shechory, M. (2005). Effects of the holding technique for restraint of aggression in children in residential care. *International Journal of Adolescent Medicine Health, 17*, 355–365.

Singh, N. N., Singh, S. D., Davis, C. M., Latham, L. L., & Ayers, J. G. (1999). Reconsidering the use of seclusion and restraints in inpatients child and adult psychiatry. *Journal of Child and Family Studies, 8*, 243–253.

Sourander, A., Aurela, A., & Piha, J. (1996). Therapeutic holding in child and adolescent psychiatric inpatient treatment. *Nordic Journal of Psychiatry, 50,* 375–379.

Sourander, A., Ellilä, H., Välimäki, V., & Piha, J. (2002). Use of holding, restraints, seclusion and time-out in child and adolescent psychiatric in-patient treatment. *European Child & Adolescent Psychiatry, 11*, 162–167.

Stirling, C., & McHugh, A. (1998). Developing a non-aversive intervention strategy in the management of aggression and violence for people with learning disabilities using natural therapeutic holding. *Journal of Advanced Nursing, 27*, 503–509.

Sugar, M. (1994). Wrist-holding for the out-of-control child. *Child Psychiatry and Human Development, 24*, 145–155.

Swanson, A. J., & Richard, B. A. (1988). Discipline and child behavior management in group care. In C. E. Schaefer & A. J. Swanson (Eds.), *Children in residential care: Critical issues in treatment* (pp.77–88). New York: Van Nostrand Reinhold.

Trieschman, A., Whittaker, J., & Brendtro, L. (1969). *The other 23 hours*. Chicago, IL: Aldine.

U.N. General Assembly (1989, November 20). *Adoption of a convention on the rights of the child*. New York: Author.

Visalli, H., McNasser, G., Johnstone, L., & Lazzaro, C. A. (1997). Reducing high-risk interventions for managing aggression in psychiatric settings. *Journal of Nursing Care Quarterly, 11*, 54–61.

Walsh, E., & Randall, B. R. (1995). Seclusion and restraint: What we need to know. *Journal of Child and Adolescent Psychiatric Nursing, 8*, 28–40.

Welch, M. G. (1983). *Holding time*. New York Fireside.

Weiss, E. M., Altimari, D., Blint, D.F., & Megan, K. (1998, October 11–15). Deadly restraint: A nationwide pattern of death. *Hartford Courant*.

Winnicott, D. W. (1960). The theory of the parent-infant relationship. *International Journal of Psychoanalysis, 41*, 585–595.

Winnicott, D. W. (1965). *The maturational process and the facilitating environment*. New York: International University Press.

Zaslow, R. W., & Breger, L. (1969). A theory and treatment of autism. In L. Breger (Ed.), *Clinical-cognitive psychology: Models and integrations* (pp. 246–291). Englewood Cliffs, NJ: Prentice-Hall.

Zaslow, R. W., & Menta, M. (1975). *The psychology of the Z process: Attachment and activation*. San Jose, CA: San Jose State University Press.

Ziegler, D. (2001). To hold or not to hold...Is that the right question? *Residential Treatment for Children and Youth, 18*, 33–44.

Ziegler, D. (2004, July/August). Is there a therapeutic value to physical restraint? [Electronic version]. *Children's Voice*, 1–6.

Modernizing Seclusion and Restraint

Kim J. Masters

Introduction

Very little fundamental change has occurred to restraint and seclusion devices and monitoring equipment since 1794, when Philippe Pinel developed humane practices for helping psychiatric patients manage episodes of violence. It is therefore not surprising that deaths continue to occur, because nowhere else in medicine do we use 350-year-old equipment to treat those who are ill. To put it another way, if we could bring Dr. Pinel to America and show him modern inventions, like the automobile, the airplane, the television, the computer, or even the electric light, he would be likely be amazed. However, show him a current piece of mechanical restraint equipment or someone doing a physical hold, or even a seclusion room, he would able to observe, "Oh, yes we used those, or we had that." Therefore the number one reason for modernizing seclusion and restraint equipment is that it may save lives. It is important to review the history of seclusion and restraint, because, while the equipment is periodically unchained and fresh in people's memory, the prevention philosophies and strategies keep being buried by loss of interest and are forgotten.

History

Dr. Pinel's Experience

Pinel began his work as the superintendent of the Bicetre Hospital in Paris, France during the French Revolution, when abuse and neglect of the mentally

ill was commonplace. It was both courageous and daring that he read his obser-
vations about the state of mental health care in Paris to the Society for Natural
History on December 11, 1794, during the Terror, when the presumption of
challenging the ideas of the Revolution could have sent him to the guillotine.
His description of asylum management issues recorded in "Memoir on
Madness" (Weiner, 1992) and refined in *Treatise on Insanity* (Pinel, 1983),
seem similar to Kesey's (1963) *One Flew Over the Cuckoo's Nest*. A reading of
Pinel's writings shows how little had really changed in the minds of those work-
ing with mental illness and its suffering over the past 200 years.

Pinel wrote:

> Public Asylums for maniacs have been regarded as places of
> confinement for such of its members as are become danger-
> ous to the peace of society. The managers of those situa-
> tions, who are frequently men of little knowledge and less
> humanity, have been permitted to exercise towards their
> innocent prisoners a most arbitrary system of cruelty and
> violence; which experience affords ample and daily proofs
> of the happier effects of a mild and conciliating treatment,
> rendered effective by steady and impassionate firmness.
> (Pinel, 1983, pp. 3–4)

His views about violence and how to treat an acutely agitated person have
a similar ring:

> A coarse and unenlightened mind, considers the violent
> expressions, vociferation, and riotous demeanor of maniacs
> [probably bipolar patients] as malicious and intentional
> insults. Hence the extreme harshness, blows and barbarous
> treatment which keepers, if not chosen with discretion and
> kept within the bounds of their duty, are disposed to
> indulge in towards the unfortunate beings confined to their
> care...Such an observer [of agitated individuals]...is dis-
> posed to allow his patients all the extent of liberty consis-
> tent with his own safety and that of others. (pp. 185–186)

Pinel's description of a humanitarian approach to a restraint has much in
common with the fundamentals of correct practice today.

> The general rule in well run hospices is to watch all phases
> of their attacks closely, anticipate their termination, and,
> generally speaking, grant as much freedom as possible to

those madmen who content themselves with mere gesticulations, loud declamations, and acts of extravagance that hurt no one. To lock up this kind of madman on the pretext of maintaining order means to impose needless constraints that provoke his rebellion and violence and render his madness more inveterate and often incurable. (Weiner, 1992, p. 732)

What was innovative in Dr. Pinel's work in the seclusion and restraint field is not that he released those afflicted with mental illness from chains—Dr. Anton Mesmer (Wikipedia, n.d.) is credited with that a quarter century before, claiming the efficacy of animal magnets. Mesmer's patients, once released, showed obvious improvement from the restoration of freedom and dignity and renewed contact with others. Dr. Pinel, however, brought the concepts of the French Revolution to the mental health hospice. Briefly summarized as "Liberty, Equality, Brotherhood," these principles mean that doctors and patients stood together, shoulder to shoulder, as brothers [or sisters], in a family, against the afflictions of mental illness. The National Alliance of the Mentally Ill (NAMI) and mental health professional organizations seem to reflect similar views in the efforts to approach restrictive interventions today from the concept of partnerships.

Restraint in 19th Century England

Dr. Pinel complained about the secrecy of mental health treatments in England just a few years before the first "burial" was dramatically reversed by subsequent public outcry about the conditions of care in madhouses in England. Roberts (1981) included the following description of the celebrated 1814 case of William Norris in his *Mental Health Timeline.*

A stout ring was riveted round his neck, from which a short chain passed to a ring made to slide upwards or downwards on an upright massive iron bar...Round his body a strong iron bar about two inches wide was riveted...which being fashioned to and enclosing each of his arms, pinioned them close to his sides...bars...passing over his shoulders, were riveted to the waist bar both before and behind.

This case and similar excesses and abuse of the mentally ill prompted a public outcry that led to Parliamentary investigations. As a result, in 1854, the Lunacy Acts were passed which set up a commission "to regulate the operation of all asylums, private as well as public" (Tomes, 1988, pp. 192–193). One of the efforts of this commission was to pressure the superintendents of asylums to use alternatives to seclusion and restraint. These strategies tended to marginalize the role of physicians because they had been defenders of the old asylum restraint practices (pp. 198–199).

Restraint in 19th Century America

In the United States, the picture was different. *Enlightened Practice* (Tomes, 1988, p. 202) supported the minimal use of seclusion. However, restraint was viewed positively. "In some shape or other, restriction is an essential element in all hospital management of insanity."[1] Therefore,

> [g]iven their premise that 'coercion is a powerful adjuvant in itself a moral instrument,' American physicians were far more comfortable with the repressive functions of the asylum buildings and regimen; it was thought that patients needed to feel physically safe and protected from the consequence of their medical disease as a first step toward regaining their self-control. (Tomes, 1988, pp. 202–203)

As a result, they ignored or resisted the teachings of Dr. Pinel and his no-restraint British counterparts. John Gray, the editor of the *American Journal of Insanity*, wrote in 1861, "We look upon restraint and seclusion, directed and controlled by a conscientious and intelligent medical man, as among the valuable alleviating and remedial agents in the care and cure of the insane."[2] Eugene Grissom, of the North Carolina State Asylum, argued, "that the moderate use of mechanical restraint was therapeutic and morally sound, that it was required by the peculiar violence of American Insanity, and that it prevented tragic accidents and injuries."[3]

All this led the English alienist (court psychiatrist) John Charles Bucknill to observe in a *Lancet* editorial in 1876, "The great stumbling-block of the American superintendents is (*sic*) their most unfortunate and unhappy resistance to the abolition of mechanical restraint."[4]

The Waning of the Restraint Intervention

In the 1880s, however, the interest in seclusion and restraint interventions waned because of the failure to alter the course of mental illness, the growing

---

1. Isaac Ray Butler, Hospital Annual Report 1863, cited in Tomes, 1988, p. 202.

2. Gray, 1861 Utica Lunatic Asylum Annual Report, p. 25, cited in Tomes, 1988, p. 206.

3. North Carolina Asylum Association meeting 1877, p. 58, cited in Tomes, 1988, p. 213.

4. John C. Bucknill, Notes on the asylum for the insane in America, *Lancet,* 18 March 1876, p. 418, cited in Tomes, 1988, p. 190.

number of mentally ill patients, the development of new technologies to treat mental illness, and in America the lack of physician involvement in the restraint abolition movement.

Implications for the 21st Century

The elements that led to the loss of momentum in the nonrestraint movement in the 19th Century have been compounded by the realities of the 21st Century, which include the use of restraint as a therapeutic endeavor, the incarceration of the mentally ill in correctional facilities, little financial and social investment in the prevention and management of distressed and aggressive behavior of the mentally ill, and the absence of new technologies in the monitoring, prevention, and modification of restrictive interventions.

Over the last few years there have been significant reductions in the use of restrictive interventions because of the dedicated work of many individuals. Unfortunately, this is somewhat the same result achieved by the Lunacy Commission. Currently, if we are following an "S"-type curve, after initial successes, increasingly more resources and efforts must be devoted to produce increasing smaller rates of restraint and seclusion reductions. This could lead ultimately to therapeutic exhaustion as it did in the past.

Current Restraint Issues

Restrictive intervention researchers, clinicians, and policy analysts are obligated to dialog, share information, and comment on the use of these strategies wherever seclusion and restraint are employed. Otherwise, it sets up the non sequitor idea that seclusions and restraints conducted inside of mental health facilities are different from those carried out in correctional facilities, schools, foster homes, and for treatment or disciplinary ends anywhere. This "anywhere" actually comprises the majority of settings where restrictive interventions are used, often with limited supervision, and creates the greatest risk to the safety and welfare of those subjected to these procedures. Some of these settings and the issues that confront the field are reviewed below.

Holding as a Therapy

In Autism. It is important to be knowledgeable about psychological strategies that emphasize holding techniques. It might seem simple to say that if a youth desires to be held, that "is not a problem," but if he does not, it is a restraint. The reality is more complex, because, particularly with traumatized children, or children with social, emotional, or developmental deficits, the wish to be held may be conflicted and ambivalent, therefore turning the hold into a restraint. Furthermore there are current treatments that emphasize holding techniques. The sensorimotor treatment approaches of Dr. Ayres require physical contacts and being confined, such as in a blanket roll (Ayres, Erwin, Mailloux, & Love, 2004). Temple Grandin, a national expert on autism, in response to her own experience with having this condition, developed a "hug" or squeeze machine, which, to anyone with a restraint background, might seem problematic (Edelson, 1996). Still, it is reported to help some autistic children who may have difficulty, for cognitive and verbal reasons, giving sustained consent for the use of the machine.

In Attachment Therapy. Restraints are employed as treatment strategies among some attachment therapists. For example in *Holding Time*, Dr. Welch writes, "Holding Time is a practical way for you as a mother to achieve a closer, more satisfying, and truly wonderful relationship with your child" (Welch, 1989, p. 17). This is also an "alternative" treatment option used by families whose adopted children have become aggressive and unmanageable. Physical holding is also promoted as part of therapy for Reactive Attachment Disorder (RAD), as a useful "bonding treatment" (Thomas, 1997).

Dateline recently produced a television story about Dr. Ron Frederici, a well-known neuropsychologist who wrote *Help for the Hopeless Child* (Frederici, 1997). He studies and treats Romanian adoptees and has adopted children of his own. The television episode aired segments of his therapy with the parents of a severely emotionally damaged adopted child who was held, prone, for 6 to 12 hour stretches, until his aggressive behavior stopped. Amazingly, as a result, he became much more cheerful and more respectful to family members and attentive to rules. Some of this holding time was televised (Talley, 2004).

On the darker side of this treatment, a child in Colorado was suffocated in a rebirthing therapy during a prolonged restraint in 2000. This was particularly distressing because a lecture the year before at a RAD conference (Masters, 1999) had warned the participants not to use physical holds to restrain children, stating it was not medically safe and could kill a child.

Professional Organization's View of Holding as a Therapeutic Tool

The American Psychiatric Association (APA) has released a position statement opposing coercive holding therapy (American Psychiatric Association, 2002). The Academy of Child and Adolescent Psychiatry (2005) has a *Practice Parameter on Reactive Attachment Disorder of Infancy and Early Childhood,* which also opposes this treatment. Despite these concerns, there is no evidence that holding as a therapy is going to stop or that there is public opposition to it. Indeed, the parents who choose such an option are desperate for help with unmanageable and ill children and mostly do not appear to see holding restraints as harmful. However, hospital regulatory agencies and many working on restraint reduction in mental health facilities perceive restraints as both undesirable and potentially physically and psychologically dangerous.

These RAD practitioners must not be ignored, in part, because they are heroes to their patients and referral sources and have a significant presence in the world of alternative therapies. They are also on the same therapeutic side of the fence as practitioners in the 1800s, like Dr. John Gray, who advocated for the use of restraint. Indeed, Holding Therapy is part of the hold/don't hold continuum, which has been an active subject of controversy for over 100 years. As recently as 1993, holding techniques had therapeutic support for use in inpatient psychiatric settings, as is described in the following excerpt from a respected text.

> Physical holding conveys the message that a person can and
> will control children when they cannot control themselves.
> Most children will not work with you on the exploration
> and expression of intense negative and frightening feelings
> unless you have convinced them that you are willing and
> able to provide them with external controls when they lose
> their internal controls. (Cotton, 1993, p. 210)

Some professionals still espouse these views today even after the *Hartford Currant* article on restraint related deaths (Weiss, Altimari, Blint, & Megan, 1998).

Historical Background of the Hold/Don't Hold Continuum

The Do Not Hold a Child viewpoint arose from a debate about the health of children that started in the 1880s when many died in orphanages. It was based on the then newly discovered germ theory of disease which stated that holding children exposed them to pathogens that ultimately killed them. As a result, medical practitioners urged people not to pick up infants or distressed children for fear of bringing about their demise. The following from Blum's (2002) work gives a flavor of this concern in a pre-antibiotic era.

- A Philadelphia physician remarked bitterly, "I had the honor to be connected with an institution in this city, in which the mortality among all infants under one year of age, when admitted...and retained there for any length of time was 100%." (pp. 32–33)

- Dr. Luther Emmett Holt of Columbia University made controlling childhood infections his focus. He led a crusade to keep kids in separate bedrooms. He wrote, "What could be worse than kissing your child?" Did parents wish, he asked, "to touch their baby with lips a known source for transmitting infection?" In foundling homes, windows were open, beds placed far apart and children touched as little as possible. (p. 33)

- Dr. John D. Watson, President of the American Psychological Association in 1915, expressed the psychological counterpart of this issue. He led a professional crusade against the evils of affection. He wrote, "When you are tempted to pet your child remember, that mother love is a dangerous instrument." According to him, too much hugging and coddling could make infancy unhappy, adolescence a nightmare—even warp the child so much that he may grow up unfit for marriage. (p. 37)

  Watson wrote a chapter on the danger of "too much mother love," in which he warned that obvious affection always produced 'invalidism' in a child, [by which he meant] becoming whiny, irresponsible, and dependent, i.e., 'a failure.' (p. 37)

  He, Holt, and others, led a generation of medical and psychology professionals in a dispassionate scientific approach to child rearing. This perspective is expressed in his 1928 bestseller *The Psychological Care of the Child and Infant*. "Parents," Watson wrote, "should participate in shaping their children through simple, objective, conditioning techniques." (p. 39)

- Government publications echoed this point of view in describing proper approaches to raising children. These professionals suggested that babies' smiles were simply conditioned responses to mothers' smiles. If a mother picks up a child who cries after falling off a bicycle, it could condition him/her to become a 'cry baby'. Locking a child in a dark room could condition the child to be afraid. For this reason, spanking was felt to be a preferable discipline technique. (p. 43)

- Clinical observations and research by physician critics like Goldfarb, Bakwin, and Spitz challenged these views. Initially, they were not heeded. William Goldfarb worked in Jewish Family Services foster homes. He wrote that the children he treated were "'like bomb escapees'—apathetic, passive...the vacuum of—[being removed from family]—was the worst thing you could inflict on a child, leaving a small boy or girl to rattle about in some empty bottle of a life." (p. 48)

Harry Bakwin, a New York pediatrician described the syndrome of loneliness in infants in which he showed that the lack of holding produced withdrawal, failure to eat, to thrive, and proneness to fevers and would dissipate when their mothers took them home (p. 36). Rene Spitz observed that infants cared for in their first year of life in a foundling home became withdrawn and apathetic and thus susceptible to infection, illness, and death. He called this condition, "hospitalism." Those, on the other hand, who were cared for by single caretakers in a detention home avoided these withdrawn states by having strong attachments to their caretakers. (pp. 36–48)

Blum's work appears in a larger book on Harry Harlow and his research on the effects of practices such as the ones espoused by Holt and Watson (2002). Harry Harlow examined the attachment patterns of monkeys raised by wire and cloth monkeys and compared them with monkeys raised by their own mothers. With this work he launched the field of affect psychology, which had largely been ridiculed by Watson. At the University of Wisconsin laboratory that he designed himself and named Goon Park, because correspondents misread its address [600 N. Park], he showed how the lack of holding created a generation of monkeys that were severely socially and emotionally damaged. In other experiments, he showed how a young monkey secluded in a chamber that prevented seeing or touching his mother, produced withdrawal, apathy, social deviancy. It also produced an inability to get along with peer monkeys that were very resistant to change.

While this work supports concerns about the effects of long-term seclusions, it also made the psychological case for the benefits of holding. In fact, in tandem with Goldfarb and Spitz's work, it completely altered child-rearing practices in this country by pointing out the primacy of mother love in healthy early primate development. In another study using a "Butler" love box (Blum, 2002, pp. 110–112), Harlow showed that a monkey consistently chose a view of his mother over a contingent food reward. This work challenged the view of Watson and others that operant conditioning explained primate decision-making strategies. However, holding does not in itself provide security or competence. The development of independence is an essential element in both these developmental tasks. Harlow observed in his cloth-mother monkey study that both the cloth- and wire-raised monkeys failed to socialize. The cloth one could comfort, but "by being so passively acceptant never nudges her charges toward other relationships and 'thereby never encourages independence in her infant and [affectionate] relationships with other infants and children.'" (Blum, 2002, pp. 196–197)

Current Implications and Debate

Restraint reduction efforts may help inform and define research efforts in understanding damaged attachment and independence forming abilities in humans. Researchers and clinicians in the restrictive intervention field have an obligation to offer a seclusion and restraint perspective to the holding therapy debate. They are in a unique position to examine what are the safe and therapeutic interpersonal boundaries and limits for children with diverse physiological and psychological backgrounds in different treatment settings, with different social and psychiatric co-morbidities. In each of these areas, the boundary between safe and unsafe containment should be explored taking into account recent research. For example, a recent review noted that from birth, psychopathic adults show both callous unemotional responses to others' suffering, and intense preoccupation with their own needs (Viding, 2004). Another recent study suggested that those with psychopathic traits had a deficit in perception of fear (Blair, Budhani, Colledge, & Scott, 2005). It would be important to understand how the behavior of psychopathic individuals during restraints or seclusions was reflected in brain pathways. Then it might be possible to make comparisons of their psychology and neural activity during restrictive interventions with those with other psychiatric illnesses, for example posttraumatic stress disorder (PTSD) and autism. Research in these areas should lead to more specificity in restraint or seclusion reduction efforts.

Juvenile Justice System

Interest in incorporating seclusion and restraint reduction strategies from psychiatric hospitals and therapeutic residential treatment centers into the juvenile justice system's correctional facilities has benefited from some of the creative efforts of participants at the 2005 Symposium Examining the Safety of High-Risk Interventions in Children and Young People. One of the presenters, Wanda Mohr has written a paper about seclusion and restraint issues in the Juvenile Justice system (Petti, Mohr, Somers, & Sims, 2001). The Substance Abuse and Mental Health Services Administration (SAMHSA) in America has also supported these efforts. There have been trauma-focused and strength-based approaches to aggression management. However, as is repeatedly acknowledged, these efforts require the active support of leadership and regulatory oversight. Unfortunately, strategies for coping with those detained in juvenile justice facilities are subject to the policies of individual states with interpretations of these policies by individual locales. For example, several years ago in South Dakota, in response to mistreatment in a juvenile correctional facility and attendant publicity, restraints were essentially prohibited as interventions with youth in the department of corrections custody.

However, in Florida until 2005, and currently in other venues, like New Jersey and Maine, there are policies for the use of restraint chairs. In the public eye, perhaps there is less concern for the welfare of those who are imprisoned because of crimes they committed, than for the suffering of those in the mental health system. Furthermore, while there are national standards developed by the National Commission on Correctional Health Care (NCCHC), only 63 out of 1,800 estimated juvenile facilities are actually accredited by them. Currently, juvenile correctional facilities have become holding tanks for many adolescents. It is estimated that 65% to 75% of incarcerated teens have psychiatric disorders (Teplin, Abram, McClelland, Dulcan, & Mericle, 2002). Having standardized, safe approaches to dealing with aggression for them and other adolescents is essential not only for humanitarian reasons, but also to lessen the risk for psychiatric and medical complications and to prevent deaths (Masters & Penn, 2005).

Current State of Physician Involvement

Physicians are not as active in this field as they are in other areas of mental illness. However, there are well known exceptions to this. Dr. Petti (Petti et al., 2001), Dr. Jensen (Schur, Sikish, Findling, Malone, Crismon, Dervian et al., 2003), and Dr. Riddle have all worked to reduce restraint use (Barnett, dos Rios, & Riddle, 2002). Additionally, Dr. Bruce Hassuk and Kathy Regan RN won the American Psychiatric Association Psychiatric Services Award in 2003 for creating an open arms seclusion and restraint elimination program at child assessment unit at Cambridge hospital in Cambridge, Massachusetts (American Psychiatric Association, 2003). Dr. Ruth Ryan worked to reduce restraints in cases with cognitive impairments (Ryan, 2001). Dr. Sandra Bloom developed a Sanctuary model (Community Works, 2006), and Dr. Bennington-Davis (Bennington-Davis, & Murphy, 2005), devised strategies that made the facility in which she was the medical director, restraint free. The sanctuary model focuses on the development of a care model that is aware of

the traumatic issues in the lives of the patients, consumers, clients, or survivors who present themselves for help to psychiatric institutions. It teaches
the staff how to develop a nonviolent therapeutic culture in their facility. It
emphasizes affect management, cognitive learning, and community gover-
nance with open communication between staff and those for whom they are
caring. Through the learning of self-discipline and learning of safe boundaries
and skills involved in developing healthy social networks, the community of
staff and patients grow together and develop hope in the future, and respect
for themselves, their achievements, and the evolving social environment they
have jointly created (Community Works, 2006).

The majority of physicians who order restraint and seclusion unfortunately are uninvolved in applying these treatment models and are instead focused
on ways, especially with medications, to end the intervention. This is a concern
because the antecedents of the restraints usually provide critical information
about ways to help patients and clients cope with the stresses involved and
would render restrictive intervention unnecessary. In addition, physician motivation to get involved with this material is undermined by the reality that they
do not have the power or influence to alter policy, influence treatment strategies, or even to be heard on national councils, while at the same time they are
responsible for carrying out national regulations and abide by training direc-
tives which they have no role in creating. Additionally, there is no financial
reimbursement to encourage physician involvement. In the United States there
are code numbers for all medical procedures that are eligible for reimbursement, and unfortunately seclusion and restraint intervention is not listed. For
physicians, seclusion and restraint work is like a form of indentured servitude;
they are ordered to attend the procedure, decide how it should be resolved,
order medication if appropriate, but at the same time have no input into the
regulations regarding these procedures and no financial recompense.

Of course, those who write policies and procedures, which are so vital in
this field, have a different perspective than those who order and are responsible for their management. The ordering physician may be concerned with the
clinical work he is leaving to complete a face-to-face interview with a
restrained or secluded person, unclear what medically is appropriate, especially if the procedure ended before his arrival, worried about its malpractice
liability, and feeling pressured to complete the interview on time or otherwise
triggering a CMS (Centers for Medicare and Medicaid Services) audit
(Martin, Fawcett, & Lee, 2004). The program administrator, on the other
hand, would more likely focus on patient safety in the broader context of a
trauma prevention initiative. On pediatric medical floors and in intensive care

units (ICU), where seclusion—rarely—and restraint—more often—is a behavioral intervention, these strength based issues may be considered by pediatric physicians as peripheral to the treatment of underlying medical disease.

Even the chapter of the *State Training Manual* on the Reduction of Seclusion and Restraint, supported by the American Association of Community Psychiatrists, does not state how its psychiatrists are involved with planning and participating in leadership roles with national restrictive intervention policy (American Association of Community Psychiatrist, n.d.). Furthermore, physicians who promote schema like the "Treatment Recommendations for Atypical Antipsychotic in Youth (TRAAY)" project focus primarily on the use of medications as a reduction strategy, which to some could appear to be justifying chemical restraint (Schur et al., 2003). Yet there is no national forum where these concerns can lead to either multidisciplinary or unified approaches to restraint reduction. Taken together this information would suggest that there is a major gulf between the approaches of the designers of sanctuary care (Community Works, 2006) and those who are called upon to order seclusion and restraint. This seems to be a similar situation to the 1880s, as described earlier.

Medical students have no training in the prevention and management of restrictive interventions. The Liaison Committee on Medical Education has felt that training should occur when the students are in places where this information is needed (J. Kay, personal communication, February 6, 2006). This effectively means that in America when a medical student graduates, she is no better informed about procedures that can traumatize, injure, or potentially kill patients, than the person one passes in the street. A model curriculum for medical students reflecting current debates and treatment strategies is needed, because most physicians will face seclusions or restraints in their careers whether it be in the emergency room, the ICU, the pediatric ward, the psychiatric unit, the geriatric unit, the residential treatment center, etc. Physicians need to be experienced in the prevention and safe application of restraints and seclusions, so their response can be guided by current standards and evolving practices.

Conflicting Views of Restrictive Interventions

This field is surrounded by social, economic, and psychological views that have different attitudes towards residents, clients, or patients than those espoused in strength based or trauma based or multisystems curricula. One might argue that this is unimportant because these are not mental health issues. However, lifetime rates of trauma have been estimated as high as 50% to 60% (Connor

& Butterfield, 2003), depression at 16% (Schatzberg, 2005), and anxiety at 9% (Lundbeck Institute, n.d.). The majority of these individuals are not residing in mental health facilities. They likely find themselves being restrained or secluded elsewhere. Furthermore, these rates do not encompass only identified patients with mental illnesses. For example many children in this country everyday are being sent to their rooms for hours or held in unmonitored restraints. How many of these are traumatized individuals incubating PTSD, depression, psychosis, etc., and are the future occupants of our emergency rooms? These are also important populations for intervention efforts.

Funding Issues

Mental health has a tradition of being under-funded, and what funds are available are spent far more on pharmacological and neuro-imaging projects than on seclusion and restraint initiatives, despite the public outcry that attended the publishing of the *Hartford Courant*'s report on restraint-related deaths (Weiss et al., 1998). Because of other needs in America, public funding for mental health is under perpetual attack. In this climate, what can prevent reductions in the limited support for restrictive intervention reduction programs?

Proprietary Issues

Another concern is the proprietary and financial aspects of some de-escalation training programs that are taught to staff to help them manage patient or client mood-driven crises. It has given birth to *therapeutic-messianism*, the belief that a proprietary seclusion and restraint training company could on its own suffice to meet the needs for empathetic emotional engagement with angry children, adolescents, and adults, while at the same time providing financial security to its developers. These programs are often unwilling to share their data about efficacy or details about their programs, because of fear that it would cause them to lose business. This attitude erects barriers for those who wish to share information, compare methods, and define the strengths and limitations of various de-escalation strategies. It also encourages concealing of adverse data and exaggeration of efficacy. Furthermore, it is not known how seclusion and restraint reduction efforts affect the course of psychiatric illnesses; which they improve, which they leave unaffected, and which, if any, they make worse.

A multidisciplinary, multiprofessional association, multiagency, and multiprogram group that promotes and reviews data for everyone in the field without regard to proprietary concerns could answer many questions including the one above. Such a group could publish data, make recommendations for future directions, and comment on results. It could also solicit funding for projects.

Fear About Modernization

Some seclusion and restraint abolition advocates fear modernization because of concern that professionals will again become comfortable with using these methods. This has not happened in the past. In the history of restrictive interventions, the equipment has not been a primary rationale for use of restrictive interventions, as shown in the history section in this chapter. Indeed, to the contrary, there has never really been any significant modernization to seclusion and restraint monitoring or equipment since Pinel's time, or for centuries before.

Tying human beings to tables or boards or locking them in rooms has been a commonplace practice throughout civilization. The most compelling reason to pursue modernization efforts is the unlikely prospect of succeeding in abolishing interventions that have been used for the last 6,000 years. Furthermore, if those who wish to prevent and manage restrictive interventions do not take the lead in this endeavor, someone else with less knowledge will.

Modernizing Restraint

Modernizing Monitoring Equipment. Potential opportunities to modernize seclusion and restraint could begin with restraint monitoring. The equipment is antiquated. Straps, locked rooms, and holding people down are techniques that were common in the earliest civilizations, 4,500 years ago. Safety monitoring of restraints today include measurement of pulse and respiration rates and blood pressure. The first two measures could have been taught to people living at the time of the Egyptian Pharaohs! Furthermore, pulse and respiration rates and blood pressure provides, at best, second hand data. Joint Commission on Accreditation of Health Care Organizations (JCAHO) sentinel event data shows that the principal risk to those restrained is suffocation induced by chest compression with resultant inability to adequately supply oxygen to blood, brain, and other body organs (Joint Commission Resources, 2002). In another study of 45 physical restraint-related deaths 29 (64%) were due to asphyxiation (Nunno, Holden, & Tollar, 2006).

Currently breathing, pulse, and blood pressure are assessed assuming that increases in any of these measures signal distress. Anxiety, anger, fear, medication effects, and baseline individual cardio-respiratory status would likely alter any readings obtained. Blood pressure cuff application and readings are nearly impossible to obtain on someone who is upset or refuses to cooperate. Portable wrist monitors may be more effective data collectors but the results are no less ambiguous because of the other factors that can cause elevations in blood pressures. Drops in blood pressure usually signal a major cardio-respiratory event, providing information that may be too late to avert a medical catastrophe. When pulse, respiration, and blood pressure checks are performed during a restraint, they are in fact more significant as a ritual, than they are as monitors that provide useful information about the person's medical condition.

Is there anything better? Yes. For well over a decade, hospitals have been using pulse oximetry to measure oxygen saturation in the medically compromised. Continuous oximetry assessment is available in ICUs. There are now reliable, inexpensive ($200 to $500 U.S. dollars), portable oximeters, which can register oxygen saturation as a spot check or continuously, when clipped for a few seconds to an earlobe, or a finger, or even a person's large toe. Some oximeters have a mechanism for indicating false positive and false negative readings. Levels less than 95% oxygen saturation require immediate reassessments and implementation of strategies to raise the oxygen saturation level. Alternative Behavioral Services has been using oximetry in all of its restraints for nine months in six hospital and residential treatment centers. Evidence is accumulating from these measurements that oximetry can detect low oxygen saturation levels before they may be clinically apparent (Masters & Wandless, 2005; Masters, 2006a, 2006b). It also appears to have an antirestraint psychological impact, because oxygenation measurements increases awareness of the potential medical dangers in carrying out restraints, particularly when baseline readings are obtained before restraints occur (Masters, 2006a, 2006b). This has allowed patients, staff, and clients to understand the potential medical complications of restraints and work towards avoiding them or ending them rapidly.

Modernizing Restraint Equipment. Modernizing other equipment devices should allow more accurate pulse and blood pressure monitoring. The technology for telemetry measurements has been available for more than a decade. We should be able to have small damage resistant transmitters, which could be placed on patients and could provide continuous readings of vital signs. The outstanding problem is how to convince those who are being restrained to keep them on. A team of nurses, psychiatrists' patient advocates, patients, and engineers should be able to develop a prototype that would be acceptable.

Current restraint equipment consists mainly of leather straps and locks. When attached to a board, they are used to move agitated patients to a unit or to a seclusion room. The boards have been called papoose or transport carriers and probably would be easily recognized by any asylum attendant working with Pinel in 1794. Alternative restraint equipment has yet to appear, but as indicated below, could provide safer options.

What provokes staff restraint interventions is the expectation or experience of assault. If a person could contain his anger, as Pinel observed, "as mere gesticulations," interventions would be aborted (Weiner, 1992, p. 732).

Distraction Aids. A relatively unsuccessful strategy for de-escalation is to encourage distressed individuals to hit punching bags or hit inflatable bats against the wall. These strategies appear to have at least as great a chance to provoke, as to contain anger. However, guided de-escalation might be a viable strategy, particularly if was multimodal: auditory, kinesthetic, motor, and visual (LeBel, 2006).

Currently, behavioral psychologists are employing the technique of Virtual Reality to treat phobic disorders. There is also preliminary experience with this technology in the treatment of PTSD and anger management (Kaplan, 2005). The justification for using virtual reality is that with a script employing guided visual, auditory, and kinesthetic information through headphones and a movie screen embedded in a headset, a person can relive distressing experiences in a controlled fashion and develop new coping strategies which can overlay existing ones. Theoretically this activity could be viewed in functional Nuclear Magnetic Resonance Scans (fMRI), or Positron Emission (PET) Scans particularly with regard to amygdala and hippocampal functioning, because these brain areas are affected by emotion, memory, and trauma. Since many people with anger issues have trauma backgrounds, virtual reality work might have a dual treatment function. While there might be a temptation to wait and see what progress other disciplines develop with virtual reality, there is ample reason to develop and spearhead research partnerships now.

Modernizing Seclusion

Seclusion modernization is also important. JCAHO data of 3,000 sentinel events that caused severe injury or death from 1995 to 2004 indicated that 124 were attributed to restraint, and only 5 to seclusion and 7 to mixed seclusion and restraint (R. Croteau, personal communication, October 20, 2003). Assuming that the total number of seclusion hours was the same as restraint hours, then, on the basis of these data, seclusion would appear to be approximately 20 times safer than restraint. Yet many restrictive intervention reduction efforts have focused on eliminating seclusion and relying on restraint. Given the data this seems highly illogical and contradictory.

Restraint deaths are mostly accounted for by suffocation and chest compression. This does not happen during seclusion because the person is not being held. One could hypothesize also that death is far less likely to result from a patient free to wander around in a locked room than from someone being forcibly held. If indeed seclusion were safer than restraint, then it would be important to discuss whether seclusion should be recommended as medically preferable procedure to restraint.

PTSD and Seclusion. There are two objections to this line of reasoning. First, PTSD symptoms can be triggered in seclusion, as Wadeson and Carpenter (1976) showed. Second, people often require transport and restraint to get them into a seclusion room.

Modernizing seclusion rooms should deal with both these concerns. It may overly restrict our understanding of anger coping to think that calming down oneself is the only function of seclusion, time out, or composure. For some, anger control may be enhanced by these measures. However, for others, engaging in an alternative activity, even a high energy one, might be an effective distraction. Perhaps, anger management rooms should be considered more broadly to be distraction chambers. A distressed person could use the chamber to play nonviolent videos, engage in aggression reduction videos or in a virtual reality exercise, or to contemplate a peaceful picture projected on a screen and listen to restful music. Since they would be voluntary, these seclusion room experiences should not provoke PTSD symptoms, require transport, or need the room door to be closed.

Composure Rooms. Composure rooms have also been developed and are described in the National Association of State Mental Health Program Directors' (NASMHPD) *Resource Manual for the Reduction of Seclusion and Restraint.* However, except for headphones they do not include technologically sophisticated distraction options (Bluebird, 2003). Allowing only for electric lights, fans, and doors that open in case of fire, seclusion rooms are little different from what Dr. Pinel used in 1794 (Gutheil & Daly, 1980). This is an international disgrace, particularly in our Western, "technology-mad" world, where there is a car in every garage and a television in every home and yet we still place leather straps on every restraint table and have locked doors barring the exit of every seclusion room.

Disco Balls and Music Distractions. Some advances in designing distraction chambers have already been described. At Focus Hospital in St. Simons Island, Georgia, a disco ball and a CD machine that played soft music were placed in the time out/seclusion room. Generally, children liked both music and lights, but adolescents preferred lights, and some wanted nothing. Seclusions using this equipment usually lasted less than 20 minutes and often patients at their request used the room as an open quiet room (Masters, 2003).

In the Netherlands, Snoezelen rooms were developed to provide a feeling of restfulness and comfort to patients with chronic illnesses and rehabilitation issues (Condell Health Network, n.d.). However, these rooms have not yet been adapted with devices like virtual reality equipment or large screens, which could engage an upset or traumatized person in the heat of an emotional crisis. One intriguing adaptation of video technology was on display at Discovery Place, Charlotte, North Carolina in the spring of 2005. A person stood in front of a screen that projected his silhouette in color as he moved or danced. It offered the ability to become absorbed in one's own movements. This is an example of using modern technology to promote awareness of personal boundaries, as well as provide for de-escalation from anger and distraction from distressing feelings. Safety is one problem with agitated and angry people using the equipment described, but that likely could be remedied by engineering strategies that would make these calming devices safe to use. Objection to this idea could stem from concern that these rooms would be a constant distraction and they would be used to escape other treatment components. How to integrate this technology with other treatments needs to be the subject of clinical study to prevent misuse and promote optimal benefits. For example, virtual reality screens and head gear might lead to successful strategies for treatment that already exist for phobias, PTSD, and anger control.

Conclusion and Recommendations for the Future

The Pinel Test. The Pinel Test provides a basis for identifying promising avenues for restrictive intervention development. It requires that any modernization in restrictive interventions: a) would have to be appropriate with a collegial provider/consumer relationship, and b) employ safer and more humane equipment than those Dr. Pinel used in his procedures. A multidisciplinary international group—including physicians—as described in this chapter, could be established then to guide "Pinel positive" interventions, direct their use, and study the impact of their implementation. This group would be charged with developing a global vision with attention to research the current use of restrictive interventions in society, and the training and education needs of practitioners, clients, and agencies.

The group would seek out research partnerships with those in allied fields; promote quality studies of modernizing efforts with restrictive interventions; provide public education; provide consultation to those using seclusion and restraint procedures, and speak out against abusive or improper use of these methods; convene periodic international conferences to promote studies and share information in the field; and seek publication of important findings in its own publications, other appropriate journals, and in the public press. Ultimately this work should become important to all of us because it would improve the understanding and ability to manage the effects of trauma and to decrease the level of violence in modern society.

References

Academy of Child and Adolescent Psychiatry. (2005). Practice parameter for the assessment and treatment of children and adolescents with reactive attachment disorder of infancy and early childhood. *Journal of the American Academy of Child and Adolescence Psychiatry, 44*, 1206–1220.

American Association of Community Psychiatrists (AACP). (no date). AACP guidelines for recover oriented services, draft 3. In National Association of State Mental Health Program Directors, (Eds.), *Resource manual for the reduction of seclusion and restrain,* (Chapter 4, item 10). Alexandria, VA: National Technical Assistance Center for State Mental Health Planning.

American Psychiatric Association. (2002, June). *Position statement on reactive attachment disorder.* Document 200205. Washington DC: Author.

American Psychiatric Association. (2003). *2003 APA Gold Award: A more compassionate model for treating children with severe mental disturbances.* Available online at http://ps.psychiatryonline.org/cgi/content/full/54/11/1529. Washington, DC: Author.

Ayres, A. J., Erwin, P. R., Mailloux, Z., & Love, J. (2004). *Inspiration for families living with the dysfunction of sensory integration.* Santa Rosa, CA: Crestport Press.

Barnett, S., dos Rios, S., & Riddle, M. A. (2002). The Maryland Youth Practice Committee for Mental Health. *Journal of the American Academy of Child and Adolescent Psychiatry, 41*, 897–905.

Bennington-Davis, M., & Murphy, T. (2005). Engaging environments. Presentation at the Symposium on Examining the Safety of High-Risk Interventions in Children and Young People, June 1–4, 2005. Abstract available online at http://rccp.cornell.edu/symposium.htm. Ithica, NY: Cornell University.

Blair, R. J., Budhani, S., Colledge, E., & Scott, S. (2005). Deafness to fear in boys with psychopathic tendencies. *Journal of Child Psychology and Psychiatry, 46*, 327–336.

Bluebird, G. (2003). Comfort rooms. In National Technical Assistance Center for State Mental Health Planning, & National Association of State Mental Health Directors, (Eds.) *National Executive Training Institute resource manual for the reduction of seclusion and restraint,* (Chapter 7, item 8). Alexandria, VA: National Technical Assistance Center for State Mental Health Planning, National Association of State Mental Health Directors.

Blum, D. (2002). *Love at Goon Park. Harlow and the science of affection.* Cambridge, MA: Perseus.

Community Works. (2006). *The sanctuary model.* Available online at www.sanctuaryweb.com/main/Sanctuary%20model.htm. Philadelphia: Author.

Condell Health Network. (n.d.). *Snoezelen sensory room offers unique therapy.* Available online at www.condell.org/libertyville/pact/snoezelen.php. Libertyville, IL: Author.

Connor, K., & Butterfield, M. (2003). Posttraumatic stress disorder. *Focus the Journal of Life Long Learning in Psychiatry, 1*(3), 248.

Cotton, N. (1993). *Lessons from the lion's den.* San Francisco: Jossey-Bass.

Edelson, S. M. (1996). *Temple Grandin's 'Hug Machine'.* Available online at www.autism.org/hugbox.html. Salem, OR: Center for the Study of Autism.

Frederici, R. (1997). *Help for the hopeless child.* Alexandria, VA: Hennage.

Gutheil, T. G., & Daly, M. (1980). Clinical considerations in seclusion room design. *Hospital and Community Psychiatry, 31*, 268–270.

Joint Commission Resources. (2002). *Sentinel event alert number 8*. Oakbrook Terrace, IL: JCAHO, 22, 1–2.

Kaplan, A. (2005, April). Virtual reality therapy beyond combat. *Psychiatric Times*, *22*(4), 10–11.

Kesey, K. (1963). *One flew over the cuckoo's nest*. New York: New American Library.

LeBel, J. (2006). Rediscovering pathways to compassionate care. *Academy of Child and Adolescent Psychiatry News, 37*(17), 50–51.

Lundbeck Institute. (no date). *Anxiety as brain disorder*. Available online at www.brainexplorer.org/anxiety/ Anxiety_Epidemiology.shtml. Skodsborg, Denmark: Author.

Martin, A., Fawcett, P. A., & Lee, T. (2004). Seclusion and restraint: "One hour rule" [Letter to the editor]. *Journal of the American Academy of Child and Adolescence Psychiatry, 43*, 1322–1324.

Masters, K. (1999, June). The medical and psychological dangers of physical restraints. Presentation at the Reactive Attachment Disorder Conference, Asheville, NC.

Masters, K. (2003). Findings from a comprehensive inpatient prevention and aggression management program. [Abstract]. Scientific proceedings of the 50th anniversary meeting of the American Academy of Child and Adolescent Psychiatry, Miami Beach, FL, 68.

Masters, K. J. (2006a, January/February). What pulse oximetry can do for you: How to improve restraint monitoring. *IANCICI's Supportive Stance, 5*(1).

Masters, K. J. (2006b). Improving restraint monitoring with pulse oximetry. *Residential Group Care Quarterly, 6*(4), 4–5. Available online at www.cwla.org/programs/groupcare/rgcqspring2006.pdf

Masters, K. J., & Penn, J. V. (2005). Juvenile justice + restrictive interventions = fragmentation. *Academy of Child and Adolescent Psychiatry News, 36*, 164, 172.

Masters, K., & Wandless, D. (2005). Use of pulse oximetry during restraint episodes [Letter to the editor]. *Psychiatric Services, 56*(10), 1313.

Nunno, M., Holden, M., & Tollar, A. (2006). Learning from tragedy: A survey of child and adolescent restraint fatalities. *Child Abuse & Neglect: An International Journal, 30*(12), 1333–1342.

Petti, T. A., Mohr, W. K., Somers, J., & Sims, L. (2001). Perception of seclusion and restraint in an intermediate-term care facility. *Journal of Child and Adolescent Psychiatric Nursing, 14*, 115–117.

Pinel, P. (1983). *A treatise on insanity* (D. Davis, Trans.) (Original work published 1806). Birmingham, AL: Sheffield, Todd.

Roberts, A. (1981). *William Norris*. Middlesex University Resource: Mental Health History Time Line. Available online at www.mdx.ac.uk/www/study/mhhtim.htm#1814. Middlesex University, England: Author.

Ryan, R. (2001, May 7). *Seclusion and restraint in the developmentally disabled*. Seminar conducted at the American Psychiatric Association Annual meeting, New Orleans, LA.

Schatzberg, A. F. (2005). Recent studies in the biology and treatment of depression. *Focus the Journal of Life Long Learning in Psychiatry, 3*(1), 14.

Schur, S., Sikish, L., Findling, R. L., Malone, R. P., Crismon M. L., Dervian, A., Macintyre II, J., Pappadopulos, E., Greenhill, L., Schooler, N., Van Orden, K., & Jensen, P. (2003). Treatment recommendations for the use of antipsychotic for aggressive youth (TRAAY) Part I. *Journal of the American Academy of Child and Adolescent Psychiatry, 42*, 132–144.

Talley, O. (Producer). (2004, June 29). *Dr. Ron Frederici on Dateline*. New York: CBS News.

Teplin, L. A., Abram, K. M., McClelland, G. M., Dulcan, M. K., & Mericle, A. A. (2002). Psychiatric disorders in youth in juvenile detention. *Archives of General Psychiatry, 59,* 1133-1143.

Thomas, N. (1997). *When love is not enough.* Evergreen, CO: Family by Design.

Tomes, N. (1988). The great restraint controversy: A comparative perspective an Anglo-American psychiatry in the nineteenth century. In R. Porter, W. F. Bynum, & W. F. Shepherd (Eds.). *The anatomy of madness: Essays on the history of psychiatry* (pp. 190–225). London: Routledge.

Viding, E. (2004). Understanding the development of psychopathy. *Journal of Child Psychology and Psychiatry, 45,* 1329–1337.

Wadeson, N., & Carpenter, W. (1976). Impact of the seclusion room experience. *The Journal of Nervous and Mental Diseases, 163,* 318–328.

Weiner, D. (1992). Philippe Pinel's "Memoir on madness" of December 11, 1794: A fundamental text of modern psychiatry. *The American Journal of Psychiatry, 149,* 725–732.

Weiss, E. M., Altimari, D., Blint, D. F., & Megan, K. (1998, October 11–15). Deadly restraint: A nationwide pattern of death. *Hartford Courant.*

Welch, M. (1989). *Holding time.* New York: Fireside.

Wikipedia. (no date). *Franz Mesmer.* Available online at http://en.wikipedia.org/wiki/Franz_Mesmer.

PART III

ENSURING SAFETY AND MANAGING RISK

CHAPTER 4

Physical Restraints

Are They Ever Safe and How Safe Is Safe Enough?

Wanda K. Mohr

DESPITE THE SUCCESS in passing legislation regulating restraints and in spite of the impressive success of some states in reducing their use, the debate concerning restraints continues with some professionals and advocates declaring that they are dangerous (Mohr, Petti, & Mohr, 2003) and others stating that they have a place in the therapeutic armament and can actually be beneficial for some individuals (Troutman, Myers, Borchardt, Kowalski, & Bubrick, 1998; Cotton, 1989). Opinions differ as to the utility or efficacy of restraints and concern has been raised about their use in psychiatric settings, particularly those settings that treat children and adolescents. This chapter analyzes the literature on physically restraining patients as viewed through Fischoff and his colleagues' (1993) concept of "acceptable risk" and discusses whether physical restraints meet the criteria of acceptable risk and constitute a safe form of intervention in the psychiatric tool kit.

The Concepts of Safety and Risk

In the increasingly litigious United States, a common denominator of a growing number of decisions facing medical professionals is the need to determine "how safe is safe enough?" Safety denotes a status that is extensively free of adverse effects or is regarded as nondangerous. Maintaining and promoting safe and competent care are key components of the ethical codes of many health care professionals (e.g., see American Nurses Association, 2001; American Medical Association, 2005). Amid growing concerns for patient safety in the complex health care arena, the Institute of Medicine called for healthcare systems to become more "safe, effective, patient-centered, timely, efficient, and equitable" (Institute of Medicine, 2003, p. 2).

Patient and staff safety are key elements in staff members' decisions to restrain potentially dangerous and out-of-control child and adolescent patients. Staff who are in a situation in which they believe that their patients are becoming violent or unsafe are faced with making a decision, in effect a choice among alternative actions. These alternative actions may have certain attendant risks. Risk is the potential harm that may arise from some present process or from some future event. It is often mapped to the probability of some event that is seen as undesirable.

The field of risk—whether it is defined as risk assessment, risk perception, risk communication, or risk management—is a relatively young one. It has no ready academic home, although scientists, engineers, social scientists, and humanists have made important contributions to the collective project. The first, and among the most crucial, conceptualizations of risk emerged from engineers who had to determine whether and under what conditions human-created systems would break down (Douglas & Wildavsky, 1982). Although engineers provided the foundation for the original understanding, risk assessment may also be applied to natural occurrences. For example, because of 50 years of data points as well as ongoing scientific investigation, the United States National Weather Service can fairly successfully predict the storm track that individual hurricanes will take as they approach North America (Monomonier, 1999).

The Acceptable Risk Model

In their monograph on risk, Fischoff, Lichenstein, Slovic, Derby, and Keeney (1993) posit that the risk associated with the most acceptable action can be conceived of as an acceptable risk. The acceptability of a risk depends on a great many factors, none of which exists in isolation. Acceptable risk problems include a threat to life or health among their consequences. In this work they analyze why acceptable risk problems are so difficult to resolve and they draw on their own experience in risk management, as well as the research literatures, to discuss the variety of methods that have been proposed for resolving acceptable risk problems. Fischoff et al. (1993) have constructed a framework or model that speaks to making decisions about risk and acceptable risk problems.

The model lists five generic complexities that characterize real world acceptable risk decisions: (a) uncertainty about how to define the decision problem (including attendant consequences of the decision); (b) difficulties in assessing the facts of the matter; (c) uncertainties about the human element in the decision-making process; (d) difficulties in assessing the quality of the decisions that are produced; and (e) difficulties in assessing relevant values.

The objective of any risk assessment is to determine the overall level of risk that the organization can tolerate for the given situation. Fischoff and his colleagues contend that the risk acceptance level is the maximum overall exposure to risk that should be accepted, based on the benefits and costs involved. If the responses to risk cannot bring the risk exposure to below this level, the activity will probably need to be stopped.

Although the *Acceptable Risk* monograph focuses primarily on technological hazards, the analysis may apply to many risks, such as the introduction of new medications or medical treatments or the risks attendant in a pest control program. The model can provide a useful heuristic to study risk and against which to compare the very real elements and contexts that characterize the clinical situation of children in mental health settings.

In the following sections, each of these complexities is discussed in view of what we know about the use of physical restraints in child psychiatric populations and whether any use of restraints is acceptable under their criteria.

Uncertainty About Problem Definition

Decision problems cannot be resolved or a decision made at all, absent a definition of the problem. The elements of such a definition involve identifying both the problem and what options exist to resolve the problem, as well as what consequences should be considered. However, what elements are involved in actual restraint and seclusion, as well as what factors are involved in the event for which the interventions take place is elusive.

Restraints and seclusion are typically performed in response to behavior that is deemed violent, disruptive, out-of-control, or dangerous to self, others or property. However, determining clear definitions of these terms and concepts is elusive. Moreover, definitions of restraint and seclusion vary widely from hospital to hospital, from state to state, and in the research literature. Even the U.S. federal government regulatory agencies cannot agree on what restraint and seclusion entail with agencies defining physical restraint in accordance with their own statutory authorities.

Definitions of violence or aggression are problematic and can vary widely. Specifically the measure of such behaviors is fraught with variability. Often, in clinical or research settings there is a single unstandardized measure to represent the construct of violent behavior. In this case the measure and the construct are one and the same, with the measure representing the ideal construct. It is presumed that the clinical and research communities have agreed on this ideal construct (in this case violent behavior), when in fact, they have not. Moreover, having a measure to exclusively represent a construct as important and multidimensional as violence is like having one kind of assessment instrument with which to make clinical decisions, regardless of patients' histories, contexts, and uniquely individual characteristics. In other words, one person's violence and aggression is not analogous to another's and, in fact, may require a different type of inquiry, evaluation, research approach, and intervention.

Thus, an operational definition of aggressive or violent behavior is critical and what constitutes the behavior must be described exactly so that everyone is consistent in identifying it. Assuming everyone agrees that punching a staff member in the face is a violent behavior, like any other behavior, this behavior may have one function or multiple functions. Child A may exhibit such behavior because she has been asked to perform a task that exceeds her capacity to perform and she has learned that hitting removes her from what she perceives to be an aversive environment. Child B may exhibit such behavior because he has found that it is a way of getting a certain attention from his peer group. Studying the behavior through a thorough functional assessment is the only way to tease out what the functions are, under what circumstances they occur, and thus to determine the most appropriate and effective ways to intervene.

Moreover, the absence of scientifically credible information and research into the issues of aggression and violence and its treatment are impediments to effective intervention and prevention efforts. A fundamental issue underlying how well we address a problem is concerned with the quality of measurement technology. High quality measures inform high quality research and practice. To develop effective interventions, high quality measures of variables that are theoretically relevant to the target interventions targeted toward the problem, are necessary (Boruch, 1997). Unfortunately in the areas of violent behavior, seclusion, and restraint, we have a wealth of theories, constructs, and ideas, but precious little in terms of measures and operational and standard definitions. Such a lack of uniformity in definitions, data elements, and attendant measurement technologies constitute a barrier to treatment and data collection. Clearly a research-based, comprehensive, and standardized taxonomy that would include problem classification, intervention, and outcome components would enhance practice, documentation, research and information management. In its absence we are left with a body of formless information based on hearsay, impression, and imprecise recollection.

What Are the Consequences?

A consequence is a description of the result or effect that will occur from carrying out a program or activity, or a long-term, ultimate measure of success or strategic effectiveness. Consequences can be intended or desirable, or unintended. Therapeutic interventions intend to be therapeutic and make people well, but they can harm as well as heal. The harm that a therapeutic intervention causes is exemplified by "iatrogenic" (care-induced) and "nosocomial" (hospital-associated) injury.

In addition to the physical harm, or death, that can befall an individual subjected to the use of the restraints, the negative impact on the psychological well-being of individuals being restrained and the culture of facilities using the restraints are also significant. Studies have been conducted on the patient's subjective experience of restraints (Steckley & Kendrick, chapter 1, this volume). The consequences of restraint or seclusion use have been documented in many research studies. Consensus emerged from these studies that the majority of patients generally viewed restraint and seclusion experiences as a punitive and coercive experience and that these experiences are counterproductive (Zun, 2003).

A number of representative studies are discussed in subsequent paragraphs, but they do not exhaust the literature on the restraint episode as experienced by patients. It should be noted that the adult literature tends to mirror that of the literature on children, adding to the strength of the points being made in this section.

Mohr, Mahon, and Noone (1998) found that children who had been restrained in inpatient psychiatric settings expressed five years later a profound alienation from staff, no understanding of the reasons for restraints, and symptoms of trauma from their own restraints as well as vicarious traumatization. Vicarious traumatization referred to the experience of seeing others restrained. Restraint served to alienate the children from clinical staff and the actual restraint experience caused direct trauma. The participants, all formerly hospitalized patients, at a five-year follow-up, recalled the event negatively and viewed it as punishment and as an event where staff used force based on power. Restraint was not recalled as a positive or therapeutic intervention. To illustrate the kinds of damage that was done to the therapeutic alliance, one of Mohr's participants stated that she would never go to a mental health professional again.

In an interesting study on unintended consequences of restraint use, Magee and Ellis (2001) found that under conditions in which physical restraint (i.e., basket-hold timeout) was applied to children, contingent on problem behavior, rates of the problematic behaviors actually increased in a sample of developmentally delayed children.

Similarly, Kahng, Abt, and Wilder (2001) evaluated a treatment for collateral self-injurious behavior (SIB) correlated with mechanical restraint. Caregivers used mechanical arm restraints to decrease hand-head SIB exhibited by a 16-year-old female with severe mental retardation. Although mechanical restraints reduced hand-head SIB, they were correlated with an increase in other types of SIB (e.g., head banging).

The above studies underscore the dangers of the unintended consequences that may come about when an intervention that is employed in a clinical setting with the intention of producing one result, in this case safety, produces a different and often conflicting result. They emphasize the real world problems that are associated with employing interventions, such as restraints, that have neither an adequate theoretical or research basis.

What Is the Hazard?

As previously noted, restraints have the potential to produce serious consequences, such as physical and psychological harm and loss of dignity. But the most serious adverse effect of restraint use is death.

In the health care literature, Evans, Wood, and Lambert (2003) conducted a comprehensive search that involved all major databases to investigate physical restraint related injury. Their findings suggest that physical restraint may increase the risk of falls, serious injury, and death. They found case reports that described sudden death and death secondary to asphyxia in restrained individuals and they discovered that retrospective investigations of death certificates and records have identified a large number of restraint-related deaths.

An important study conducted by Nunno, Holden, and Tollar (2006) recorded 45 child and adolescent fatalities related to restraint in residential (institutional) placements in the United States from 1993 to 2003. Unfortunately, the data reported by Nunno, Holden, and Tollar had to be accessed through news media reports, as there is no systematic way of reporting such data, suggesting that those data are disproportionately low.

Mohr, Petti, and Mohr (2003) searched the electronic databases Medline, Cinahl, and PsycINFO, reviewing the areas of forensics and pathology, nursing, cardiology, immunology, psychology, neurosciences, psychiatry, emergency medicine, and sports medicine to ascertain what literature was available on the topic of death proximal to restraint use. They identified asphyxiation as the most common reported cause of restraint-related death, but also found death by aspiration, blunt trauma to the chest (commotio cordis), malignant cardiac rhythm disturbances secondary to massive catecholamine rush, thrombosis, rhabdomyolosis, excited delirium with overwhelming metabolic acidosis, and pulmonary embolism to be conditions implicated in deaths proximal to physical restraint use.

In addition, they suggested that the potential adverse effects of restraints might be increased with the use of psychotropic medications, with children being particularly susceptible to certain drug class effects. For example, among the drugs commonly used for treatment of pain, tricyclic antidepressants have the highest anticholinergic properties and can also impact adrenergic transmission (McFee, Mofenson, & Caraccio, 2000). The peripheral anticholinergic effects of tricyclic antidepressants, which reduce sweating, can interfere with normal thermoregulatory responses during a period of intense activity, such as fighting against staff or restraints. This can lead to hyperthermia. Children, by virtue of their small size, are particularly vulnerable to this effect. Moreover, children are particularly susceptible to commotio cordis (blunt trauma to the chest resulting in a malignant ventricular fibrillation) because of their thin chest walls (Link, 2003). Unfortunately rapid defibrillation does not necessarily save these children from death (Weinstock, Maron, Song, Mane, Estes, & Link, 2006).

In response to the alarm raised by the media, advocates, and professionals at the numbers of restraint deaths, manufacturers marketed a restraint chair to correctional facilities, asserting that it was a "more humane" way of restraining violent and out-of-control youth in juvenile justice facilities. Because the individual is restrained in an upright, sitting position, the manufacturers suggested that it would be a less traumatizing and safer method of restraint. This assertion, as with those made by the vendors of many aggression-management programs, however, had no research studies supporting such claims (Cusac, 2000). Amnesty International raised concerns about using a restraint chair with juveniles in correctional facilities and a later report found that during a two year period, from 2000 to 2002, at least four persons died after being restrained using the restraint chair (Amnesty International, 2002). Between 1994 and 2000, 11 deaths were linked to using the restraint chair (Cusac, 2000). The cause of death in these cases included excessive force used during the restraint, stroke, cardiac arrest, blood clots, and asphyxia. In addition, medical complications from its use included permanent nerve damage and spinal compression, resulting in loss of upper body mobility (see Project NoSpank, 2006a, 2006b).

Finally, P. Day (2002), in a meta-analysis for the New Zealand Health Technology Assessment (NZHTA) Clearing House for Health Outcomes and Health Technology Assessment, concluded that the quality of the evidence about the safety of restraints as employed by law enforcement and health care professionals was very low. The overall evidence for the safety of physical restraint use actually indicated that its use might be contributory to serious adverse effects in behaviorally disturbed individuals.

If one surveys the psychiatric literature, the incidence of death seems to be a relatively rare event. However, in the absence of any sustained data collection across diverse settings, deaths associated with restraint use may not be as rare as a first impression might suggest. There are several reasons for this. Only recently have government agencies required facilities to report such deaths. Also, in surveying the Lexus Nexus databases, the deaths that are gleaned from such a search do not all occur in psychiatric facilities that are governed by the Joint Commission on Accreditation of Healthcare Organizations (JCAHO) or the Center for Medicare and Medicate Services (CMS) regulations. There are myriad "therapeutic boarding schools," behavior modification schools, boot camps, and wilderness camps in which deaths have occurred. These deaths have only come to light as a result of media scrutiny and the attention of plaintiff attorneys. Finally, there are deaths that have occurred proximal to restraint use in police custody. For example, O'Halloran and Frank (2000) reported on 21 asphyxial deaths occurring during prone restraint; 18 of these occurred in police custody or during an altercation with police. These restraint deaths do not appear in any database concerned with gathering statistics on adverse effects of restraint use.

Difficulty in Assessing Facts

Assessing the facts of a situation presumes that individuals are aware of how to recognize those facts and that they can agree on them. As social psychologists have demonstrated repeatedly throughout many years, eyewitnesses to events are extraordinarily unreliable as to what they report (Hastie, Ostrom, Ebbeson, Wyer, Hamilton, & Carlston, 1980). Principal among the factors germane to witnessing are perception, memory, communication, and candor. Even trained observers, e.g., law enforcement officers, can make erroneous identifications and evaluation in exigencies of the moment (Loftus & Doyle, 1997).

Systematic observation and fact-finding process are based on the premises that observers or witnesses can reconstruct the truth based on perception, memory, and recollection. But the capacity of the human sensory organs to perceive is limited. Perceptions are molded by expectation, sometimes known as "mind set" or "set." People perceive what they expect to perceive and what they think is expected of them. Witnesses want to live up to the expectations of the system, as well as their expectations of themselves. Rosenhan (1973) demonstrated this quite dramatically in his classic study "On Being Sane in Insane Places." In the Rosenhan study, several sane individuals had themselves admitted to various psychiatric facilities and on admission they complained of hearing voices and no other symptoms. Thereafter, they were instructed to act "normally" and not mention voices again. They each found themselves admitted with a severe diagnosis, labeled as "crazy," and all of their actions and behaviors were described in the medical record as being derived from their presumed pathology.

Moreover, observers are also influenced in their perceptions by biases, prejudices, interests, and motives. Psychologists have learned that perception is a decision-making process, one that is influenced by attitudes, background, abilities, environment, and the way that the witness' perception is tested. The same is true for memory (Loftus & Doyle, 1997).

Another problematic consideration with assessment of facts has to do with communication, candor, and the use of psychiatric jargon to describe behaviors (Olson & Mohr, 2002). Jargon is the specialized language of a trade or profession that functions as a kind of shorthand means of communication between members of the professional group. Jargon can often be efficient and descriptive as a means of communication, but it can often be obfuscatory, pretentious, and can be employed to make the ordinary seem extraordinary or profound. Psychiatric jargon, as opposed to data based observations, is not theory-neutral because it is an *interpretation* of behavioral events.

An important assumption that underlies the way in which most mental health providers use psychiatric jargon is that the label, qualifier, or descriptive term means the same thing to all practitioners and is consistently applied to the same phenomenon. This assumption creates serious barriers to attaining accurate and reliable assessments, recording of progress, and reliable treatment outcomes, simply because it is flawed. For decades there has been little agreement among mental health practitioners regarding the basic events of psychopathology, psychotherapy, and psychiatric interventions. Assessments, labels, problems, and interventions are defined differently depending on the disciplinary lens or level of education through which they are viewed. This reality can distort the clinical picture.

As a way of knowing—an epistemology—a discipline uses distinctive analytic tools, concepts, methods, units of analysis, and its own specialized terminologies and forms of communication. This becomes especially apparent as a barrier to interdisciplinary work when assumptions of mutual understanding across perspectives cannot be made. An example of this is the case when a clinical behavioral psychologist shares an applied behavioral analysis with a physician who is concerned with Lithium levels and their effects on explosive behavior and a registered nurse who sees his role as maintaining a therapeutic and reasonably harmonious milieu. Identification of mutually shared concepts across perspectives with three such divergent approaches may seem unattainable unless the two professionals find a common ground on which they can agree. While all three are important goals, a narrow focus through the lens of a single perspective can provide a very narrow view of a complex situation and thereby also limit the range of possible therapeutic interventions.

Unfortunately, we cannot even assume that all staff are talking about the same constructs and events and attaching different words or labels to them. Fifty years ago, Carl Rogers (1957) concluded not only do practitioners apply different labels to the same phenomena, but they also apply the same label to different phenomena.

Ideally, jargon terms should be followed by an objective observation that justifies using that term, in other words, data. Thus, if a note in the chart indicates that a particular patient was secluded or restrained because he was engaging in "aggressive behavior and that he was a threat to himself or others" it is incumbent on the professional who makes such a note to describe the aggressive behavior (for example, was the patient kicking or choking someone or merely cursing loudly and making obscene or threatening gestures) and then to justify why these behaviors constituted a threat such that it became necessary to subject the patient to a potentially deadly intervention. The term *aggressive behavior* is subject to multiple interpretations, as is being a threat to oneself or others, and is often used as a shorthand way to justify restraining a patient. These terms should be described and defined operationally by the professional who is recording the events in the medical record. An operational definition of aggressive behavior would justify the use of the label as to what the person making the entry really means. It would break down the term to a series of discrete and objective descriptive observations. Accuracy in communication is important in a legal-historical sense, because all that remains of a person's hospitalization and in assessing the relevant facts that transpire during that hospitalization is the medical record and the inaccurate and unreliable memories of all who are concerned with his care (Mohr, 2006).

In addition to using a data-based language that provides an accurate picture of the patient's treatment, psychiatric professionals and staff are charged with being nonjudgmental. However, too often the medical record can say more about how the staff views the patient, than about her condition. Mohr and Noone (1997) conducted a study in which they coded a total of 4,321 entries made by registered nurses in psychiatric medical records. The number of non-pejorative adjectives used to describe patients was outnumbered by pejorative adjectives that presented a negative connotation of the patient, by three to one.

In a second example, Mohr (1999) studied over 500 medical records and described nine categories of entries made by registered nurses or other staff. Only 1% of entries reflected any kind of positive assessment of patients. In contrast more than 20% of entries emerged under categories designated as pejorative, inane, punitive, and nonsensical. In view of the above studies, a reliance on the observation of staff as expressed in their language must be viewed as flawed and colored by values, perceptions, and role expectations. As their perceptions, expectations, and values can distort objective assessment and observation, so they might color staff's attitude and subsequent behavior with respect to patients. Thus, once a child is labeled as "aggressive" or "a trouble maker" they may tend to be scrutinized that way and treated accordingly.

Uncertainty About the Human Element

Those who provide care for people with psychiatric problems must understand the content of the subject matter, the patients with whom they work, and the nature of the environment in which they work. One of the major challenges and uncertainty in psychiatric settings is finding appropriate, educated, and experienced staff. Working with psychiatric patients is challenging, demanding, and often frustrating. Although physicians are the professionals in psychiatric settings who most often order restraints, it is up to the nursing staff to assess patients and carry out the ordered intervention. An examination of the kinds of educational requirements required of medical and other staff reveals that they are woefully inadequately prepared to assess and deal with aggressive behavior. School and residency training for psychiatrists does not include training on crisis response or crisis de-escalation techniques (NAMI, 2003). Likewise nurses receive little in the way of exposure to the issue of aggression and aggressive management in their educational programs (Mohr & Anderson, 2001) and there is little content on the subject in most nursing textbooks.

In addition, the stability of the workforce is a further source of uncertainty. The quality of care in psychiatric settings rests primarily in the hands of nurses and nursing assistants/mental health aides. National data on turnover in psychiatric facilities are not available, but if the data on nursing home and long-term care facilities are any indication, it is quite high (Banaszak-Holl & Hines, 1996). A recent report in *New York City Voices* stated that the annual staff turnover in psychiatric facilities in New York State was as high as 54% (Saperia, 2002). In one study (Ito, Eisen, Sederer, Yamada, & Tachimori, 2001) 44.3% of the nurses surveyed intended to leave their jobs in psychiatric facilities within the year. These numbers are of concern because they suggest turbulent workplace environments, uncertainty, lost productivity, low morale, and potentially detrimental influences on the quality of care delivered to patients (Argote, Insko, Yovetich, & Romero, 1995).

As posited in the above studies, the quantity and quality of the human element and the potential for staff to render educated care, as well as continuity of care is compromised both by lack of education and by lack of a stable workforce.

Uncertainty About the Quality of Decision Making

Another issue to be considered in ascertaining facts is whether staff actually know how to recognize potentially violent situations in order to act upon them. The literature suggests otherwise. Morrison (1993) asked expert psychiatric nurse practitioners to compare the seriousness of violent incidents. Although the group had similar educational backgrounds and the same disciplinary lens, they were in considerable disagreement within and between groups regarding the seriousness of the incidents. Likewise, in another study Holzworth and Wills (1999) demonstrated that nurses show considerable individual differences in making strategic recommendations for 80 hypothetical patients.

In reviews of factors contributing to the use of restraint, the common belief is that the use of restraints is dictated by the behavioral presentation of the patient at the time a restraint is applied (Delaney, 2002). However, the central factor contributing to the use of restraints lies in the individual staff's perceptions of the seriousness of the behaviors displayed and that much inconsistency is present in the evaluations of behaviors across staff (Mohr & Anderson, 2001).

All of the above points raise serious questions, not only about the ability of staff to agree upon facts and observations and make evaluative judgments of potentially violent situations needing intervention, but also their ability to accurately communicate these facts.

Difficulty in Assessing Relevant Values

Each person, staff member, professional, or patient has a code of values that we hold individually and jointly with some culture or subculture. This code may be implicit or explicit, but it is often reflected in our behaviors. Values underlying behaviors are beliefs about a condition or circumstance that have meaning and importance. Groups of people hold multiple beliefs that are compatible and support each other. They often take these for granted and believe them to be true. Shared values are the means by which people are brought into organizational or group subcultures. Subcultures are meaning systems, modes of expression or life styles developed by groups in subordinate structural positions in response to dominant meaning systems, and which reflect their attempt to solve structural contradictions arising from the wider societal context (Trice & Beyer, 1993). Most often this is done by "learning the ropes" and being immersed in the subculture.

The difficulties in assessing values in a psychiatric organization have to do with differing subcultural values, some of which may be in conflict. Problems may arise between staff who see their role as that of police-manning and milieu control (see Morrison's 1992 study on "The Tradition of Toughness") and patients who perceive of themselves as autonomous and oppressed individuals (Mohr, 2003).

In any such contradictory situation, there is bound to be conflict with those in power who have been socialized into their police-manning role, taking that role to extremes. The social psychology literature says much about sharing of values and socialization into such subcultures. In 1971, a team of psychologists designed and executed an unusual simulation that used a mock prison setting, with college students role-playing prisoners and guards to test the power of the social situation to influence behavior (Zimbardo, Haney, Banks, & Jaffe, 1973). The research, known as the Stanford Prison Experiment (SPE), has become a classic demonstration of situational power in influencing individual attitudes, values, and behavior. So extreme, swift, and unexpected were the transformations of character in many of the participants that this study, planned to last two-weeks, had to be terminated by the sixth day. The SPE has become one of psychology's most dramatic illustrations of how good people can be transformed into perpetrators of evil, and healthy people can begin to experience pathological reactions, traceable to situational forces.

Likewise, the hierarchy that exists in psychiatric hospitals creates further uncertainty with institutional values and staff members' penchant to obey their superiors creating further uncertainty and a clash of values. Stanley Milgram's experiments are not often discussed outside of the psychology arena, but their results have held up for almost 50 years.

Milgram (1974) conducted the most widely cited obedience experiments in history. Conducted in the 1960s they were intended to measure the willingness of a participant to obey an authority who instructs the participant to do something that may conflict with the participant's personal conscience. In Milgram's experiments, people were directed to administer shocks of increasing intensity and pain to subjects. The experiment included 40 participants, of which 27 (65%) administered the experiment's final 450-volt shock, though many were quite uncomfortable in doing so. No participant stopped before the 300-volt level. Milgram himself and other psychologists around the world later performed variants of the experiment with similar results. Blass (1999) performed a meta-analysis on the results of repeated performances of the experiment (done at various times since, in the United States and elsewhere). He found that the percentage of participants who are prepared to inflict fatal voltages remains remarkably constant, between 61% and 66%, regardless of time or location.

Given this body of work, it is clear that there is uncertainty about the values of different members of a psychiatric institution, a potential malintegration of organizational and personal values, and inevitable anxiety that may result from such incongruity. Encounters between patients and staff may become painful and disruptive as both seek to assert what is of value to them.

Discussion

Despite their long history as an intervention in psychiatric settings, restraints are interventions without sound theoretical bases or research foundation.

David Day (2002) concluded that the theoretical paradigms used to support restraint use are outdated and found that there is very limited empirical evidence to support the therapeutic utility of restrictive measures or research that could be used to inform practice. Others have noted these same observations (Martin, 2002; Selekman & Snyder, 1996). Employing such an understudied intervention is at best a dubious enterprise.

Moreover, one cannot take comfort from trainings on safe restraint use. In a case series report of 63 cases involving restraint death, Rubin, Dube, and Mitchell (1993) found that the vast majority of restraint deaths occurred while restraints were correctly applied. This implies an inherent danger in the use of physical restraints.

I began this chapter intending to answer the question of are restraints safe. Given the evidence examined through an acceptable risk framework, the answer must be "no." The acceptability of any intervention technology should depend on the acceptability of its consequences for individual recipients of those interventions. In this light, a technology should be acceptable to an individual if it creates an acceptable balance of personal risks and benefits. So far as the literature suggests in this area, the risks outweigh the benefits and restraints are an unsafe technology.

But it is not sufficient to simply conclude that restraints are not a safe technology for patients. The risks of not using physical restraint in contrast are possible serious injury to the behaviorally disturbed person, to others around them, or to property. Although there has been abundant literature addressing the possible harms of physical restraint use, little has been written examining the benefits of its use (Connick, Palat, & Pugliese, 2000). Because safety concerns (i.e., keeping staff and patients safe) are usually invoked as the ostensible reason for the use of physical restraints, a critical analysis also necessitates determining whether the reduction or elimination of restraint use is unsafe. A brief look at facilities that have reduced or eliminated the use of restraints would suggest that those measures have not compromised patient or staff safety.

Under the leadership of Charles Currie, Pennsylvania reduced restraint use by 90% in six years (from 1996 to 2002); staff and patient injury rates dropped by 74% (See: http://alt.samhsa.gov/seclusion/SRMay5report7.htm; Pennsylvania Patient Safety Reporting System, 2005). Since Pennsylvania's success, others have reported similar reductions. LeBel and colleagues (2004) reported dramatic reductions in restraint and seclusion use on children and adolescent units using a system strength-based approach. Likewise, others have reported substantial reduction of restraint and seclusion use on their units with no greater rates of injury for staff or patients, when a strong commitment to reduce coercive interventions was made by institutional leadership (Sullivan, Besmen, Barron, Rivera, Curley-Casey, & Marino, 2005; McCue, Urcuyo, Lilu, Tobias, & Chambers, 2004; Donovan, Plant, Peller, Siegel, & Martin, 2003). Only one report stated that injury rates for staff increased when a restraint reduction program was initiated (Khadivi, Patel, Atkinson, & Levine, 2004). In that case it was unclear as to how well the staff was supported by way of resources and training. Indeed resources and workload are considerable factors in staff injury. On behalf of the Hospital Employees' Union, Vancouver, BC, Canada, Cohen and his colleagues (2004) examined injury rates, pain, burnout, and self-reported health in an intermediate care psychiatric institution. They found that facilities with low injury rates had better staff-to-resident staffing ratios and that the differences in staffing reflected differences in how organizations prioritized and allocated resources. They concluded that workload is an important determinant of injuries and that increased staffing levels correlate with decreased injuries.

The emerging literature on restraint reduction is dramatic and promising and it challenges long held assumptions about safety. Fischoff et al. (1993) assert that if a hazard is articulated as having been associated with a particular technology, evaluating options directed at each stage of the hazard evolution should be assessed. These include modifying desired outcomes, changing the technology, and preventing initiating events. There are alternatives and options that can become part of the professional tool kit in addressing the issue of aggressive and potentially violent behavior. Although there are no empirically tested programs to support restraint and seclusion reduction and elimination, the National Association of State Mental Health Program Directors (NASMHPD, 1999) has suggested alternative options. These include culture change, approach to restraints as an intervention, and a public health model of prevention. The model includes the following: primary prevention (organizational leadership accountability, empowering strength-based culture, well-trained staff), secondary intervention (knowing triggers and using trauma-informed strategies, creative/innovative early interventions to de-escalate conflict) and tertiary intervention (if intervention is necessary), which will allow for the least traumatic treatment experience, early release, and active debriefing of staff and consumers in order to minimize risk of harm. NASMHPD suggests that feedback from each stage needs to inform the next stage and support ongoing prevention.

The NASMHPD model is promising and intuitively attractive. In the absence of a literature that tests multiple models of restraint reduction and aggression management, our patients deserve nothing less than a commitment to such best practice models in pursuit of interventions that are therapeutic and "safe enough."

References

American Medical Association. (2005). *Code of medical ethics current opinions with annotations, 2004–2005.* Chicago, IL: Author.

American Nurses Association. (2001). *Code of ethics with interpretive statements.* Washington, DC: Author.

Amnesty International. (2002). *Amnesty International Report: USA–The restraint chair: How many more deaths? (AI Index AMR 51/31/2002).* Available online at http://web.amnesty.org/library/index/ engamr510312002.

Argote, L., Insko, C., Yovetich, N., & Romero, O. (1995). The effects of turnover and task complexity on group performance. *Journal of Applied Social Psychology, 25*(6), 512–529.

Banaszak-Holl, J., & Hines, M. A. (1996). Factors associated with nursing home staff turnover. *The Gerontologist, 36,* 512–517.

Blass, T. (1999). The Milgram paradigm after 35 years: Some things we now know about obedience to authority. *Journal of Applied Social Psychology, 25,* 955–978.

Boruch, R. (1997). *Randomized experiments for planning and evaluation: A practical guide.* Thousand Oaks, CA: Sage.

Cohen, M.,Village, J., Ostry, A. S., Ratner, P. A., Cvitkovich, Y., & Yassi, A. (2004). Workload as a determinant of staff injury in intermediate care. *International Journal of Occupational & Environmental Health, 10*(4), 375–383.

Connick, C., Palat, M., & Pugliese, S. (2000). The appropriate use of physical restraint: Considerations. *Journal of Dentistry for Children, 67,* 256–262, 231.

Cotton, N. (1989). The developmental-clinical rationale for the use of seclusion in the psychiatric treatment of children. *American Journal of Orthopsychiatry, 59,* 442–449.

Cusac, A. (2000, April). The devil's chair [Electronic version]. *The Progressive,* 1–12. Available online at www.progressive.org/mag_cusacchair.

Day, D. M. (2002). Examining the therapeutic utility of restraints and seclusion with children and youth: The role of theory and research in practice. *American Journal of Orthopsychiatry, 72,* 266–278.

Day, P. (2002). What evidence exits about the safety of physical restraint when used by law enforcement and medical staff to control individuals with acute behavioural disturbance? *NZHTA Tech Brief Series 2002.* Christchurch, NZ: Department of Public Health and General Practice Christchurch School of Medicine.

Delaney, K. R. (2002). Developing a restraint reduction program for child/adolescent inpatient treatment. *Journal of Child and Adolescent Psychiatric Nursing, 14,* 128–140.

Donovan, A., Plant, R., Peller, A., Siegel, L., & Martin, A. (2003). Two-year trends in the use of seclusion and restraint among psychiatrically hospitalized youths. *Psychiatric Services, 54*(7), 987–993.

Douglas, M., & Wildavsky, A. (1982). *Risk and culture: An essay on the selection of technical and environmental dangers.* Berkeley, CA: University of California Press.

Evans, D., Wood, J., & Lambert, L. (2003). *Patient injury and physical restraint devices: a systematic review. Journal of Advanced Nursing, 412*(3), 274–282.

Fischoff, B., Lichenstein, S., Slovic, P., Derby, S. L., & Keeney, R. L. (1993). *Acceptable risk.* U.K.: Cambridge University Press.

Hastie, R., Ostrom, T. M., Ebbeson, E. B., Wyer, R. S., Hamilton, D. L., & Carlston, D. E. (1980). *Person memory: The cognitive basis of social perception.* Lawrence Erlbaum Associates.

Holzworth, R. J., & Wills, C. E. (1999). Nurses' judgments regarding seclusion and restraint of psychiatric patients: A social judgment analysis. *Research in Nursing and Health, 22,* 189–201.

Institute of Medicine. (2003). *Keeping patients safe: Transforming the work environment of nurses*. Washington, DC: National Academy Press.

Ito, H., Eisen, S. V., Sederer, L. I., Yamada, O., & Tachimori, H. (2001). Factors affecting psychiatric nurses' intention to leave their current job. *Psychiatric Services, 52,* 232–234.

Kahng, S. W., Abt, K. A., & Wilder, M. (2001). Treatment of self-injury correlated with mechanical restraints. *Behavioral Interventions, 16*(2), 105–110.

Khadivi, A. N., Patel, R. C., Atkinson, A. R., & Levine, J. M. (2004). Association between seclusion and restraint and patient-related violence. *Psychiatric Services, 55*(11), 1311–1312.

LeBel, J., Stromberg, N., Duckworth, K., Kerzner, J., Goldstein, R., Weeks, M., Harper, G., LaFlair, L., & Sudders, M. (2004). Child and adolescent inpatient restraint reduction: a state initiative to promote strength-based care. *Journal of the American Academy of Child & Adolescent Psychiatry, 43*(1), 37–45.

Link, M. S. (2003). Mechanically induced sudden death in chest wall impact (commotio cordis). *Progress in Biophysics & Molecular Biology, 82,* 175–86.

Loftus, E. F., & Doyle, J. (1997). *Eyewitness testimony: Civil and criminal, 3d ed.* Charlottesville, VA: Lexis Law Publishing.

Magee, S. K., & Ellis, J. (2001). The detrimental effects of physical restraint as a consequence for inappropriate classroom behavior. *Journal of Applied Behavior Analysis, 34,* 501–504.

Martin, B. (2002). Restraint use in acute and critical care settings: changing practice. *American Association of Colleges of Nursing Clinical Issues, 13,* 294–306.

McCue, R. E., Urcuyo, L., Lilu, Y., Tobias, T., & Chambers, M. J. (2004). Reducing restraint use in a public psychiatric inpatient service. *Journal of Behavioral Health Services & Research, 31*(2), 217–224.

McFee, R., Mofenson, H., & Caraccio, T. (2000). A nationwide survey of the management of unintentional-low dose tricyclic antidepressant ingestions involving asymptomatic children: implications for the development of an evidence-based clinical guideline. *Journal of Toxicology: Clinical Toxicology, 38*(1), 15–19.

Milgram, S. (1974). *Obedience to authority.* New York: Harper & Row.

Mohr, W. K. (1999). Deconstructing the language of psychiatric hospitals. *Journal of Advanced Nursing, 29*(5), 1052–1059.

Mohr, W. K. (2003). The substance of a support group. *Western Journal of Nursing Research, 25*(6), 676–700.

Mohr, W. K. (2006). Psychiatric records. In P. Iyer, B. J. Levin, & M. A. Shea (Eds.), *Medical legal aspects of medical records* (pp. 691–705). Tuscon, AZ: Lawyers & Judges Publishing Company Inc.

Mohr, W. K., & Anderson, J. A. (2001). Faulty assumptions associated with the use of restraints with children. *Journal of Child and Adolescent Psychiatric Nursing, 14*(3), 141–151.

Mohr, W. K., Mahon, M. M., & Noone, M. J. (1998). A restraint on restraints: The need to reconsider restrictive interventions. *Archives of Psychiatric Nursing, 12*(2), 95–106.

Mohr, W. K. & Noone, M. J. (1997). Deconstructing progress notes in psychiatric settings. *Archives of Psychiatric Nursing, 11*(6), 325–332.

Mohr, W. K., Petti, T. A., & Mohr, B. D. (2003). Adverse effects associated with the use of physical restraints. *Canadian Journal of Psychiatry, 48,* 330–337.

Monomonier, M. (1999). *Air apparent: How meteorologists learned to map, predict, and dramatize weather.* Chicago, IL: University of Chicago Press.

Morrison, E. F. (1992). The tradition of toughness. *Image, 20*(4) 222–234.

Morrison, E. F. (1993) Towards a better understanding of violence in psychiatric settings: Debunking the myths. *Archives of Psychiatric Nursing, 7*(6), 328–335.

National Association of State Mental Health Program Directors (NASMHPD). (1999). *NASMHPD position statement on seclusion and restraint.* Alexandria, VA: National Technical Assistance Center for State Mental Health Planning.

National Alliance for the Mentally Ill. (2003, May). *Seclusion and restraint taskforce report.* Arlington, VA: NAMI Policy Research Institute.

National Institute of Medicine. (2001). *Crossing the quality chasm: A new health system for the 21st Century.* Washington, DC: National Academy Press.

Nunno, M., Holden, M., & Tollar, A. (2006). Learning from tragedy: A survey of child and adolescent restraint fatalities. *Child Abuse & Neglect: An International Journal, 30*(12), 1333–1342.

O'Halloran, R. L., & Frank, J. G. (2000). Asphyxial death during prone restraint revisited: A report of 21 cases. *American Journal of Forensic Medicine and Pathology, 21,* 39–52.

Olson, J. N., & Mohr, W. K. (2002). The lost art of accuracy: A contextual approach to assessment. *Journal of Psychosocial Nursing and Mental Health Services, 40*(10), 38–45.

Pennsylvania Patient Safety Reporting System. (2005, March). Changing the culture of seclusion and restraint. *Patient Safety Authority, 2*(1), 22–26. Available online at www.psa.state.pa.us/psa/lib/psa /advisories/march_2005_advisory_v2_n1.pdf

Project NoSpank. (2006a). *Children prosecuted in the juvenile justice system. Plain talk about spanking.* Available online at www.nospank.net/ai-rpt3.htm. Alamo, CA: Parents and Teachers Against Violence in Education (PTAVE).

Project NoSpank. (2006b). *Summary of Amnesty International's recommendations to U.S. authorities.* Available online at www.nospank.net/ai-rpt8.htm. Alamo, CA: Parents and Teachers Against Violence in Education (PTAVE).

Rosenhan, D. (1973). On being sane in insane places. *Science, 179,* 250–258.

Rogers, C. (1957). The necessary and sufficient conditions of therapeutic personality change. *Journal of Consulting Psychology, 21,* 90–103.

Rubin, B. S., Dube, A. H., & Mitchell, E. K. (1993) Asphyxial deaths due to physical restraint. A case series. *Archives of Family Medicine, 2*(4), 405–408.

Saperia, P. A. (2002). Governor's budget gives mental health short shrift. *New York City Voices, 7*(1). Available online at www.newyorkcityvoices.org/2002janmar/20020318.html.

Selekman, J., & Snyder, B. (1996). Uses of and alternatives to restraints in pediatric settings. *American Association of Colleges of Nursing Clinical Issues, 7,* 603–610.

Sullivan, A. M., Besmen, J., Barron, C. T., Rivera, J., Curley-Casey, L., & Marino, D. (2005). Reducing restraints: alternatives to restraints on an inpatient psychiatric service—utilizing safe and effective methods to evaluate and treat the violent patient. *Psychiatric Quarterly, 76*(1), 51–65.

Trice, H. M., &. Beyer, J. M. (1993). *The Cultures of Work Organizations.* Prentice Hall: Upper Saddle River, NJ.

Troutman, B., Myers, K., Borchardt, C., Kowalski, R., & Bubrick, J. (1998). Case study: when restraints are the least restrictive alternative for managing aggression. *Journal of the American Academy of Child & Adolescent Psychiatry, 37*(5), 554–558.

Weinstock, J., Maron, B. J., Song, C., Mane, P. P., Estes III, N. A., & Link, M. S. (2006). Failure of commercially available chest wall protectors to prevent sudden cardiac death induced by chest wall blows in an experimental model of commotio cordis. *Pediatrics, 117*(4), 656–662.

Zimbardo, P. G., Haney, C., Banks, W. C., & Jaffe, D. (1973, April 8). The mind is a formidable jailer: A Pirandellian prison. *The New York Times Magazine,* Section 6, pp. 38.

Zun, L. S. (2003). A prospective study of the complication rate of use of patient restraint in the emergency department. *Journal of Emergency Medicine, 24*(2), 119–124.

CHAPTER 5

Risk and Prone Restraint

Reviewing the Evidence

David Allen

The truth must dazzle gradually
Or every man be blind.

—Emily Dickinson (1830–1886)

Introduction

This chapter deals with the contentious subject of prone restraint. Along with the use of pain compliance procedures (that is, evasive or restrictive procedures that are dependent on the deliberate infliction of pain for their effectiveness), facedown floor restraint is the most controversial type of physical intervention utilized in human care services. As such, its use generates strong feelings amongst both its critics and proponents alike. The chapter will explore various aspects of risk in relation to prone restraint and then try to locate this risk within a broader array of personal and organizational variables.

Restraint and Risk

By definition, intervening physically to help calm and control challenging behaviors is a risky business. These risks impact both on the person being restrained and the persons implementing the restraint. They include both physical risk (injury or death) and emotional risk (traumatization both during and following the restraint episode).

It would be logical to assume that an inverse relationship exists between the degree of control offered by a restraint hold and the potential risk it presents. In other words, the more controlling and restrictive the hold is, the more intrusive it is likely to be and, consequently, the greater the risk it is likely to pose. The risks and the effectiveness of physical intervention techniques therefore need to be considered in tandem.

It has been suggested (Allen, 2002, p. 84) that there are five questions that need to be asked regarding risk and physical intervention procedures.

- How effective is the technique concerned; that is, what degree of control does it offer over very disturbed behavior?

- How technically complex is the procedure to execute; that is, how many separate steps does it involve and how many of these steps require carers to make sophisticated judgments, for example, how much pressure to exert in applying a hold?

- What is the potential for harm to the child or adult being restrained; that is, is the procedure likely to cause physical pain, muscular-skeletal damage, respiratory distress, emotional distress, and so on?

- What is the potential for harm to carers? Again, concerns here may relate to physical damage (e.g., back injury while applying holds, injury from ineffective holds) and emotional consequences (e.g., posttraumatic stress).

- What is the margin for error? To what extent are any risks inherent within a certain procedure exacerbated if the technique is performed incorrectly?

An ideal technique is one that is safe for both those with whom it is used and those who apply it; it offers a high degree of control over challenging behavior and poses few or no risks to the physical or emotional health of either party. Most techniques are not ideal however. A technique may be safe for the carers applying it, but unsafe for those receiving it; in other words, it may offer a high degree of control, but pose significant risk to the person being restrained. Conversely, it may be safe for service users,[1] but unsafe for carers because it is ineffective and fails to achieve control over behavior. Finally, it may be unsafe for both parties in that it is both ineffective and risky.

Two assumptions will now be made in relation to prone restraint. First, although comparative data on the effectiveness of different restraint forms are conspicuous by their absence, it would be reasonable to state that prone restraint is probably generally regarded as the position that affords the highest degree of control over a service user's challenging behavior. Second, given that prone restraint typically involves taking a person from a standing position, lowering him to the floor, and then applying the restraint hold, it may also be

---

1. This general term will be used throughout to describe the consumers of mental health, mental retardation, and other human care services. Carer is also common terminology used in the United Kingdom and will be used throughout to describe caregivers.

assumed that prone restraint is relatively complex operation to perform. A reasonable initial conclusion would therefore be that prone restraint is effective but potentially hard to execute. Having made these assumptions, the material that follows will look at prone restraint from the perspective of physical harm, emotional harm, and harm arising from inaccurate application.

Physical Harm

Routine data on injuries sustained during physical interventions are almost impossible to obtain. A limited number of published studies show variable impacts of training in physical interventions on staff and service user injuries, indicating that injuries can decrease or increase post-training (Allen, 2001). In a survey of 560 adult users of New York's mental health services, 26% reported being physically injured during a restraint or seclusion (Sundram, Stack, & Benjamin, 1994). In the United Kingdom, a study of nursing staff working in regional secure and intensive psychiatric units reported that 27% of respondents were injured during physical intervention training, and that 19% of staff and 11% of service users were injured in the last episode of restraint in which respondents were involved (SNMAC, 1999).

The latter figures are particularly alarming and pose questions both about the techniques taught and the methods employed to teach them. In this instance, the approach in question was Control & Restraint, a method originally devised for use in the U.K. prison service. It was introduced into the Special Hospital Service following a restraint death in 1979, and from there cascaded down into a whole variety of care services supporting many different service user groups (including children), initially with little or no modification. Certainly at the time that the study was conducted, the approach was one that favored the use of prone restraint. Alarmingly, a Department of Health initiated review of restraint use in the U.K. health service somehow managed to conclude that "simple, *police derived*, reflexive skills appear to be the most effective of any training approach in this country" (Bleetman & Boatman, 2001, p. 3; emphasis added).

Interesting though these results are, the data do not exist that would allow for any kind of analysis as to whether specific techniques or certain training brands pose greater injury risks *in general*. This is not the case with the material that follows, where somewhat more specific conclusions can be drawn.

The most extreme outcome of restraint for service users is of course death. One United Kingdom review (Simpson & Freeman, 2000, p. 2) stated, "...deaths in restraint do occasionally occur." Unfortunately, restraint deaths in both law enforcement and care services are far more common than this statement might suggest. In the United States, Ross (1998) reported 61 deaths involving law enforcement between 1988 and 1997. O'Halloran and Frank (2000) reported another 21 fatal cases involving restraint by the police between 1992 and 1996, and Stratton, Rogers, Brickett, and Gruzinski (2001) reported an additional 18 cases. A series of articles in the *Hartford Courant* (Weiss, Altimari, Blint, & Megan, 1998) newspaper reported 142 deaths in U.S. care services during a 10-year period; the National Alliance for the Mentally Ill (NAMI) (2000) reported 12 deaths to the publication of the *Courant* report, the Joint Commission on Accreditation of Healthcare Organizations (JCAHO) (1998) reported 20 deaths, and Morrison, Duryea, Moore, and Nathanson-Shinn (2002) described 7 deaths. In addition, Nunno, Holden, and Tollar (2006) recently reported on a series of 45 child restraint-related deaths.

A similar pattern, albeit on a smaller scale, is evident in the United Kingdom—Leigh, Johnson, and Ingram (1998) reported on 16 deaths in police custody between 1990 and 1996; the Police Complaints Authority (2002) an additional 9 deaths between 1998 and 1999; and the Police Leadership and Powers Unit (2001) 6 deaths between 1999 and 2000. Patterson, Bradley, Stark, Saddler, Leadbetter, and Allen (2003) reported on 12 deaths in U.K. care services between 1979 and 2000; an additional 4 deaths have been identified in health or social care services since that paper first appeared.

Given the serious consequences of using restraint incorrectly, there is an ethical and scientific imperative to establish the factors that heighten risks of restraint injury and death. There are three broad types of literature that help identify the particular risks associated with the application of different types of restraint. These are case series data that look at relatively large samples but in fairly superficial detail (such as the *Hartford Courant* database), forensic case studies that typically consist of between one and six detailed individual analyses of restraint death, and a small experimental literature that tests out the physiological impact of restraint application. The key question to answer from studying the results from this literature is whether or not there is any evidence for a particular restraint form being more frequently associated with restraint fatality. Each of these literature streams will be examined in turn.

The case series reported by Leigh et al. (1998); the *Hartford Courant* (Weiss et al., 1998); NAMI (2000); Morrison et al. (2002); and Patterson et al. (2003) allow the type of restraint involved to be identified in 148 restraint fatalities. The combined data from these 5 studies is shown in Figure 5-1.

As clearly seen, prone restraint is by far the most frequent form of physical intervention associated with restraint death. Mechanical restraint, typically

FIGURE 5–1: Summed Data from 5 Studies (n = 148)

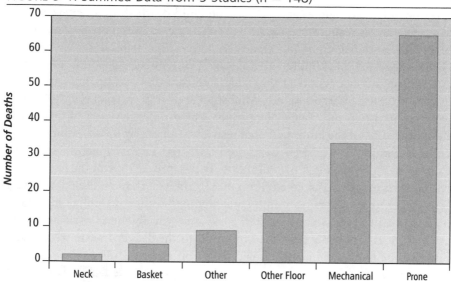

(Weiss et al., 1998; NAMI, 2000; Leigh et al., 1998; Patterson et al., 2003; Morrison et al., 2002)

FIGURE 5–2: U.S. Child Deaths 1993–2003 (Nunno et al., 2006)

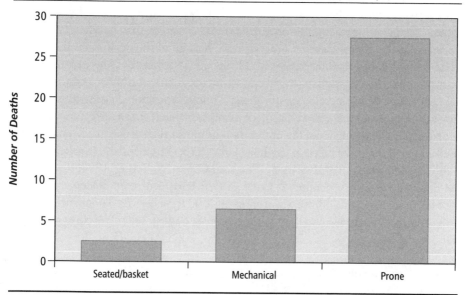

involving the restraint of elderly persons via ties, restraint vests, etc., also features significantly. Nunno et al.'s study on child death showed an even clearer profile in this respect (see Figure 5-2). Whether children are at greater risk of restraint related injury or fatality is a question of interest. Weiss et al. (1998) suggested that children are four more times likely to be restrained than adults. The Skinner report (1992) suggested that physical restraint was used in 74% of U.K. children's homes. Almost 89% of staff interviewed by Hayden (1997) stated that they felt that restraint was a necessary part of residential care; over 90% of the latter had used restraint and nearly 63% within the previous six months. Children comprised 26% of fatalities in the *Hartford Courant* sample, although overall they only comprised 15% of the population within the care settings studied. Presumably, the fact that children are smaller (and therefore easier to restrain) is one factor that may determine high rates of restraint use (Weiss et al., 1998). This same variable may mean that they are more at risk of being restrained by adults as the discrepancy in weight: size ratio will be more dramatic than with adult-on-adult restraint.

Forensic case studies will be considered next. Belviso, De Donno, Vitale, and Introna (2003) cited references dating back to the 1830s that examined the phenomenon of traumatic asphyxia (suffocation as a result of the compression of the thorax or abdomen). The term *positional asphyxia* is now more commonly used to describe fatalities that appear to arise from mechanical interference with pulmonary functioning due to the adoption of particular body positions. Bell, Rao, Wetli, and Rodriguez (1992) defined positional asphyxia as occurring when the following three criteria are met: the person is found in a position that interferes with pulmonary gas exchange or there is a verifiable history of the person having been in that position; their inability to escape from the position must be explained (for example, due to entrapment[2] or substance intoxication); and other possible causes of death must be excluded at postmortem. Although positional asphyxia can occur for a variety of reasons, there has been significant interest in recent years in positional asphyxia arising from the application of physical restraint (see Kumar, 1991; Bell et al., 1992; O'Halloran & Lewman, 1993; Mirchandani, Rorke, Sekula-Perlman, & Hood, 1994; Pollanen, Chiasson, Cairns, & Young, 1998; Ross, 1998; Milleken, 1998; Hick, Smith, & Lynch, 1999; Park, Korn, & Henderson, 2001; O'Halloran, & Frank, 2000; Stratton et al., 2001; Siebert & Thogmartin, 2000; Hem, Steen, & Opjordsmoen, 2001; Morrison & Sadler, 2001; Belviso et al., 2003; Di Nunno, Vacca, Costantinides, & Di Nunno, 2003; O'Halloran, 2004).

---

2. As an example, Boglioli & Taff (1995) wrote a paper on positional asphyxia that referred to "The Santa Claus Syndrome," a term derived from the fact that some cases of positional asphyxia have been reported in burglars who became stuck in chimneys during attempted robberies.

Compression of the thorax and abdomen need not necessarily be unique to prone restraint. For example, it could occur in basket holds (in which the service users arms are held across their chest in an 'X' shape by a carer who is holding them from behind) or in a seated position if the person's chest is forced forward towards their knees. In analyzing the forensic case studies, it is again possible to clearly identify the type of restraint used in just over 100 of the cases reported; the summed data from 11 studies are shown in Figure 5-3. Once again, prone restraint is clearly the most common restraint form reported in fatalities.

Both the above forms of data are of course correlational rather than causal; this means that it cannot be inferred that the restraint position actually caused the death of the restrained person. A further problem arises in interpreting these data in the absence of any information on base rates of training in different types of restraint procedure. Thus, the apparent correlation between prone restraint and restraint death would be entirely spurious if this form of restraint was by far the most commonly taught restrictive procedure on physical intervention training programs across the world. Under these conditions, an apparent correlation would be almost inevitable. Similarly, if the only vehicles allowed on the road were Greyhound buses, there would be an inevitable correlation between pedestrian road deaths and the use of such buses. These qualifications aside, it would appear foolish in the extreme not to take note of the association, albeit correlational, between prone restraint and restraint fatality. The more precise nature of this association will be explored further shortly.

Experimental studies on the impact of restraint are few in number (Reay, Flinger, Stilwell, & Ward, 1988; Roeggla, Wagner, Muellner, Roeggla, Hirscl, & Roeggla, 1997; Chan, Neuman et al., 2004; Chan, Vilke et al., 1997; Chan, Vilke, & Neuman, 1998; Schmidt & Snowden, 1999; Cary, Roberts, Cumin, & Adams, 2000; Parkes, 2000), and for informed consent and safety reasons experimental studies on children are nonexistent. Children, by reason of their psychosocial developmental needs, and their anatomical and physiological immaturity, especially in their respiratory functions demand a separate and rigorous research agenda. The results from these adult studies are generally equivocal—some claim quite major effects on cardiovascular functioning, others claim little or no effect from placing participants in restraints. In the studies that show limited impact, the physiological restraint sequelae are usually dismissed as not significant. However, as Patterson et al. (2003) note, these studies lack ecological validity on at least three counts.

First, they have mostly concentrated on one particular form of the prone restraint—the hobble (or hog tie), a very particular form used for some time

FIGURE 5–3: Summed data from Forensic Case Studies

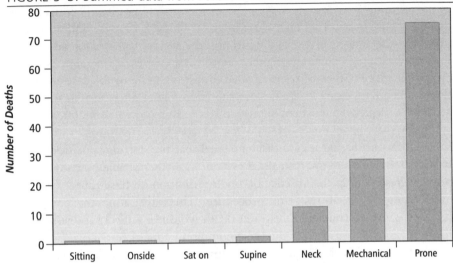

(DiNunno et al., 2003; Stratton et al., 2001; Ross, 1998; O'Halloran & Lewman, 1993; O'Halloran & Frank, 2000; O'Halloran, 2004; Hick et al., 1999; Pollanen et al., 1998; Siegert & Thogmartin, 2000; Morrison & Sadler, 2001; Park et al., 2001)

within North American police forces. The studies have generally not focused on forms of restraint in use within care services for children, and therefore the generalizations of the results from these studies is thus limited primarily to adults.

Second, the rigor of application of restraint in the experimental conditions bears little or no resemblance to available descriptions of restraint in practice. Patterson et al. (2003) comment, for example, that in the study by Cary et al. (2000), participants had 165 lb. sandbags placed on their backs while placed in a prone restraint position. The study concluded that there was no impact on recovery rates. Patterson et al. compared the weight applied in this study with the estimated weight placed on the back of the service user in one U.K. fatality that involved the application of restraint by several staff. In that case, it was calculated that the weight on the person's back was equivalent to 697 lb. Risks are likely to be significantly increased with children, where the weight and size discrepancy between those being restrained and those implementing the restraint will be considerable, and where pressure is applied to the abdomen (as young children are primarily abdominal breathers). Furthermore, although several studies included an element of exercise in an attempt to mimic the stresses of a restraint episode; the levels of exercise were controlled so as to remain within safe limits.

Finally, unhealthy subjects were typically screened out of the research samples in order to reduce risk. While this makes sense from a risk management perspective, it represents a significant variation from clinical practice, where many of those restrained will present with health problems or developmental conditions that may increase risk in restraint (see below).

To summarize the above there are strong suggestions from both case series data and forensic case studies that there is some association between the use of prone restraint and heightened risk of restraint death. The experimental studies that have been conducted have failed to produce definitive evidence, but are themselves weak in terms of validity. Despite evidence of a link between prone restraint and positional asphyxia, the following conclusions must be drawn.

- Not all prone restraint results in death (if it did, a pandemic of restraint death would be expected given the apparent frequency of use of this procedure).

- Not all restraint deaths occur in the prone position (the most recent U.K. death, for example, occurred in a seated position and basket holds clearly figured in the *Hartford Courant* database).

- While prone restraint is undoubtedly a high-risk procedure, it is therefore neither a necessary or sufficient condition for restraint death.

Given that this is the case, the key question would therefore appear to be "What factors moderate risk in prone restraint?" In other words, what additional factors have to be present to elevate the risks in prone restraint to the point that the health of the restrained person is seriously compromised. In addition to helping to highlight the types of restraint most commonly involved in restraint death, the forensic case studies have helped identify a number of other variables that appear to increase risk. Patterson et al. (2003) summarized these factors.

Given that positional asphyxia occurs as a result of the inability of the essential mechanics of the respiratory system to function, it should come as no surprise that people with existing cardio vascular difficulties are at higher risk. People who are overweight are also at greater risk because, during prone restraint, excess adipose tissue is forced upwards into the body cavity, thus further reducing the ability of the diaphragm and intercostal muscles to expand and contract. This in turn prevents the operation of the "bellows" system that draws into and expels air from the lungs. Acute psychiatric disturbance (in the form of agitated delirium—a condition in which the sufferer experiences extreme motor agitation, rapid loss of body weight, reduced blood pressure, rapid pulse, and hypothermia) has been put forward both as a contributory factor and alternate explanation for restraint death. It has also been suggested that cocaine use features strongly in persons who present with agitated delirium.

Finally, prescribed drugs could also play an important role, given that the side effects of a number of psychoactive drugs include an adverse impact on cardiovascular functioning. The use of rapid tranquilization during restraint poses particular problems in this respect (Royal College of Psychiatrists, 1998), as it carries the risk of loss of consciousness and oversedation. The use of benzodiazepines in rapid tranquillization is associated with respiratory depression or arrest; chloromazine has similar risks.

These findings need to be linked back the principal criticism of the experimental literature—the ethically necessary use of healthy subjects. Most people who experience restraint are certainly not healthy. Children and adults with intellectual disabilities and challenging behavior, for example, have a high probability of being restrained (Emerson, 2002). It is well established that people with intellectual disabilities in general are at high risk of the kind of secondary health problems known to increase restraint risk (Hamilton-Kirkwood, Ahmed, Allen, Deb, Fraser, Lindsay, McKenzie, Penny, & Scotland, 2001; van Schrojenstein Lantman-de Valk, 2005). This problem is likely to be even greater amongst those people with intellectual disabilities who are the *most* likely people to be restrained (as the prevalence of challenging behavior is positively correlated with the presence of secondary health disabilities). Furthermore, 60% to 70% of this group will be in receipt of psychotropic medications, significant numbers of which carry the side effects described above. Respiratory problems are common in children in general, and preexisting conditions like scoliosis, kyphosis, and juvenile rheumatoid arthritis can all elevate restraint risks. Additional risks also arise from the fact that the bones of the major limbs and joints may not be fully formed.

Long-term users of mental health services show similarly poor general health profiles. The Disability Rights Commission (2005) found, for example, that primary health care patients with a diagnosis of schizophrenia or bipolar disorder were much more likely to suffer from diabetes, ischemic heart disease, stroke, hypertension, and epilepsy when compared to primary health care patients without mental health problems. People with schizophrenia were also found to be more likely to have problems of obesity.

A further possibility therefore is that the risk of certain restraint positions, and of prone restraint in particular, increases to significant degree if these additional personal risk factors are present. Unfortunately, unlike the participants in the experimental studies, few service users have a health screen to establish whether or not they are fit to be restrained.

Braverman (2002) has written cogently about the general need to adopt a systemic perspective when analyzing workplace violence. The same systemic perspective needs to be adopted when considering the use of restraint. Inquiries into restraint death (Morrison et al., 2002; NSCSHA, 2003) have suggested that there are a number of systemic variables that increase risks in restraint use. These include:

- unclear policies and procedures,

- absence of proactive interventions to minimize or eliminate challenging behaviors,

- inadequate care planning that fails to consider alternatives to restraint;

- use of restraint as a form of punishment (rather than simply as a reactive strategy for managing out-of-control behaviors),

- organizational culture (for example, a culture of racism was heavily implicated in the death of David Bennett in England in 1998),

- poor staffing ratios and staff competencies,

- inadequate training (both proactive and reactive), and

- wrong type of training (training in restraint needs to be tailored to the challenges presented by the service user population in question; Morrison et al. [2002], in an analysis of seven restraint fatalities, make the point that "Staff did everything by the book. The problem is that the book is wrong").

Aside from the last two variables, which directly impact upon safety, the influence of the other factors is more subtle. In behavioral terms, they might best be described as setting events. They set the scene for things going wrong by increasing the probability that they will. Lack of clear guidance and standards for staff means that performance will be improvised, highly variable, and staff-led, rather than management-led. The absence of proactive strategies to prevent violence creates a breeding ground for aggressive acts. In a service that may be characterized by subtle racism, the "care" responses that people get will be determined by the color of their skin rather than their clinical need. The actual outcome will be determined by the more specific factors described earlier (i.e., the type of restraint used and the characteristics and health profile of the service user), together with the performance errors such as those described later in the chapter.

Emotional Harm

A number of writers have highlighted the fact that restraint can be an emotionally as well as physically challenging life event. The British Medical Association (2001) stated that the use of restraint could cause "substantial psychological morbidity, including demoralization and feelings of humiliation." Brase-Smith (1995) reported that mechanical restraint precipitated flashbacks to sexual trauma and provoked feelings of domination, vulnerability, and loss of dignity for rape victims. The U.S. General Accounting Office (U.S. GAO, 1999) stated that 50% of women within psychiatric services in one U.S. state had a history of physical or sexual abuse, and again suggested that the use of restraint often resulted in a reexperiencing of the trauma and treatment set back.

Similarly, Gallop, McCay, Guha, and Khan (1999) wrote that women who had previously experienced sexual abuse reported fear, anxiety, rage, and powerlessness in relation to restraint use. Mohr, Petti, and Mohr (2003) reported similar findings. The latter authors stated that children and adolescents who had been restrained experienced nightmares, intrusive thoughts, avoidance responses, and marked startle responses. Seeing others restrained reawakened such emotional responses that persisted over a period of five years. In this retrospective study by Sundram et al. (1994), 40% of respondents reported psychological abuse during restraint or seclusion. One respondent referred to being called "a piece of shit" and a "white bitch" (p. 12). Other comments included, "It was very scary to be in restraints" and "I was only 9 years old and was never scared of adults (before this)" (p. 14).

As with the material on general injuries arising from restraint, it is not possible to be specific about the emotional impact of prone restraint. The U.K. Department of Health (1996) nevertheless concluded that floor restraint was "a position of general vulnerability" that was "highly traumatic for young people who had been sexually abused." It is also apparent that some particular forms of floor restraint in which the restrained person is straddled by carers may be of particular concern in this respect. It is nevertheless probable that all forms of restraint have the capacity to generate negative emotional consequences for service users.

A small of number of studies (e.g., Sequeira & Halstead, 2004; Hawkins, Allen, & Jenkins, 2005) have also examined the impact on carer stress arising from restraint use. These qualitative studies, though small in both scope and number, provide clear evidence that traumatization from restraint use can be a two-way process:

I almost wet myself the first time that I actually had to restrain somebody…it was that…I was like 'Wahay, what's going on' and I almost actually wet myself…em…yeah it was definitely quite frightening. The first one was anyway. (Sequeira & Halstead, 2004, p. 6)

We are here to reassure them, to calm them down in a soft, caring, professional way but if they don't respond to that you tend to get angry—I mean I'm only human—if I get injured, it's that sort of human reaction…if you are holding them down, pinning them down to the floor, for large amounts of time you get angry, you get frustrated. (Sequeira & Halstead, 2004, p. 7)

During the intervention, my level of stress rises as the service user struggles more and more. You don't always get rid of that stress at the same time that the service user does. That can make it difficult to let go and actually stop the restraint. (Hawkins et al., 2005, p. 29)

I felt quite drained yesterday…I got home, sat there and felt a huge amount of relief that the incident was all over. Yesterday I was physically and emotionally drained after the intervention. (Hawkins et al., 2005, p. 30)

The need to provide emotional support to staff that are supporting very challenging service users often goes unrecognized in services. It is interesting to speculate as to whether this failure to manage staff stress is in itself a precipitant for the overzealous use of physical intervention procedures and a contributing factor to service user abuse (Baker & Allen, 2001).

Harm Arising from Incorrect Application

Exponents of what Leadbetter (2002) has termed "high tariff" techniques often defend their training on the naïve premise that goes something like "As long as my technique is performed accurately, it is perfectly safe." While techniques may be correctly performed in the classroom, under field conditions optimum performance will be elusive. Factors influencing this outcome will include levels of carer stress, carer attributions for service user behavior (and particularly whether they blame the person for their behavior), level of available carer resources, date since last training refresher, quality of training, training recall, and the physical ability of those executing the restraint—a volatile and complex mix. As Bleetman & Boatman (2001) observed, "Trainers need to be aware of the educational constraints in teaching defensive and control skills to staff who are unfit, inexperienced, and poorly motivated" (p. 3). Rather than assuming that a technique will be performed correctly, it is therefore safer to assume that it will not.

This being the case, is it possible to identify additional factors that heighten risk if added to prone restraint? It has been suggested that the following physical actions all exacerbate risk:

- the immobilization of the hands behind the back;
- the application of additional pressure/weight to the back, neck, or trunk area;
- the obstruction of the mouth or nose; and
- specific pressure on the vagus or carotid nerve.

Some training approaches may actually advocate some of the above as a bona fide aspect of physical intervention training. For example, in the documentation of one training approach in the United Kingdom, which was recently reviewed by this author, staff were specifically told to "lie across the residents (sic) trunk." Hopefully, such blatant bad practice is the exception rather than the rule and most reputable trainers will advise against such moves. However, in the melee of many restraint episodes, modifications to previously taught practice creep in (and often become part of established practice). Some of these modifications may resemble the actions referred to above. Risk is then again escalated if they are employed and, in conjunction with the use of higher risk restraint positions, such as prone, and in service users who are already physically compromised, this risk may prove fatal.

In addition to corruptions of taught restraint moves, there are three other factors identified in restraint fatality inquiries that appear to increase risk. These are:

- *Long restraint duration*
  It is self-evident that protracted restraint is likely to heighten any physiological concerns. This has been highlighted in one recent high-profile U.K. inquiry which included the recommendation that: "Under no circumstances should any patient be restrained in a prone position for a period longer than three minutes" (NSCSHA, 2003, p. 67).[3]

---

3. Although the Westminster Government rejected this specific recommendation, it is of interest to note that the devolved Wales Assembly Government has issued a recent policy on restraint use that states that 'Under no circumstances, should any individual be restrained in a face down position' (WAG, 2005, p. 6).

- *Inadequate monitoring of vital signs*
  The same inquiry drew attention to the obvious need to ensure that carers are able to effectively monitor vital signs during restraint episodes. In the case of prone restraint, this may include the requirement for an additional staff member, not involved in the restraint, to undertake this specific role (NSCSHA, 2003).

- *Misinterpretation of vital signs*
  Mohr et al. (2003) drew attention to the fact that carers may commonly misinterpret signal signs. Typically this involves viewing respiratory failure as a sign of calming or a reluctance to release the person as they may be "play acting" and likely to reengage in violence if the restraint hold is released prematurely.

Conclusions

As George Orwell might have said, "All restraints are dangerous but some restraints are more dangerous than others." It is extremely hard to argue that prone restraint does not fall into the latter category. In terms of the classification of risk presented at the start of this chapter, prone is probably best described as a form of restraint that may be (relatively) safe for the carers applying it, but unsafe for those receiving it. It is therefore one of the risk variables in the complex equation of restraint injury and fatality (Day, 2002). Supporters of this form of physical intervention nevertheless strive to make the argument that this is not the case, and they do so principally on the basis of the fact that definitive research is lacking. This is undoubtedly true, and the fact that training in restraint is market-led rather than evidence-based is a shared international scandal. When the highly intrusive and risky nature of restraint is considered, it is all too apparent that the present evidence base is wholly inadequate and that there is a particular need for high-quality, independent research into the biomechanics and physiological sequelae of controversial physical holds.

From another perspective however, the dangers of restraint holds such as prone are self-evident. To return to the Greyhound bus analogy, we probably do not need to construct a more robust evidence base to show that stepping out in front of one of these vehicles will be bad for your health. Death may not result every time someone does so, but if conditions are right (velocity of vehicle, frailty of pedestrian, etc.), it will. We accept from experiential evidence that this is so. Should the same case not hold for prone restraint? Do we really need experimental data to show that holding someone who is demonstrating significant resistance facedown on the floor, often for prolonged periods, carries substantial risk? Probably not. Do we have clear evidence that prone restraint in itself is a necessary condition for restraint death? No, we do not. What we do have is a cumulative body of evidence that suggests that, in combination with other factors, which are themselves not uncommon, this form of restraint carries very real and very significant risks.

As Wright, Gray, Parkes, and Gournay (2002) observed: "In a health care context, it is not necessary to prove that a single factor directly causes death; that it increases the risk of death is sufficient for it to be relevant to training and practice" (p. 55). A definitive view about the risks of prone restraint may actually not be achievable, as ethical concerns will almost certainly preclude realistic, ecologically valid research. The contention of this chapter is that there is already sufficient concern, if not sufficient evidence, to suggest that there needs to be a change in the training and practice of prone restraint. However, as the quote from Dickinson at the start of the chapter suggests, the truth often dawns slowly, and some powerful lobbies in both North America and the United Kingdom continue to resist the view that prone restraint is inherently dangerous. How many more people have to die or be injured before this particular truth shines more brightly?

Rather than just pursuing a primarily negative line of trying to establish beyond doubt the risks associated with obviously highly intrusive procedures, future research needs to focus on the development of procedures that produce the best fit in terms of minimizing risk and maximizing effectiveness. This is vital as, in order to effectively proscribe the use of controversial interventions, it will be necessary to have equally effective but more ethical and less risky alternatives in place. When that day dawns, progress really will have been made. It will come more quickly if key stakeholders invest their time and efforts in collaborative working and problem solving rather than in efforts to defend practice that is increasingly indefensible.

References

Allen, D. (2001). *Training carers in physical interventions. Research towards evidence-based practice.* Kidderminster: British Institute of Learning Disabilities.

Allen, D. (2002). Devising individualised risk management plans. In D. Allen, (Ed.), *Ethical approaches to physical intervention. Responding to challenging behaviour in people with intellectual disabilities* (pp. 71–88). Kidderminster: British Institute of Learning Disabilities.

Baker, P., & Allen, D. (2001). Physical abuse and physical interventions in learning disabilities: An element of risk? *Journal of Adult Protection, 3*(2), 25–31.

Belviso, M., De Donno, A., Vitale, L., & Introna, F. (2003). Positional asphyxia. Reflection on 2 cases. *American Journal of Forensic Medicine and Pathology, 24*(3), 292–297.

Bell, M. D., Rao, V. J., Wetli, C. V., & Rodriguez, R. N. (1992). Positional asphyxiation on Adults: A series of 30 cases from the Dade and Broward County Florida Medical Centre Examiner Offices from 1982 to 1990. *American Journal of Forensic Medicine and Pathology, 13*(2), 101–107.

Bleetman, A., & Boatman, P. (2001). *An overview of control and restraint issues for the health service.* London: Department of Health.

Boglioli, L. R., & Taff, M. L. (1995). The 'Santa Claus Syndrome' entrapment in chimneys. *Journal of Forensic Sciences, 40*(3), 499–500.

Brase-Smith, S. (1995). Restraints: Retraumatization for rape victims? *Journal of Psychosocial Nursing, 33,* 23–28.

Braverman, M. (2002). Prevention of violence affecting workers: a systems perspective. In M. Gill, B. Fisher, B., & V. Bowie, (Eds.), *Violence at work: Causes, patterns and prevention* (pp. 114–131). Cullumpton, Devon: Willan Publishing.

British Medical Association (2001). *The medical profession & human rights: Handbook for a changing agenda.* London: Author.

Chan, T. C., Neuman, T., Clausen, J., Eisele, J., & Vilke, G. M. (2004). Weight force during prone restraint and respiratory function. *American Journal of Forensic Medicine and Pathology, 25*(3), 185–189.

Chan, T. C., Vilke, G. M., & Neuman, T. (1998). Re-examination of custody restraint and positional asphyxia. *American Journal of Forensic Medical Pathology, 19*(3), 201–215.

Chan, T. C., Vilke, G. M., Neuman, T., & Clausen, J. L. (1997). Restraint position and positional asphyxia. *Annals of Emergency Medicine, 30,* 578–586.

Cary, N. R. B., Roberts, C. A., Cumin, A. R. C., & Adams, L. (2000). The effects of simulated restraint in the prone position on cardio-respiratory function following exercise in humans. *Journal of Physiology, 525*(Suppl.), 30–31.

Day, P. (2002). What evidence exists about the safety of physical restraint when used by law enforcement and medical staff to control individuals with acute behavioural disturbance? *NZHTA Tech Brief Series, 1,* 3.

Department of Health. (1996). *Taking care. Taking control.* London: Crown Copyright.

Di Nunno, N., Vacca, M., Costantinides, F., & Di Nunno, C. (2003). Death following atypical compression of the neck. *American Journal of Forensic Medicine and Pathology 24*(4), 364–368.

Disability Rights Commission. (2005). *Equal treatment: Closing the gap. Interim report of a formal investigation into health inequalities.* London: Author.

Emerson, E. (2002). The prevalence of use of reactive management strategies in community-based services in the UK. In D. Allen, (Ed.), *Ethical approaches to physical intervention. Responding to challenging behaviour in people with intellectual disabilities* (pp. 15–28). Kidderminster: British Institute of Learning Disabilities.

Gallop., R., McCay, E., Guha, M., & Khan, P. (1999). The experience of hospitalisation and restraint of women who have a history of childhood sexual abuse. *Health Care for Women International, 2*(4), 401–416.

Hamilton-Kirkwood, L., Ahmed, Z., Allen, D., Deb, S., Fraser, W., Lindsay, W., McKenzie, K., Penny, E., & Scotland, J. (2001). *Health evidence bulletins—Wales. Learning disabilities (Intellectual Disability).* Cardiff: Department of Information Services.

Hawkins, S., Allen, D., & Jenkins, R. (2005). The use of physical interventions with people with intellectual disabilities and challenging behavior: The experience of service users and staff members. *Journal of Applied Research in Intellectual Disabilities, 18,* 19–34.

Hayden, C. (1997). *Physical restraint in children's residential care.* University of Portsmouth: Social services Research and Information Unit, No. 37.

Hem, E., Steen, O., & Opjordsmoen, S. (2001). Thrombosis associated with physical restraints. *Acta Psychiatrica Scandinavica, 103*(1), 73–76.

Hick, J. L., Smith, S. W., & Lynch, M. T. (1999). Metabolic acidosis in restraint-associated cardiac arrest: A case series. *Academic Emergency Medicine 6*(3), 239–243.

Joint Commission on Accreditation of Healthcare Organizations. (1998). *Sentinel Alert 8.* Illinois: Author.

Kumar, A. (1991). Sudden unexplained death in a psychiatric patient—A case report: The role of phenothiazines and physical restraint. *Medicine, Science and the Law, 37*(2), 170–175.

Leadbetter, D. (2002). Good practice in physical intervention. In D. Allen, (Ed.), *Ethical approaches to physical intervention. Responding to challenging behaviour in people with intellectual disabilities* (pp. 114–133). Kidderminster: British Institute of Learning Disabilities.

Leigh, A., Johnson, G., & Ingram, A. (1998). *Deaths in police custody: Learning the lessons. Police Research Series Paper 26.* London: Home Office Police Research Group.

Milleken, D. (1998). Death by restraint. *Canadian Medical Association Journal, 158,* 1611–1612.

Mirchandani, H., Rorke, L. B., Sekula-Perlman, A., & Hood, I. C. (1994). Cocaine-induced agitated delirium, forceful struggle, and minor head injury. *American Journal of Forensic Medicine and Pathology, 15*(2), 95–99.

Mohr, W. K., Petti, T. A., & Mohr, B. D. (2003). Adverse effects associated with physical restraint. *Canadian Journal of Psychiatry, 48*(5), 330–337.

Morrison, A., & Saddler, D. (2001). Death of a psychiatric patient during physical restraint. Excited delirium—a case report. *Medicine Science and the Law, 41*(1), 46–50.

Morrison, L., Duryea, P. B., Moore, C., & Nathanson-Shinn, A. (2002). *The lethal hazard of prone restraint: Positional asphyxiation.* Oakland, CA: Protection & Advocacy Inc.

National Alliance for the Mentally Ill. (2000). *Cries of anguish: A summary of reports of restraint and seclusion received since the October 1998 investigation by the* Hartford Courant. Available online at www.nami.org/update/hartford.html. Arlington, VA: Author.

Norfolk, Suffolk & Cambridgeshire Strategic Heath Authority (NSCSHA). (2003). *Independent inquiry into the death of David Bennett.* Cambridge: Author.

Nunno, M., Holden, M., & Tollar, A. (2006). Learning from tragedy: A survey of child and adolescent restraint facilities. *Child Abuse & Neglect: The International Journal, 30*(12), 1333–1342.

O'Halloran, R. L. (2004). Reenactment of circumstances in deaths related to restraint. *American Journal of Forensic Medicine and Pathology, 25*(3), 190–193.

O'Halloran, R. L., & Frank, J. G. (2000). Aphyxial death during prone restraint revisited: A report of 21 cases. *American Journal of Forensic Medical Pathology, 21*(1), 39–52.

O'Halloran, R. L., & Lewman, L. V. (1993). Restraint asphyxiation in excited delirium. *American Journal of Forensic Medical Pathology, 14,* 289–295.

Park, K. S., Korn, C. S., & Henderson, S. O. (2001). Agitated delirium and sudden death. *Prehospital Emergency Care, 5*(2), 214–216.

Parkes, J. (2000). Sudden death during restraint: a study to measure the effect of restraint positions on the rate of recovery from exercise. *Medicine Science and the Law, 40*(1), 39–44.

Patterson, B., Bradely, P., Stark, C., Saddler, D., Leadbetter, D., & Allen, D. (2003). Deaths associated with restraint use in health and social care in the UK. The results of a preliminary survey. *Journal of Psychiatric and Mental Health Nursing, 10*, 3–15.

Police Complaints Authority. (2002). *Safer restraint. Report of a conference held in April 2002 at Church House, Westminster.* London: Author.

Police Leadership and Powers Unit. (2001). *Deaths in police custody. Statistics for England & Wales, April 1999 to March 2000.* London: Home Office.

Pollanen, M. S., Chiasson, D. A, Cairns, J. T., & Young, J. G. (1998). Unexpected deaths related to restraint for agitated delirium: a retrospective study of deaths in police custody and the community. *Canadian Medical Association Journal, 158*, 1603–1637.

Reay, D. T., Flinger, A. D., Stilwell, A. D., & Ward, R. J. (1988). Effects of positional restraint on saturation and heart rate following exercise. *American Journal of Forensic Medical Pathology, 1*, 16–18.

Roeggla, M., Wagner, A., Muellner, M., Roeggla, H., Hirscl, M. M., & Roeggla, G. (1997). Cardiovascular consequences to hobble restraint. *Weiner Klinische Wochenschrift, 109&110*, 359–361.

Ross, D. L. (1998). Factors associated with excited delirium deaths in police custody. *Modern Pathology, 11*(11), 1127–1137.

Royal College of Psychiatrists. (1998). *Management of imminent violence: Clinical practice guidelines to support mental health services. Occasional Paper OP41.* London: Royal College of Psychiatrists Research Unit.

Sequeira, H., & Halstead, S. (2004). The psychological effects on nursing staff of administering physical restraint in a secure psychiatric hospital: 'When I go home, it's then I think about it'. *British Journal of Forensic Practice, 8*(1), 3–18.

Schmidt, P., & Snowden, T. (1999). The effects of positional restraint on heart rate and oxygen saturation. *Journal of Emergency Medicine, 17*(5), 777–782.

Siebert, C. F., & Thogmartin, J. R. (2000). Restraint related fatalities in mental health facilities: Report of two cases. *American Journal of Forensic Medicine and Pathology, 21*(3), 210–212.

Simpson, S., & Freeman, M. (2000). *Addressing the prone position in control and restraint—Examining the literature.* Devon Partnership, Cornwall Health Community & Plymouth Community Trusts: SWACRI .

Skinner, A. (1992). *Another kind of home—A review of residential childcare.* Edinburgh: HMSO.

Standing Nursing and Midwifery Committee (SNMAC). (1999). *Mental health nursing. Addressing acute concerns.* London: Author.

Stratton, S. J., Rogers, C., Brickett, K., & Gruzinski, G. (2001). Factors associated with sudden death of individuals requiring restraint for excited delirium. *American Journal of Emergency Medicine, 19*(3), 187–191.

Sundram, C. J., Stack, E. W., & Benjamin, W. P. (1994). *Voices from the front line: Patients' perspectives on restraint and seclusion use.* Schenectady, New York: New York State Commission on Quality of Care for the Mentally Disabled.

U.S. General Accounting Office. (1999). *Mental health: Improper restraint or seclusion use places patients at risk.* Available online at http://www.gao.gov/archive/1999/he99176.pdf.

van Schrojenstein Lantman-de Valk, H. M. J. (2005). Health in people with intellectual disabilities: Current knowledge and gaps in knowledge. *Journal of Applied Research in Intellectual Disabilities, 18,* 325–333.

Wales Assembly Government. (2005). *Framework for restrictive intervention policy and practice.* Cardiff: Author.

Weiss, E. M., Altimari, D., Blint, D. F., & Megan, K. (1998, October 11–15). Deadly restraint: A nationwide pattern of death. *Hartford Courant.*

Wright, S., Gray, R., Parkes, J., & Gournay, K. (2002). *The recognition, prevention and therapeutic management of violence in acute in-patient psychiatry. A literature review and evidence-based recommendations for good practice.* London: Institute of Psychiatry.

CHAPTER 6

Learning from the Research

Martha Holden
and Dale Curry

Introduction

In the early 1980s, under a grant from the National Center on Child Abuse and Neglect, Cornell University developed the Therapeutic Crisis Intervention (TCI) crisis prevention and intervention curriculum for residential care facilities as part of the Residential Child Care Project (RCCP). The RCCP supports vigorous and ongoing in-house evaluation of TCI training and implementation efforts through testing participants' knowledge and skills, a certification program, formal assessment, and direct monitoring of agencies' use of high-risk interventions. The RCCP seeks to maintain a leadership role in discovering new knowledge, establishing new approaches to knowledge dissemination, and developing innovative programs to enable child caring agencies to serve children, youth, and families more effectively by building strong linkages among research, outreach activities, and evaluation efforts. These relationships are viewed as cyclical: research leads to the development of innovative and effective outreach programs, which are carefully evaluated. Evaluation activities contribute directly to the adaptation and improvement of outreach programs and may also contribute to new research. In-house and external evaluations have been essential in modifying intervention strategies and protocols to improve the TCI System's effectiveness for a wide range of organizations (see Figure 6-1).

Since the curriculum's inception there have been four major revisions. The revision process has generally included five major components: (1) examining the evaluation results and research conducted by the RCCP, (2) reviewing

FIGURE 6–1: Research Practice and Evaluation Cycle

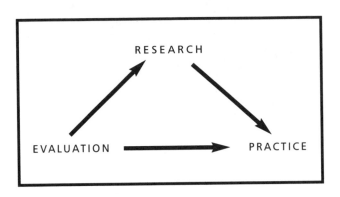

related literature and research, (3) conducting surveys of organizations using the TCI System, (4) talking to other crisis management training providers, and (5) convening a group of experts for consultation and review. This chapter primarily addresses the second component—the critical research that was used to inform and modify the 5th edition of the TCI curriculum.

An independent study published by Bell and Stark (1998) indicated that there was little agreement among the raters (TCI trainers) on what errors were severe, moderate, or unacceptable when scoring individual performance on conducting physical restraint techniques. These findings helped guide curriculum changes, learning activities, and skills testing. The findings from the study identified six areas of concern.

1. There was little agreement among the raters (TCI trainers) on what errors were severe, moderate, or unacceptable when scoring individual performance on conducting physical restraint techniques.

2. There was greater consistency when the raters used measuring instruments to assess performance.

3. Counting and prioritizing errors was not the key to effectively measuring someone's ability to competently perform any physical restraint.

4. The physical techniques involved a series of complex actions performed over a short period of time and a large number of errors could be made in carrying out the restraints.

5. The rating of seriousness of errors did not necessarily follow safety concerns or ability to complete the holds.

6. The study suggested that the training, evaluation, and registration methodology currently used by the RCCP was not adequate for TCI trainer skill maintenance.

This chapter outlines how the RCCP team took the lessons learned from the Bell and Stark study and applied these findings and other relevant research to the redevelopment of the TCI training curriculum.

What Was Learned from the Skill Maintenance Research

Since there was not a large body of research and evaluation on skills retention in physical restraint training, one method of examining skills retention was to review the literature in areas that are analogous. The literature on Cardiopulmonary Resuscitation (CPR) training and skills retention seemed to hold promise for how people learned and maintained physical skills. The CPR literature cites disturbingly rapid deterioration of skills after training regardless of use patterns on-the-job (Fosel, Kiskaddon, & Sternbach, 1983; Deliere & Schneider, 1980; Friesen & Stotts, 1984). Even medical specialties that frequently use CPR on-the-job such as emergency medical technicians and emergency room physicians and nurses had no better skill retention than those who used CPR infrequently (Gass & Curry, 1983).

The retention problem was examined from two perspectives: how individuals learned the skill and how they tried to maintain the skill. Researchers found that medical specialties learned CPR equally well with a variety of instructional methods over a variety of time frames (Moser & Coleman, 1992). For example, self-training with video seemed to work the same as live lecture-demonstration in increasing knowledge and practical skills to mastery levels immediately after training. However skills dropped off quickly with every training method except deliberate over-training, an intensive training technique requiring six to eight hours of training and trainer-level mastery of the subject matter (Yakel, 1989; Tweed, Wilson & Isfeld, 1980). Researchers found that the process of random retesting four to six months after training resulted in higher skill retention levels when subjects were tested again several months later. Higher retention levels resulted from subjects participating in a short refresher course that included skills practice and error correction (Yakel, 1989; Fosel et al., 1983).

What Was Learned from TCI Implementation Research

From 1994 through 1998, the RCCP conducted two major studies to evaluate and monitor the impact of the TCI System on residential child care facilities (Nunno, Holden, & Leidy, 2003). Impact was measured by monitoring critical incidents, staff knowledge, confidence and skill levels, and the consistency of staff intervention pre- and postimplementation. Results from the study indicated that the implementation of TCI was successful in substantially reducing critical incidents, significantly reducing documented physical restraint episodes, and increasing staff knowledge, confidence, and consistency in crisis intervention agencywide. The study also showed that, although knowledge levels remained high and were stable, high posttraining skill levels deteriorated or shifted without refresher training, corrective feedback during practice sessions, and organizational support.

What Was Learned from Motor Skills Training Research

Motor skills appear to be learned in phases (Fitts & Posner, 1967). Before performing complex motor skills, the training participant must understand why each movement is important to the performance of the entire motor skill. This is especially important when participants are learning continuous and complex motor skills. Learning to execute a physical restraint successfully on the job requires the individual to make continuous adjustments and corrections based on feedback received internally (from the muscles) and externally (from the child and the environment). After learning the procedure and the goal of the skill, the learner must learn each part of the skill correctly and then integrate each part into the total skill. This requires practice with corrective feedback. In the final phase of learning, the skill becomes automatic. While practice is considered the key element of motor skill training, practice alone does not ensure successful use of the skill. Informative feedback must accompany the practice so that the learner can correct errors and improve performance.

According to Gagne and Medsker (1996), the three factors that affect retention are: (1) the level of learning at the end of training, (2) the layoff period between training and retraining, and (3) rehearsal during the layoff period. The best predictor of retention is how well the learner has learned the skill. Overtraining or saturation learning (continued practice after the desired level of performance has been reached) enhances retention. The longer the period is between refresher training or retraining, the greater the probability of a decrease in retention. Rehearsing the skills is most effective when the rehearsal resembles the actual task and is combined with feedback for error correction.

What Was Learned from Transfer of Learning Research

Ultimately, effective utilization of skills on the job is desired. *Transfer of learning* has been described as the application of learning (knowledge, skills, and attitudes) acquired in a training setting to the job (Curry, Caplan, & Knuppel, 1994). Baldwin and Ford (1988) developed a useful overall framework for examining transfer of learning that can help to promote competence in using crisis prevention and intervention. They emphasized the importance of individual trainee characteristics, the work environment, and the training design. For example, one of the most important individual factors is what a trainee already knows. Similarly, environmental factors such as organizational support, the organizational value of training, administrative support, supervisory support, coworker support, and opportunity to use training have been found to promote transfer of learning (Brittain, 2000; Curry, 1996; Holton, Bates, Seller, & Carvalho, 1997; Tracey, Tannenbaum, & Kavanagh, 1995). Interventions to promote effective on-the-job practice incorporate individual and organizational/environmental elements into the training design.

A large body of research has been conducted on four areas of training design, or transfer principles (identical elements, general principles, stimulus variability, and response availability), that are relevant to training in crisis intervention (Baldwin & Ford, 1988; Curry, 1996; Goldstein, Lopez, & Greenleaf, 1979). Salomon and Perkins (1989) condense these four transfer principles to two major areas: (1) low road transfer and (2) high road transfer. Curry (2006a; 2006b) articulated the transfer recommendations specific to child and youth care training based on these researched principles.

Low Road Transfer

This type of transfer occurs via incremental learning involving varied and extensive practice that gradually extends to ever-widening situations. The learner may overlearn certain crucial content to the extent that it is displayed almost automatically when cued by the appropriate situation. The training and development professional may initially design the training and the transfer situations to be as similar as possible (identical elements) but gradually extend the learning and practice opportunities to include a wide variation of potential situations.

Unfortunately, it would appear that most training programs rarely design training that would involve this type of approach (it is usually very difficult to get administrative support to provide the required amount of learning and practice time), even though it is essential for certain types of skills (e.g., physical restraint). Many existing training programs involve insufficient opportunity for practice. Even when role-plays are included in training, they are often not used adequately for skill rehearsal by all of the participants. Learning a skill to the level of "automaticity" usually requires extensive practice time. It involves what is sometimes described as moving from conscious competence to unconscious competence, from controlled to automatic processing (Curry, 2001; Ormrod, 1990).

During the transition to this level workers may be described as having conscious competence. The worker has the knowledge and skill to perform a task, but the performance does not happen automatically. The worker may have to be reminded or cued by the trainer, supervisor or competent colleague to utilize the knowledge or skill already stored in long-term memory. Also, whenever the worker performs the skill, it may not be fluid. The worker may have to think about it while performing.

According to Miller (1956) short-term memory can only contain a limited amount of information (seven plus or minus two chunks). Therefore, a worker may sometimes have to rely on notes or cues from others. Interaction with youth necessitates that the worker keep one's goal, strategy, and information regarding the youth in active working memory. In addition, attending to what the youth is saying and doing so well while monitoring one's own behavior as part of an interactional exchange may overtax one's cognitive processing abilities. For example, during a life space interview, the worker may lose sight of the goal of the interview and may be unsure of his interview techniques at each step, sometimes not using the most appropriate response.

Anxiety can also limit the amount of information that can be maintained within short-term, active memory as well as the retrieval of information from long-term memory into active memory (Ormrod, 1990). Over-reliance on notes or long pauses trying to remember what to do next may adversely affect the worker's credibility with youth. In a noncrisis situation, the result is a less efficient and often less effective interactional process when compared to the performance of a more experienced practitioner. Without support in a crisis situation, negative transfer may occur, potentially resulting in harmful behavior.

As a learner progresses toward automatic processing, the worker's understanding and performance in a competency area begins the transition from a collection of relatively isolated information and facts to a recognition of "if, then" procedures. The worker begins to recognize that certain situations require specific actions or reactions. The worker also begins to recognize the underlying patterns/structure of behavior rather than responding surface features. With practice, performance steps consolidate and begin to require less active short-term memory, characteristic of highly competent practitioners. Performance now appears as a fluid, "effortless" activity. The worker uses little active, short-term memory while conducting the skill. She no longer has to "think" about the skill while performing (unconscious competence). It has been learned to the level of automaticity. Short-term memory is freed up and the worker can consciously focus on other activities such as self-monitoring (reflective practice) (Anderson, 1985; Curry, 2001).

Implications for crisis intervention training based on this approach include:

1. *Identify concrete common crisis situations so that skills that can be practiced in the training and work environments.* Practice the demonstration of skills with real case scenarios (or as close to real as possible while ensuring the safety of the learners). Learners need the opportunity to demonstrate skills and not just discuss cases.

2. *Identify and practice key skills to the level of automaticity (including nonmotor skills).* Some behaviors should be overlearned to the extent that a worker routinely employs them with little conscious effort. For example, a worker may routinely use reflective listening when interacting with youth.

3. *Practice with application in mind.* Make connections between the learning and doing situations. For example, ask a learner to adapt a role-play to make it as similar as possible to a typical work situation. You may ask them to choose another role player that most reminds them of someone in their work situation.

4. *Provide prompts, cues, and learning and application aides until a skill is fluidly performed.* These aides can be used both in the classroom setting and the application setting.

5. *Provide coaching, performance feedback, and emotional support until fluidly performed.* Rackham (1979) warns of a results dip that often occurs when learning new skills. Performance can temporarily decrease until a new skill is adequately learned. A worker's confidence and sense of efficacy may also decrease. Thus, a worker may revert back to previous behavior without adequate support.

6. *Increase the types of crisis intervention practice scenarios to include increasingly ever-widening situations.* This may involve the use of a variety of individuals and settings that workers encounter. Since the

amount of time permitted in training is limited, a practice and participant feedback plan must be developed and implemented that extends beyond the training setting.

7. *Use distributed practice with gradual removal of practice.* Integrate the practice into the work environment. This may involve the use of trainers and coaches in team meetings, etc. Encourage supervisors and others within the work environment to promote practice through discussion, practice, and problem solving in team meetings.

High Road Transfer

While low road transfer strategies encourage the learning of key skills to the level of automaticity (to the extent that a behavior occurs almost automatically, with little conscious effort), high road transfer involves very deliberate, conscious (mindful) thinking about the learning and implementation of a skill. The ability to think about, monitor, and guide how one learns and applies learning on the job has been described as metacognition or metacompetence (Bernotavicz, 1994; Curry & Rybicki, 1995). Learning skills to the level of automaticity frees up the limited amount of conscious short-term memory available to an individual and potentially increases the opportunity for learners to use metacognitive skills to promote application of ethical problem solving. More frequently, however, the tendency for most individuals is that automaticity inhibits analytical reflection. Examples in everyday life include learning about culture and family. Family and cultural knowledge are usually learned so well (to the level of automaticity) that most of us lose conscious awareness of the powerful family and cultural norms and values that guide our day-to-day behavior. This often becomes a barrier for many professionals in their attempts to become culturally competent. This invisible learning can affect (in a positive or negative manner) how child and youth care workers deal with many potential crisis situations. Thus, reflective practice (high road learning) must be encouraged.

High road transfer also involves the use of abstract principles (e.g., rules, labels, prototypes, schematic patterns). Transfer occurs by purposefully using general rules or principles that underlie the subject matter. One of the differences between experts and novices is that experts classify problems on the basis of abstract concepts, patterns, and principles compared with novices who tend to focus on specific parts of a problem (often the surface features) (Anderson, 1985; Chi, Feltovich, & Glaser, 1981). Implications for transfer of learning based on the high road approach include:

1. *Train underlying principles of child and youth care that transcend context.* Help learners recognize these underlying principles (mindful abstraction). For example, emphasize that behavior is an expression of need (need for closeness/connection or distance/independence).

2. *Help workers become aware of things they have learned so well that they are no longer conscious of the learning.* For example, help workers to identify their intervention style (e.g., directing, listening, teaching, relating, structuring). Help workers become aware of family and cultural learning that may continue to impact their child and youth care practice.

3. *Train assessment and decision-making strategies that can be used with many different types of problems.* Use of the Stress Model of Crisis and the Crisis or Conflict Cycle are examples (see Holden et al., 2001, for examples).

4. *Utilize parallel processing.* For example, have the learners examine how the trainer-trainee, the supervisor-supervisee, the worker-youth relationship, and the parent-child relationships are similar regarding the use of power. Also, when discussing how the environment affects the behavior of youth, examine how it also affects the behavior of youth workers.

5. *Use a variety of case examples for each crisis intervention principle to strengthen a learner's understanding of the principles.*

6. *Provide examples of when a principle applies and when not.* Helping workers differentiate when and when not to use physical restraint is a key competency.

7. *Help learners cognitively store information with retrieval in mind.* Identify potential crisis situations that are likely to occur. Help learners identify cues that will signal the worker that a potential crisis situation may exist.

8. *Train metacognitive skills.* Help the training participants learn how to learn and apply application principles. Help them learn to monitor and guide their practice. For example, provide suggestions and application aides that can serve as reminders to workers on the job that a case situation may have similarities to one that was previously discussed in training. Help them learn to recognize opportunities to use new skills and how to monitor their performance. Suggest that learners keep an application log to reflect on application of learning. Have them monitor their use of the four questions: What am I feeling

now? What does this young person feel, need, or want? How is the environment affecting the young person? How do I best respond?

9. *Help participants plan for application of learning.* Help them think about how to overcome barriers to application as well as strategies to prevent or reverse the process of backsliding into old habits.

10. *Train strategies for dealing with ill-defined problems.* While common child and youth care situations can often be effectively replicated (at least in case study discussion) within training, workers should also be trained to solve problems that may require outside sources of information such as libraries and evidence-based practice websites.

To effectively promote the application of learning in child and youth care practice settings, training and development professionals need to incorporate both low and high road transfer approaches. Utilization of both approaches helps to encourage practice by workers who are not only able to perform at a proficient level, but can conceptualize and articulate what it is that they do so well. These workers may be described as "reflective practitioners" who can also communicate effective practice principles, strategies, and techniques to others.

These workers recognize the underlying structure to certain situations rather than just the surface features. Low road transfer approaches may facilitate a worker's intuitive understanding but insufficiently help a worker to competently conceptualize and articulate these abstract concepts to others. Reflective practitioners are able to perform proficiently as well as conceptually understand and monitor the performance process (metacognition).

In addition to emphasizing individual strategies that promote low and high road transfer, it is clear that interventions must extend beyond the classroom setting and involve key persons within the transfer milieu.

An Ecological Model for Promoting Application of Learning on the Job

Curry, Caplan, and Knuppel (1994) describe a basic but comprehensive model that can be used to guide individual, environmental, and training design transfer interventions (including low and high road approaches) into a comprehensive transfer plan. Broad and Newstrom (1992) and Wentz (2002) also advocate a similar approach. They emphasize that key persons (e.g., worker, coworker, supervisor, trainer) at key times (before, during, and after formal training) can help or hinder transfer effectiveness. They suggest the utilization of a transfer matrix for transfer assessment and intervention that can be applied to any training. Table 6-2 provides a brief illustration of how the model could be applied to crisis prevention and intervention training. Many additional before, during, and after transfer strategies that incorporate both low and high road approaches can be included to help a child and youth care training and development professional achieve training and transfer objectives. According to the model, the total number and strength of factors in each cell promoting (driving forces) and hindering (restraining forces) transfer determines the amount of transfer of learning. The model can be used as a template to place over any existing training program to assess factors that affect transfer and develop an effective plan for transfer intervention and evaluation by increasing driving forces and decreasing restraining forces. Wentz (2002) also recommends using the model when things seem to go wrong in training, moving from blaming to learning. This approach involves a paradigm shift from viewing training as an event that occurs during the training session to an intervention influenced by context including key individuals before, during, and after training.

The Redevelopment of TCI

Although many of the learning and transfer principles discussed have already been incorporated into the TCI System (e.g., use of mnemonic devices to facilitate retention), additional and fundamental changes were indicated. For example, in order to strengthen and improve the delivery of the TCI System to residential organizations, the RCCP team concluded that it was necessary to shift an organization's crisis prevention and management focus from a training intervention to a system's approach that would help support the increased demands placed on agencies to reduce the need for physical restraint and maintain staff member's skill levels to execute high risk interventions with a minimum of risk to the child and the staff member. Changing the focus from TCI as a training curriculum to a crisis prevention and management system was a major element of the redevelopment.

In 2001, the TCI curriculum and system was redeveloped and reintroduced to new organizations as well as agencies already using TCI with an emphasis on a system's approach to crisis prevention and management. Key modifications in the system based on the research were included in seven main areas.

1. Five domains were identified (leadership, clinical oversight, supervision, training, documentation/critical incident monitoring) as critical organizational components affecting the prevention and management of crises (Nunno et al., 2003). Recommendations and implementation standards pertaining to each domain were developed.

TABLE 6–2: Transfer Matrix

PERSON	BEFORE	DURING	AFTER
Learner	Identify relevant cases that pertain to crisis prevention and intervention training.	Think about how you will recognize opportunities to prevent crisis situations when you are on the job.	Meet with your supervisor to help you identify how you can use your new learning in potential crisis situations.
Trainer	Meet with various personnel to identify relevant case scenarios for later use in training.	Help learners make cognitive connections from in-class discussion to real work situations by helping them identify a case to apply newly learned skills.	Send an e-mail reminding learners to meet with their supervisors to facilitate application. Meet with learners for a follow-up "booster shot" session to discuss application of learning and refresh skills.
Supervisor	Meet with worker to emphasize the importance of crisis prevention and intervention.	Attend the training with the entire team.	Lead a discussion during a team meeting regarding ways that the training could be incorporated into daily practice.

Adapted from: Curry, D., & McCarragher, T. (2004). Training ethics: A moral compass for child welfare practice. Protecting Children, 19, 37–52.

2. The training curriculum was revised based on R. M. Gagne's instructional design model to include methodology specific to teaching motor skills (Gagne, Briggs, & Wager, 1992; Driscoll, 2000).

3. The physical restraint techniques were redesigned with fewer steps allowing them to be learned and maintained more easily. A more emphatic and clear determination was made to help trainers assess whether a deviation within a physical restraint was a safety concern.

4. Standards were raised in relation to practice, overtraining or saturation learning, refreshers, and retesting for the TCI Training of Trainers course and direct TCI training.

5. Evaluation was embedded in the training with corrective feedback built in throughout the training event (McCowan & Weganast, 1997).

6. The training instruments were redesigned and expanded to include a written knowledge test, a verbal skills/interviewing test, and a physical skills test. The instruments were tested for validity and reliability.

7. A certification process was developed for TCI trainers that required mastery of verbal skills, physical skills, and decision-making skills measured through a testing process.

Measuring Physical Performance

One of the keys to measuring performance in physical restraints is to assess whether an adult can safely secure a child on the floor following a sequence of steps, while making adjustments for the size of the child, the way in which the child struggles, and the immediate location of the restraint.

The assessment standard shifted from determining a series of mechanical and physical errors to a standard of overall safety and security. Within this context the testing instruments identified functional stages and tasks within a physical restraint, and then identified the essential skills necessary to execute those tasks that are critical to overall safe performance of physical restraints.

Following this standard, a move or procedure was unacceptable if it had the potential to result in injury or prohibited the person from completing the restraint as prescribed. Even the most "expert" demonstrators vary in the way they execute the physical restraints in both movement and their use of cues. If the person restraining is too precise or has too many little nuances, the person restraining cannot be flexible to adjust the hold to varying conditions during a real restraint. With a resisting child, the adult must follow restraint steps that are simple, flexible, and basic. Again, the essential context is to do nothing that hurts the child and the restrainers or prohibits the completion of the restraint.

Instrument Design

In order to accomplish the goal of instrument development, the RCCP team identified the functional steps and tasks within a physical restraint. These steps were categorized into functional skills that were critical to overall safe performance. In addition, safety violations were identified and noted so that any person violating a safety concern would not pass the competency test. Since Cornell-based TCI instructors are the only individuals that instruct in the TCI train-the-trainer curriculum for agency trainers, it is imperative that Cornell-based TCI instructors are in complete agreement on restraint safety violations. Biannual clinics and retreats are held to ensure complete instructor safety rating reliability.

Improving TCI Skill Acquisition and Retention in TCI Organizations

As part of the overall TCI trainer credentialing process, guidelines were established for TCI trainers to follow to improve their participants' skill mastery, retention, and effective transfer of learning from the classroom to the work place.

1. *Allow sufficient time to practice during the training session.* During the training of trainers program, there are eight hours of physical restraint practice. Eight hours is also the minimum practice time recommended for the direct training. The longer the training and practice time devoted to skill mastery the longer the retention of the skill. The trainer should determine mastery levels using the steps outlined in the TCI curriculum.

2. *Build in refresher courses.* Refreshers should be conducted on a regular basis. The TCI System recommends four times a year or, as a minimum, every six months. Ensuring that *all* trained direct care staff take part in refresher training complete with error correction feedback may require the development of an organizational expectation.

3. *The competence of trainees to perform skills, both verbal and physical, should be assessed at the completion of the training and during refreshers.* Checklists for physical restraint techniques and life space interviewing skills to assist in this process of determining skill levels are included in the TCI course material.

4. *The minimum recommended length of the TCI course in the direct training format is four days, but a five-day offering is highly recommended.* There is often a trade-off between the amount of time necessary to sufficiently learn and practice skills and the amount of time realistically available to leave the job to attend training. A four- or five-day agenda will allow for adequate practice time, and allows for discussion of relevant issues surrounding the utilization of all techniques learned. Agendas for a four- and five-day course are distributed during the train-the-trainer week. It is a given that in order for learners to achieve mastery, adequate practice time and evaluative feedback for the initial learning of all TCI skills whether they are the life space interview, active listening, or any of the physical restraint methods must be provided. It should also be recognized that continuous learning and practice must occur in the transfer setting(s).

Conclusion

Calling upon a growing knowledge base that has implications for the training and development of staff using high-risk interventions with youth, this chapter has illustrated the importance and provided examples of research informing practice and practice informing research. Furthermore, this cyclical process suggests a transformation in how training and development activities should be viewed, expanding from a traditional view of intervention with individuals to include intervention with systems. Failure to successfully implement training and development interventions in the private business sector may result in a significant amount of unrealized financial return in worker learning. Misapplication of high-risk interventions in youth care settings can result in increased risk of harm or death to youth or youth care providers. An ongoing collaborative effort among various critical stakeholders including workers, supervisors, administrators, training and development professionals, and evaluation/research personnel is essential.

References

Anderson, J. R. (1985). *Cognitive psychology and its implications (2nd ed.)*. New York: Freeman.

Baldwin, T. T., & Ford, K. J. (1988). Transfer of training: A review and directions for future research. *Personnel Psychology, 41*, 63–105.

Bernotavicz, F. (1994). A new paradigm for competency-based training. *Journal of Continuing Social Work Education, 6*, 3–9.

Bell, L., & Stark, C. (1998). *Measuring competence in physical restraint skills in residential child care: Social Work Research Findings No. 21*. Edinburgh, Scotland: The Scottish Office Central Research Unit.

Brittain, C. R. (2000). *The effect of a supportive organizational environment on transfer of training in child welfare organizations*. Unpublished Doctoral Dissertation. University of Denver, Denver, CO.

Broad, M. L., & Newstrom, J. W. (1992). *Transfer of training: Action-packed strategies to ensure high payoff from training investments*. Reading, MA: Addison-Wesley.

Chi, M., Feltovich, P., & Glaser, R. (1981). Categorization and representation of physics problems by experts and novices. *Cognitive Science, 5*, 121–152.

Curry, D. (2001). Evaluating transfer of learning in human services. *Journal of Child and Youth Care Work, 15&16*, 155–170.

Curry, D. (2006a). Integrating training into practice. *Residential Group Care Quarterly, 6*(3), 5–7.

Curry, D. (2006b). Training intervention strategies to promote application of ethics learning in practice settings. *CYC-Online, The International Child and Youth Care Network, 84*.

Curry, D., & McCarragher, T. (2004). Training ethics: A moral compass for child welfare practice. *Protecting Children, 19*, 37-52.

Curry, D., & Rybicki Sr., M. (1995). Assessment of child and youth care worker trainer competencies. *Journal of Child and Youth Care Work. 10*, 61–73.

Curry, D. H. (1996). *Factors affecting the perceived transfer of learning of child protection social workers.* Unpublished Doctoral Dissertation. Kent State University.

Curry, D. H., Caplan, P. & Knuppel, J. (1994). Transfer of Training and Adult Learning (TOTAL). *Journal of Continuing Social Work Education, 6,* 8–14.

Deliere, H., & Schneider, L. (1980). A study of cardiopulmonary resuscitation skill retention among trained EMT-A's. *The EMT Journal, 4*, 57–60.

Driscoll, M. (2000). *Psychology of learning for instruction.* Boston: Allyn and Bacon.

Fitts, P., & Posner, M. (1967). *Learning and skilled performance in human performance.* Belmont CA: Brock-Cole.

Fosel, M., Kiskaddon, R. T., & Sternbach, G. (1983). Retention of cardiopulmonary resuscitation skills by medical students. *Journal of Medical Education, 23*, 184–191.

Friesen, L., & Stotts, N. (1984). Retention of basic cardiac life support content: The effect of two teaching methods. *Journal of Nursing Education, 23*, 184–191.

Gagne, R. M., & Medsker, K. L. (1996). *The conditions of learning, training applications.* Orlando, FL: Harcourt Brace College Publishers.

Gagne, R. M., Briggs, L. J., & Wager, W. W. (1992). *Principles of instructional design.* Belmont, CA: Wadsworth Thomason Learning.

Gass, D., & Curry, L. (1983). Physicians' and nurses' retention of knowledge and skills after training in cardiopulmonary resuscitation. *Canada Medical Association Journal, 128*, 550–551.

Goldstein, A., Lopez, M., & Greenleaf, S. O. (1979). Introduction. In A. P. Goldstein & F. H. Kanfer (Eds.), *Maximizing treatment gains: Transfer enhancement in psychotherapy.* New York: Academic Press.

Holden, M. J., Mooney, A. J., Holden, J. C., Kuhn, I. F., Sockwell-Morgan, C., Taylor, R., et al. (2001). *Therapeutic Crisis Intervention* (5th ed.). Ithaca, NY: Family Life Development Center, Cornell University.

Holton, E. F., Bates, R. A., Seller, D. L., & Carvalho, M. B. (1997). Toward construct validation of a transfer climate instrument. *Human Resource Development Quarterly, 8*, 95–113.

McCowan, R. J., & Weganast, D. P. (1997). *Embedded training evaluation: Blending training and assessment.* Buffalo, NY: SUC Buffalo.

Miller, G. A. (1956). The magical number seven, plus or minus two: Some limits on our capacity for processing information. *Psychological Review, 63*, 81–97.

Moser, D. K., & Coleman, S. (1992). Recommendations for improving cardiopulmonary resuscitation skills retention. *Heart & Lung, 21*(4), 372–380.

Nunno, M. A., Holden, M. J., & Leidy, B. (2003). Evaluation and monitoring the impact of a crisis intervention system on a residential child care facility. *Children and Youth Services Review, 24*(4), 295–315.

Ormrod, J. E. (1990). *Human learning: Theories, principles, and educational applications.* Columbus, OH: Merrill.

Rackham, N. (1979). The coaching controversy. *Training and Development Journal, 39*, 12–16.

Salomon, G., & Perkins, D. N. (1989). Rocky roads to transfer: Rethinking mechanisms of a neglected phenomenon. *Educational Psychologist, 24*, 113–142.

Tracey, J. B., Tannenbaum, S. I., & Kavanagh, M. J. (1995). Applying trained skill on the job: The importance of the work environment. *Journal of Applied Psychology, 80*, 239–252.

Tweed, W., Wilson, E., & Isfeld, B. (1980). Retention of cardiopulmonary resuscitation skills after initial over-training. *Critical Care Medicine 8*, 651–653.

Wentz, R. M. (2002). Learning from funny and outrageous training stories. *Training and Development in Human Services, 2,* 34–40.

Yakel, M. (1989). Retention of cardiopulmonary resuscitation skills among nursing personnel: What makes the difference? *Heart & Lung, 18*, 520–525.

PART IV

REDUCING
RESTRAINTS
THROUGH
ORGANIZATIONAL
CHANGE

Adopting a Public Health Model to Reduce Violence and Restraints in Children's Residential Care Facilities

Brodie Paterson,
David Leadbetter,
Gail Miller, and
John Crichton

Introduction

The concept of "frames" has a long history in the social sciences. Erving Goffman (1974) contended that we use frames in order to make sense of our life experience. In his description, frames are internal cognitive structures consisting of systems of classification and rules of interpretation. We make sense of our experiences on an ongoing basis by continually relating them to known patterns in the form of pre-existing stable frameworks that are already present in our culture or memory. Perception and the construction of meaning and understanding are based on these preorganized patterns. Frames exist, however, not only at the level of the individual but also at a societal level where the process of framing encompasses the selection of some aspects of a perceived reality and the promotion of a particular problem definition in such a way as to construct a particular causal interpretation, moral evaluation, or treatment recommendation (Entman, 1993). How we tend to understand and respond to any given social phenomenon is the product of an interaction between our cognitive frameworks and those frames that are dominant in our society. This process of making sense of our experiences occurs at both a conscious and unconscious level.

This chapter proposes that the societal frame that has dominated explanations of aggression and violence in residential services for children can be characterized as "individualistic." Within this frame, violence results from the child's pathology or character deficits and/or the staff's skill deficits or character flaws (Leadbetter, 2003). The limitations associated with this individualistic frame and the implications for the use of physical restraints by staff with children in care as a response to violence will be examined in this chapter. The advantages of adopting the public health model to reframe the problem of workplace violence also will be explored (Paterson, Miller, & Leadbetter, 2006).

Using the term "public health" in a book on residential child care risks alienating those professionals and practitioners who see themselves as operating primarily within a psychosocial or social educational model. The relevance of the public health model, however, will be illustrated with reference to a story that may be familiar to some readers.

In 1854, John Snow, an English physician, successfully traced the source of an outbreak of cholera in London to a communal water pump in Broad Street in Soho. The water supplied by the pump had become contaminated with fecal matter from cholera victims and was continually recycling the then fatal disease.

Snow was alerted to the fallacy of the prevalent explanation of how cholera was transmitted not only by the cluster of cases around that particular pump but also by a case that had occurred several miles away in an affluent area of London. He was able to trace this particular case back to the contaminated water taken from the pump in Broad Street. In order to establish that water was the cause of the cholera outbreak, Snow had to make a conceptual leap in rejecting the opinion of the day that blamed miasma (foul air) for causing cholera. Snow's insight into how cholera was transmitted ultimately led, through massive investment in the provision of clean drinking water and sewerage, to the effective elimination of cholera from the developed world.

The lesson derived from the example provided by the story of Snow's Broad Street pump is that "prevention is always better than cure." Moreover, in updating the prevention model, Sethi, Marais, Seedat, Nurse, and Butchart (2004) state that prevention has three distinct dimensions, as follows, when applied in the context of violence prevention:

- *Primary*: action taken to prevent violence before it occurs;

- *Secondary*: action taken to prevent violence when it is perceived to be imminent; and

- *Tertiary*: action taken when violence is occurring and after it has occurred to prevent or reduce the potential for physical and psychological harm to the parties involved and to inform primary and secondary prevention strategies. The notion of prevention in this context is in the public health sense of preventing or reducing harm.

This chapter will use this primary, secondary, and tertiary prevention framework as the basis for an exploration of how the public health model can be used in practice to reduce levels of aggression and violence, and therefore restraints, in residential treatment facilities. Restraint can, where used under rigorous oversight, play a critical role in keeping both staff and children safe in situations of violent crisis. Attempts to reduce the use of restraint, though, have been associated in some settings with decreases in violence towards staff (Murphy & Bennington-Davis, 2005). This suggests that the causes and therefore the solutions to both may share certain causal factors.

Primary Prevention

The notion of primary prevention posits that attributing responsibility for violent behavior solely to individual characteristics of the child or staff neglects the extent to which many aspects for the cause of violence are actually beyond the control of the individual. Causation has to be understood, then, as multiply determined. Of course, causes of aggression and violence by the child, for example, do exist at the level of the individual, such as genetic factors, social and cognitive skills, and unique experiences with neglect or abuse, and the ensuing trauma and dysfunctional attachment patterns. These causal factors are often described as "internal" to the child.

It has been known for more than 50 years, however, that there also is a relationship between residential staff behavior and agency culture and the rates of violence and the use of coercive interventions, such as physical restraints (Stanton & Schwartz, 1954). The behavior and characteristics of young people who use residential services are, in fact, poorer predictors of rates of violence and restraint use than are agency philosophy and staff beliefs about the reasons for violence in children and youth (de Cangas, 1993).

Violence and its concomitants in restraint or seclusion happen not in isolation but in a context comprised of interpersonal relationships themselves influenced by organizational culture and philosophy. The primary prevention of violence requires, therefore, that attention be paid to agency culture and its effect on workplace climate because violence can only be fully understood and prevented when it is seen as part of the agency culture (Gilligan, 2000).

Recognition of the Problem

Before an exploration of the cultural dimensions of coercion, restraint, and violence within an agency can be undertaken, the agency must first recognize it has a problem. Unfortunately, a number of organizations remain locked into coping strategies that use techniques described as "avoidance" or "denial"

(Leadbetter, 2003). Avoidance can be seen where the organization seeks to steer clear of any recognition of the issue, for example, by adopting No Touch policies or discouraging the reporting of violent incidents or restraint in order to pretend that a significant problem does not exist.

A more common yet problematic approach is denial. Denial in this organizational context accepts the existence of violence but explains it as a function of consumer pathology and staff skills deficits. This explanation clearly adheres to the individualistic frame (Leadbetter, 2003) and effectively blames the parties directly involved, abnegating any form of collective organizational responsibility (Fisher, 2003).

This tendency to individualize responsibility for violence within organizations can also be seen when organizations frame their response to workplace violence within policy documents. Content studies of such documents confirm the prevalence of a tendency to present behavioral management in highly individualistic terms (Johnstone, 1988). This observation is not a criticism of the need for services to acknowledge the unique needs of each child through such practices as individualized assessment and treatment care planning. This is both good practice and a core requirement of almost all regulatory agencies irrespective of the setting.

It is, instead, to suggest that, where policies place responsibility on workers to anticipate, manage, and recover from the child's aggressive behavior, these policies can serve to downplay and obscure the significance of the role of the organization (Fisher, 2003). A "good" organizational strategy for managing violence, for example, will link the organization's statement of philosophy to clear goals for the reduction of violence that, in turn, are linked to ongoing initiatives, each of which is subject to evaluation. A "bad" organizational strategy, for example, may consist solely of a Management of Violence or Restraint Policy largely comprising statements instructing staff on how they should respond to imminent or actual violence.

Organizational Responses to Violence

The International Labour Organization has advocated that organizations seeking to respond to the issue of violence in the workplace should adopt what it has termed *high road* approaches (Chappel & DiMartino, 1998). High road approaches are based on the concept of the "smart" (i.e., learning) organization (Senge, Kleiner, Roberts, Ross, Roth, & Smith, 1999). The organization is understood as an active entity that learns through continual reflection on its performance (Birleson, 1999). In the context of violence and restraint prevention, this reflection starts with the development of an explicit statement of the organization's philosophy and values and encompasses every aspect of an organization's role in addressing the issue of workplace violence. Such philosophies are contained within an organization's vision statement (Murphy & Bennington-Davis, 2005, p. 5). For example:

- to create a place of absolute safety and respect for the staff and the young people we serve;

- to work in an environment where restraint and seclusion are unnecessary and where the alternatives of respect, kindness, safety, and education replace them.

The means by which such values are transmitted into practice, however, is not left to chance. A project management model, informed by theories such as the Balanced Scorecard model (Niven, 2003), can be used to establish whose expectations must be met (Dowd, 1999). This approach provides a set of principles along with the techniques for analyzing and improving an organization's performance in four general areas: financial performance, customer care, organizational learning, and internal processes. The balanced scorecard model breaks down high-level strategies into four aspects: objectives, measurements, targets, and initiatives. Data collection systems are then applied to monitor the behavior of staff and senior managers. These behaviors include those of staff toward each other as well as those of direct care staff toward children.

Once a specific objective to decrease the use of restraints has been set, indicators are put into place to establish baselines that allow targets to be set; for example, a 50% reduction in the use of restraint over the next 12 months. Initiatives to achieve these targets are then developed. These initiatives might include a directive for senior management to attend to the scene after every episode of a restraint, and the use of regular clinical supervision to ensure that the organization consistently delivers on its values in both its dealings with its staff and the children. The exact nature of the initiatives, of course, should reflect the local context (McKenna & Paterson, 2006). When the Balanced Scorecard approach is linked to the idea of the learning organization the desired result is a virtuous cycle of restraint reduction initiatives informed by reflection. Such an approach once activated, can also help an organization to remain true to its philosophy and values irrespective of short-term pressures such as those resulting from changes in personnel that can occur (Birleson, 1999).

Root Causes of Violence in Organizations

At this point, before embarking on the various initiatives to reduce violence and restraint through the public health model, it is necessary to establish a solid understanding of the root causes of violence in residential settings. If these potential sources of violence are not recognized and addressed as part of a systematic preventative strategy then the strategy is fundamentally flawed. Therefore, a brief discussion of some of the more commonly recognized root causes of violence in the workplace will be discussed and some solutions will be offered.

Child and Staff Interactions. Research across various settings consistently suggests that conflict between the child and staff is often an antecedent to aggression and violence and that such conflict is often unrelated to the pathology of the individual. Such conflict occurs most often where staff act as aversive stimuli, that is, staff are involved in an experience that the child perceives as unpleasant, such as preventing her from fulfilling a particular wish, denying access to some form of resource, making an activity demand, or criticizing or shaming the child, perhaps in front of the child's peers (Whittington & Wykes, 1996). Violence described as unprovoked can instead represent what is a delayed or even displaced response by the child to such aversive stimuli (Whittington & Wykes, 1996).

Negative Organizational Climates and Staff Reactions. The autonomy of residential staff is often restricted by explicit or implicit demands that control over children be exercised in order to meet cost and time pressures (Paterson et al., 2006). Direct care staff, particularly those at the lowest point in an organizational hierarchy, can experience high levels of "negative role stress" as a consequence of their limited autonomy and conditions of work that can include exposure to aggression directed towards them by children (Karasek & Theorell, 1990). Negative role stress can increase a staff member's likelihood of being a victim of violence (Hurrell, Worthington, & Driscoll, 1997).

One mechanism to explain the relationship between negative role stress and victimhood is that the member of staff disempowered by her hierarchy, may unconsciously displace her needs for control and self-esteem into their relationships with children and, in seeking to compensate, over-control children and, by doing so, evoke conflict. The feelings of futility and hopelessness evoked by the discrepancy between the worker's expectations of her work role and the reality she may experience can, as a result of displacement, also find their expression in overt or covert hostility directed at other workers (Paterson et al., 2006).

Constructive organizational cultures address these potential causes of violence by creating and maintaining norms of supportiveness and by actively promoting positive interactions with others. The organization's approach to getting the job done is not to sacrifice the emotional needs of staff to meet the requirements of the agency but, instead, to consider meeting the higher-order satisfaction needs of staff as an integral part of their long-term strategy; a strategy whose effects will ultimately reduce rates of violence in the longer term (Belbin, 1981).

Status and Power Inequities Among Staff. Settings, such as children's residential homes or inpatient services, are often characterized by inequalities of power both between children and staff and between the different professional and paraprofessional groups that comprise the staff complement. These inequalities are readily evident, for example, in differences in status reflected in income and benefits. Such inequalities provide fertile ground for conflict because they provide the conditions for an abuse of power (Peacock, 2002) and can all too readily foster the development of what they have described as "toxic" organizations (White, 1997; Wyatt & Hare, 1997). A toxic organization's central dynamic is marked by shame and humiliation accomplished via bullying (White, 1997). This creates a defensive posture in those bullied and can lead to a widespread toxic culture characterized by demands for submissiveness from both staff and children that leads interactions with others to be approached not as opportunities for collaboration and mutual growth but as potentially threatening events (Cooke & Szumal, 2000).

Where the individualistic frame continues to provide the dominant explanation for violence, a dichotomy in staff responses to violence by children can sometimes be observed. On the one hand, where the judgment by staff is that violence has been a consequence of pathology, and therefore illness, the result is a focus on *care and treatment.* On the other hand, where their judgment attributes responsibility for such violence instead to character failings, the result is a search for a *means of punishment,* which, in some circumstances, physical restraint can provide (Crichton, 1999). Staff can, and almost inevitably will, at some point, question the nature of the management strategy to be adopted in response to violence by individual children (Goren & Curtis, 1996). These disagreements can be productive when, for example, they lead to greater reflection on the needs of a particular child and how these needs are being met. But where the disagreements are the result of differing attributions of responsibility for violent episodes, these disagreements can lead to differing beliefs about responding to violence (Goren & Curtis, 1996).

Counteraggression and Avoidance. Repeated situations where staff are exposed to violence, and their causal attribution places responsibility with the child's character failings, can lead to one of two types of staff responses. Some staff may adopt a counteraggressive response in their routine dealings with the child. Other staff may seek to minimize their contact with the child who has previously been violent or to avoid situations where conflict may arise (Maier & Ryebroek, 1995). Neither response is helpful in seeking to reduce violence or restraint. The former because it serves to legitimize controlling, if not punitive, interactions that can reinforce the existing negative stereotypes held by staff. The latter because it leads to reduced levels of positive engagement and increased frustration in children. Both increase rather than decrease the potential for alienation between children in care and residential staff (Fisher, 2003).

Unfortunately, rather than take the necessary action to address negative organizational culture and its behavioral manifestations, for example, by promoting job enrichment, reducing negative role stress, and promoting cultures of respect, a more common reaction, driven yet again by the individualizing frame, has been to send staff on a training course in the prevention and management of violence. Such training has almost invariably focused on secondary and tertiary prevention and concentrated on developing staff skills in conflict resolution, de-escalation and physical intervention skills, and post-incident support (Leadbetter & Paterson, 2004). These are usually delivered in the form of standardized crisis management systems that are often heavily marketed to managers unfamiliar with the complexities of violence management. The effect is to apply a solution in the form of a "product bought off the shelf" to a problem whose roots lie in the processes involved in how the organization delivers its services rather than to the maladaptive or inappropriate behavior of any one individual (McKenna & Paterson, 2006).

Use of Depersonalizing Language. It is not uncommon in some settings to encounter descriptions of children's violent behavior by staff as "acting up," "acting out," or "kicking off." The use of such terms establishes a barrier between staff and children, allowing staff to maintain an emotional distance from the actual emotions of the child, whether of anger, fear, or loss. The easy response is to ban these forms of language use as inappropriate and seek to punish any staff found using them. The more challenging approach is to acknowledge the purpose served by such language in depersonalizing the strong emotions they are exposed to as a defense strategy against the phenomena of burnout and recognize the need for the organization to promote alternative positive coping strategies, for example, by regular clinical supervision. By establishing and addressing the root causes of aggressive and violent behavior rather than focusing merely on eliminating it as undesirable, positive cultural change can be achieved.

Nonproductive Staff and Organizational Responses to Violence: Training Without Broad Organizational Change

Training can play a valuable role in enhancing staff's abilities to recognize and avert conflict situations, to deal more safely with physical violence, and to respond more constructively in how they provide postincident support. In a review of the research on aggression management training, Allen (2000) concluded that such training could generate a range of positive outcomes including reductions in violent incidents and injuries. Allen also observed, however, "[U]nfortunately, the research indicates that none of the above outcomes can be guaranteed from training, and negative results have also been observed in each of the above areas" (p. 23). Such results are readily explained because, even where the relevant model has "face validity" in the context, if the root causes of violence have not been understood and addressed, the influence of aggression management training on rates of violence is likely to be marginal. Sections of the unregulated training industry that has emerged in child care over the last two decades in their promotion of training in the "short-term management of violence" as a one-stop solution to the problem of workplace violence may indeed have perpetuated the dominance of individualistic explanations and allowed organizations to remain in denial. The result in some settings of the application of such training solutions might have been an increased rather than a decreased risk to the welfare of children and staff from violence (Health and Safety Executive, 2006).

Before any training for direct care staff is undertaken, the question of whether broader cultural change is necessary must be considered. In this context, the culture of organizations is exemplified by the local norms modeled by senior management. A cultural assessment of the agency can provide information about where and when to intervene to deliver change in order to achieve violence reduction (Burke, 1994). This assessment can then inform a training needs analysis that includes all workers from the executive director down. The training strategy ultimately adopted may include the need to revisit core professional values, collaborative approaches to care planning, and the use of structured risk assessment and management plans (Harchik, Sherman, Sheldon, & Strouse, 1992). In addition, advanced training in such therapeutic approaches as cognitive behavioral psychotherapy and psychosocial interventions should be considered. The organization must ensure that staff have the necessary skills to deliver the focused, structured, evidence-based interventions that have the possibility of averting violence before it occurs (Goldstein, Glick, & Gibbs, 1998). Assuming that such skills necessarily exist simply belies the reality of some children's services.

Moreover, when the issue of who needs training is raised the training needs of managers, whether at the executive or board level, are often not considered. This is a fundamental mistake because, although senior managers or board members may not require training in physical interventions, they will have other training needs (National Health Service Education Scotland,

2006), such as recognition of their role in promoting a constructive culture, positive leadership skills, the provision of clinical supervision, how to support staff exposed to violence, and training in techniques of root cause analysis.[1]

Secondary Prevention

A Functional Analysis of Behavior

Given the emphasis in this chapter on the need to adopt a public health model, because of the tendency for the individualistic frame to overemphasize secondary and tertiary prevention, reference to secondary prevention will be brief. As stated earlier, secondary prevention concerns action taken to prevent violence that is perceived to be imminent but has not yet taken place. Depending on the context, secondary prevention may be planned or unplanned. In some situations, violence by children can involve highly predictable patterns of responses. Knowledge of such patterns garnered through a functional analysis can allow the planning of proactive, positive interventions to prevent violence. This planning, where practical, should be done in conjunction with the child, enabling early recognition of indicators that he is not coping and knowledge of his preferred coping strategies to be incorporated into crisis support plans.

In other instances the child may not be well known to an organization, such as when a child has only recently been admitted to the residence. In such situations, staff must follow broad guidelines on violence prevention strategies, such as conflict resolution and de-escalation, while using clinical judgment to identify an effective response, compatible with the relevant legal and ethical principles applicable to their setting (Paterson, Leadbetter, & Tringham, 1999).

Tertiary Prevention

Strategies to Manage Violence

Within the context of tertiary prevention, violence is either happening or has happened; staff have been unable to prevent its occurrence and are now focused on reducing the risk of violence causing physical and psychological harm to the child. Strategies to manage immediate violence will vary depending on risk assessment and organizational policy but may also include withdrawal by staff,

---

1. Root cause analysis refers to an approach to incidents, developed originally to investigate aircraft crashes, that identifies the role played by the individual and the organization in incident causation and examines the interactions between the various systems (Anderson & Fagerhaugh, 1992).

the removal of other children who may be at risk of assault, or whose presence is either provoking violence or the implementation of physical interventions such as "blocking" or "breakaway" strategies.[2] Such techniques reflect the presumption that holding or restraining children should not be automatic responses to violent behavior by children (Delaney, 2001). Serious or prolonged violence may, however, necessitate physical intervention in the form of physical or mechanical restraint, seclusion, or medication (Delaney, 2001). These interventions often involve immediate care staff, senior personnel, and a response team where such an approach is practical. There must, however, be clear protocols in place detailing the nature of the response expected by each member of the team.

Becoming a Learning Organization

Once the immediate crisis has passed, organizations could do several things in order to remain consistent with the requirement for becoming a learning organization and to adopt a public health model. Five key steps are essential:

1. *Review the incident* for whatever lessons need to be learned organizationally. The purpose is to avert or manage similar situations better and reduce the potential for aggression and violence.

2. *Review the care of the individual concerned* so whatever actions necessary in relation to the individual's care or support plan are taken to avert future crisis and enhance the management of crisis.

3. *Review the actions of staff involved* so any acts or omissions that may have contributed to the incident or detracted from its successful management are identified, recorded, and addressed. This does not necessarily mean an "investigation" by management, unless serious misconduct is alleged or suspected, and is sometimes best carried out through peer review if a positive and supportive culture exists. In some instances, however, where a supportive culture does not yet exist and "staff attitudes might themselves be a problem" (Horton, 2001, p. 7), any investigation of alleged wrongdoing should therefore involve an external representative, such as a child advocate.

---

2. Blocking strategies involve physical techniques designed to reduce the likelihood of staff experiencing injury during and assault. Breakaway strategies involve physical techniques designed to enable staff to remove themselves from a threat.

4. *Promote positive outcomes for the child involved* since violence or restraints can evoke strong feelings in both victim and perpetrator creating a volatile emotional situation. Immediate management of the circumstance will focus on ensuring safety and preventing re-ignition of violence in a situation that may remain volatile. When it is judged appropriate, a structured debrief with the child may be conducted that seeks to explore the antecedents (i.e., the relationships between feelings, behavior, and alternative coping strategies) that might be used to deal with similar situations in the future. These coping strategies can then be practiced later on in controlled simulations, such as in role plays, thus forming part of primary prevention and helping to avoid future crises (Neizo & Lanza, 1984).

5. *Put in place flexible supports* so staff involved in such incidents can access at their discretion a range of supports that may include occupational health, employee assistance programs, and various forms of Pastoral support. There are some suggestions that pre-incident, rather than post-incident, support may be the most important determinant of whether an individual develops or does not develop a pathological reaction to exposure to violence and there have been criticisms that "stand alone" post-incident support can actually be harmful (Health and Safety Executive, 2006). Consequently, there remains some debate about how we can best support staff exposed to violence, particularly postincident (Paterson, Leadbetter & Bowie, 1999). What is unquestionably not in doubt is that support should be there.

Conclusion

Too many organizations providing residential care services to children and youth continue to believe that their violence and restraint levels are at the lowest that can be achieved and that their current strategies based around secondary and tertiary prevention represent an acceptable response. The public health approach challenges such complacency in asserting that the roots of violence in our services can lie in the failures of organizations to:

• promote constructive workplace cultures;

• understand and thus meet the needs of the children they serve and their staff;

• understand the significance of the nature of the relationships between staff and children;

- understand the importance of resolving conflicts between staff members and within staff teams;

- understand and respond to the emotional impact of exposure of aggression and violence on staff;

- recognize the role of trauma in pathology and the negative impacts of trauma on both children and staff; and

- acknowledge the potential for abuse associated with inequalities of power and to seek to ensure that children and staff are treated with dignity and respect.

Nevertheless, as this book has illustrated in celebrating examples of successful initiatives, each of these failings is amenable to remedy. What is missing in some services is the courage shown by Snow to make a conceptual leap when faced by the evidence of the role of the water pump. The individualistic frame allows organizations to stay within the comfort zone provided by victim blaming with responsibility for solving the problem of violence firmly allocated to their training opportunities. Whether we are dealing with a potentially toxic organization, a dysfunctional and conflicted team, or our own relationships with those children with whom we work and the sources of the emotions present in these relationships, confrontation and self-reflection are never easy. Reflecting on and confronting the existence of a problem is invariably the first step toward its eventual resolution.

As an overarching framework, the public health model is sufficiently flexible to accommodate a broad range of different types of interventions and treatment programs, whether behavioral, attachment, or trauma-focused. Reframing the problem of violence and restraint reduction using the public health model does not, therefore, require the abandonment of such programs. Rather it requires reflection upon how we understand the task of violence prevention in ways that should focus our attention differently. It does not suggest that interventions that engage with individual pathology in the form of intra-psychic issues, such as the impact of trauma, are unimportant. Indeed, it emphasizes the need for children to have access to skilled and qualified staff who are equipped to engage in appropriate treatments in settings that facilitate rather than hinder such work. In stressing primary prevention, however, the public health model suggests that such interventions should be complemented by interventions that seek to transform the organization's culture so that its function as a therapeutic agent is accorded equal status (Paterson et al., 2006).

References

Allen, D. (2000). *Training carers in physical interventions: Research towards evidence based practice.* Kidderminster: British Institute for Learning Disabilities.

Anderson, B., & Fagerhaug, T. (1992) *Root cause analysis: Simplified tools and techniques.* New York, ASQ Publishers.

Belbin, M. (1981), *Management teams—Why they succeed or fail.* London: Heinemann.

Birleson, P. (1999). Turning child and adolescent mental-health services into learning organizations. *Clinical Child Psychology and Psychiatry, 4,* 265–274.

Burke, W. W. (1994). Diagnostic models for organization development. In A. Howard (Ed.), *Diagnosis for organizational change: Methods and models* (pp. 53–84). New York: Guilford Press.

Chappel, D., & DiMartino, V. (1998). *Violence at work.* Geneva: International Labour Office.

Cooke, R. A., & Szumal, J. L. (2000). Using the organizational culture inventory to understand the operating cultures of organizations. In N. M. Ashkanasy, C. P. M. Wilderom, & M. F. Peterson (Eds.), *Handbook of organizational culture and climate* (pp. 147–162). Thousand Oaks, CA: Sage.

Crichton, J. H. M. (1999). Staff response to disturbed behaviour in group homes for adults with a learning disability. *Criminal Behaviour and Mental Health, 9,* 215–225.

de Cangas, J. P. C. (1993). Nursing staff and unit characteristics: Do they affect the use of seclusion? *Perspectives in Psychiatric Care, 29*(3), 15–22

Delaney, K. (2001). Developing a restraint-reduction program for child/adolescent inpatient treatment. *Journal of Child and Adolescent Psychiatric Nursing, 14*(3), 128–140.

Dowd, J. F. (1999). Learning organizations: An introduction. *Managed Care Quarterly, 7*(2), 43–50.

Entman, R. M. (1993). Framing: Towards clarification of a fractured paradigm. *Journal of Communication, 43*(4), 51–58.

Fisher, J. A. (2003). Curtailing the use of restraint in psychiatric settings. *Journal of Humanistic Psychology, 43*(2), 69–95.

Gilligan, J. (2000). *Violence: Reflections on our deadliest epidemic.* London: Jessica Kingsley Publishers.

Goffman, E. (1974). *Frame analysis: An essay on the organization of experience.* New York: Harper and Row.

Goldstein, A. P., Glick, B., & Gibbs, J. C. (1998). *Aggression replacement Training: A comprehensive intervention for aggressive youth.* Chicago: Research Press.

Goren, S., & Curtis, W. J. (1996). Staff members' beliefs about seclusion and restraint in child psychiatric hospitals. *Journal of Child and Adolescent Psychiatric Nursing, 9*(4), 7.

Harchik, A. E., Sherman, J. A., Sheldon, J. B., & Strouse, M. C. (1992). Ongoing consultation as a method of improving performance of staff members in a group home. *Journal Applied Behavioural Analysis; 25,* 599–610

Health and Safety Executive. (2006). *Violence and aggression management training for trainers and managers: Research Report RR440.* London: Health and Safety Executive.

Horton, J. (2001, July 25). No protection. *Guardian Society Pages*, p. 7.

Hurrell, J.J., Worthington, K.A., & Driscoll, R.J. (1997). Job stress, gender and workplace violence: Analysis of assault experiences of state employees. In G. R. VandenBos, & E. Q. Bulatao (Eds.), *Violence on the job,* (pp. 163–171) Washington, DC: American Psychological Association.

Johnstone, S. (1988). Guidelines for social workers coping with violent consumers. *British Journal of Social Work, 18,* 377–390.

Karasek, R., & Theorell, T. (1990). *Stress productivity and the reconstruction of working life.* New York: Basic Books.

Leadbetter, D. (2003). *CALM associates training manual.* Menstrie: CALM Training, Scotland.

Leadbetter, D., & Paterson, B. (2004). Developing an agency approach to safe physical intervention. *Nursing & Residential Care, 6*(6), 280–283.

Maier, G. J., & Ryebroek, G. J. (1995). Managing counter transference reactions to assaultive patients. In B. S. Eichelam, & A. C. Hatwig, (Eds.), *Patient violence and the clinician,* (pp. 73–104). Washington, DC: American Psychiatric Press.

McKenna, K., & Paterson, B. (2006). Locating training within a strategic organizational response to aggression and violence. In D. Richter, & R. Whittington (Eds.), *Violence in mental health settings causes consequences management* (pp. 231–251). New York: Springer Verlag.

Murphy, T., & Bennington-Davis, M. (2005). *Restraint and seclusion: The model for eliminating their use in health care.* Marblehead, MA: HCpro.

National Health Service Education Scotland. (2006). *Standards for training in the prevention and therapeutic management of violence in adult mental health settings.* Available online at www.nes.scot.nhs.uk/docs/news/ FINAL_DOC_FOR_PUBLICATION_NOV05.doc. Edinburgh, Scotland: National Health Service Education Scotland.

Neizo, B. A., & Lanza, M. (1984). Post violence dialogue: Perception change through language restructuring. *Issues In Mental Health Nursing, 6,* 245–254.

Niven, P. R. (2003). *Balanced scorecard: A step-by-step guide for government and nonprofit agencies.* New York: Wiley.

Paterson B., Leadbetter D., & Bowie V. (1999). Supporting nursing staff exposed to violence at work. *International Journal of Nursing Studies, 36*(6), 479–486.

Paterson, B., Leadbetter, D., & Tringham, C. (1999). Critical incident management: Aggression and violence case study. In D. Mercer, T. Mason, M. McKeown, & N. McCann (Eds.), *Forensic mental health care planning, directions and dilemmas* (pp. 139–145). Edinburgh: Churchill Livingstone.

Paterson, B., Miller, G., & Leadbetter, D. (2006). Beyond Zero Tolerance: A varied response to workplace work place violence. *British Journal of Nursing, 14*(15), 811–815.

Peacock, R. (2002). Macro and micro links between interpersonal violence and violence in broader society: An integrated etiological perspective. *Acta Criminologica, 15*(3), 39–44.

Senge, P., Kleiner A., Roberts C., Ross R., Roth G., & Smith, B. (1999). *The dance of change: The challenges of sustaining momentum in learning organizations.* New York: Doubleday/Currency.

Sethi, D., Marais, S., Seedat, M., Nurse, J., & Butchart, A. (2004). *Handbook for the documentation of interpersonal violence prevention programmes.* Geneva: World Health Organization, Department of Injuries and Violence Prevention.

Stanton A. H., & Schwartz, M. S. (1954). Some covert effects of communication difficulties in a psychiatric hospital. *Psychiatry, 17,* 27–40.

White, W. L. (1997). *The incestuous workplace: Stress and distress in the organizational family.* Center City, MN: Hazelden.

Whittington, R., & Wykes, T. (1996). Aversive stimulation by staff and violence by psychiatric patients. *British Journal of Clinical Psychology, 35,* 11–20.

Wyatt, J., & Hare, C. (1997). *Work abuse: How to recognize and survive it.* Rochester, VT: Schenkman Books.

CHAPTER 8

Leadership's and Program's Role in Organizational and Cultural Change to Reduce Seclusions and Restraints

David Colton

Introduction

Acceptance of seclusion and restraint by employees of behavioral health care organizations exists along a continuum, which helps to shape and is shaped by the organization's culture. In some organizations seclusion and restraint are viewed as forms of external control which provide no therapeutic benefits, have little if any empirical support as a clinical practice, and may lead to additional trauma and harm (e.g., Mohr & Anderson, 2001). This contrasts with viewpoints that describe these interventions as a "necessary evil" to impose when all other approaches to helping the youth maintain self-control have been attempted and failed or as an action that when implemented properly can be a part of the continuum of available therapeutic interventions (e.g., Antoinette, Iyengar, & Joaquim, 1990; Troutman, Myers, Borchardt, Kowalski, & Bubrick, 1998).

The culture of an organization consists of "shared basic assumptions...that has worked well enough to be considered valid and, therefore, to be taught to new members as the correct way to perceive, think, and feel in relation to problems" (Schein, 2004, p. 17). Consequently, making the transition from one viewpoint to the other can be a challenging process, as it may require questioning and testing personal beliefs, values, and past actions. To use the terminology of psychologist Kurt Lewin, we may need to "unfreeze" our existing belief system in order to consider alternative explanations (Burnes, 2005).

As difficult as it may be to question beliefs, it may be even more challenging to change our behaviors. The term "paradigm shift" has been coined to describe a metamorphosis in what we believe in *and* what we do in response to new ideas. Paradigm shifts can be challenging and they can make us uncomfortable. As behavioral health care organizations take action to address the use of seclusion and restraint they are finding that this indeed involves a transformation of existing values, belief systems, and actions to entirely new ways of thinking about and delivering treatment. This entails structural, process and cultural change, and making this transformation can be challenging as well as threatening to treatment staff, which can have a profound effect on the ability of the organization to initiate and sustain this transition.

Models of Organizational Change

For this study, organizational change was defined as activities that attempt to modify structural, process, or cultural elements. The change process can be planned and systematic, for example, by articulating goals to reduce or eliminate restrictive interventions and then by formulating a strategic plan that addresses many of the factors that contribute to seclusion and restraint reduction (Colton, 2004). On the other hand, change can be an emergent process, without a clear or written document that describes the process. In such organizations seclusion and restraint reduction may take longer due to the lack of a clear focus and sense of direction. In some cases, change can be a reactive or even chaotic process where there is no plan or leadership resulting in different department/divisions within the organization addressing the change process in their own way, at their own pace, and with a different understanding of the results to be achieved.

To understand the transformation of the organization's culture, it is important to identify the approach that the organization uses to carry out the change process. This reflects a number of intangible attributes such as management's ability to lead, communicate, and coordinate the change process, as well as an understanding of interpersonal dynamics. For example, employees may be supportive, neutral, or resistive to change. This response may be overt or covert, it may be a reflection of an individual's ability to accept and adapt, or may represent a collective response/defense to change. Ultimately, the organization's ability to implement and sustain changes in structure and process will depend on how well the intangible attributes and thus cultural change occurs.

> To the extent that change initiatives are values-based, they
> may clash with cultural patterns of values, thought, and
> action already in place. If already-existing cultural patterns
> are inconsistent with new values and cultural implications
> of systematic change initiatives, then defensiveness, with-

> drawal, and distortion of important information may result. These effects can powerfully inhibit an organization's ability to implement successful, durable systematic change.
> Moreover, another result of these effects is that organizational learning—learning that could focus attention on these effects as potential problems—is likely to be prevented. (Dooley, n.d., p.1)

When structural and process changes become embedded it is *assumed* that cultural change will also occur. In relation to reduction of seclusion and restraint, cultural change might be reflected by the decisions, language, and actions staff use to guide and support children in crisis situations. For example, when a child is escalating, preseclusion/restraint reduction language and actions might be based on a culture of "keeping the environment safe" by ensuring that staff are in control of the situation. The child is given the choice of going to his room or to time out. Such actions can quickly escalate into power struggles and increase the perceived need for external control. In response to structural change such as a new program model and staff development curriculum, staff approach the situation and implement the process differently, such as by allowing the child to cool down in place and by being physically present, but not engaging the child unless he is ready to interact. Cultural change would occur when staff are comfortable with these new approaches and implement them as the preferred style.

The change process does not occur immediately; organizations that report success in reshaping their culture and climate indicate that this is a multiyear process. Dooley (n.d., p.2) suggests that, "systematic change requires a transition period of at least three to five years." The 99% reduction in the use of restraints reported by Millcreek Behavioral Health Services was attained over a four-year period (JCAHO, 2004). Collins (2001) refers to this as the "fly wheel" principle, as it takes many actions over many years to propel change within the organization. Gladwell (2002) uses the term "tipping point," a concept from the field of epidemiology that suggests small changes will have little or no effect on a system until a critical mass is reached. Then a further small change "tips" the system and a large effect is observed.

Conceptualizing Change

Prechange Condition. Several ways of conceptualizing the change process have been presented in the literature and as reflected in Table 8-1 there is considerable overlap between these models. Although the process is not necessarily linear, there is agreement that a prechange condition exists in which the

TABLE 8–1: Stages of Organizational Change

Colton[1] (2004)	Duck (2001)	Gordon (1999)	Kotter (1996)
No action / no discussion	Stagnation	Increase forces for change	Overcome complacency
Espoused	Preparation	Decrease forces against change	Establish a sense of urgency / Create a guiding coalition / Development of vision and strategy / Communicate the vision
Intermittent / inconsistent action	Implementation	Select the most appropriate change agent	Empower employees for broad-based action
Action	Determination	Implement the most effective intervention strategies	Support short term wins as a means to long term change and success
Sustained action / maintenance	Fruition	Evaluate and institutionalize organizational change	Be aware of forces that will hinder change / Be aware of the impact of cultural change

1. *Adapted from Prochaska and DiClemente (1984).*

members of the organization are unaware of a problem or need for change, or resist the threat of change. For example, in this stage "there is no formal consensus within the organization that a problem exists and if some members think there may be a problem there is no concerted effort or intention to address the problem" (Colton, 2004, p. 8). Kotter (1996) notes that complacency often contributes to a sense that everything is okay and there is no urgent need to change the status quo. In the *Change Monster* (2001), Duck notes that during periods of stagnation, the organization gets good at ignoring the data. For example, practitioners may come to accept staff injuries as the price of working with emotionally disturbed children, rather than considering how the treatment process, programs, and level of staff skills may be contributing to the problem.

Preparation and Selection of Strategies. Once organizational members recognize the need to tackle a problem or change existing practices there is a period of preparation that might involve communicating the problem to the organization, building support for change, and initiating planning. Depending on the level of leadership, this stage may flow fluidly, or may be inconsistent or intermittent with a flurry of activity followed by periods of inaction and inertia. Here again, the organization must confront the readiness of its workforce to accept and implement change.

> Once a company has recognized that it is, in fact, in a state
> of Stagnation, and its leaders, after diagnosing the areas
> and degree of Stagnation, have determined that they want
> to change the business rather than dump it, the next step is
> to develop a strategy that will bring them to success. Strategy, by definition, must lead the current reality. Developing
> a sound strategy is not easy; executing it is even more difficult because the beliefs, habits, and attitudes of an organization—its culture—usually lag behind the current reality.
> In other words, the culture is defined by one set of circumstances—usually some earlier reality—but when the reality
> changes the culture does not. (Duck, 2001, p. 77)

One aspect that is often difficult for leaders to confront is their own role in this stage of the process and their responsibility for ensuring that there is a structure to support the change process. For example, Collins (2001) notes that prior to creating a vision and developing a strategy it is incumbent on leaders to obtain the *right* people to support the process. Although it is healthy to be open to and consider different perspectives, it is important that the organization's leaders support the new vision. If a member of the management team believes that seclusion is an appropriate therapeutic option she may be less likely to actively support the change process and may overtly or covertly work against it. The organization's leaders must be willing to confront this, such as determining how that member can be brought on board or by making the difficult decision of asking the individual to leave.

Action taken during the preparation stage has a significant impact on the effectiveness of activities subsequently taken during the action/implementation phase. For example, most organizations engage in some form of strategic or tactical planning, such as creating and communicating a vision, clarifying goals and objectives, and identifying actions that need to be implemented to foster change. A good strategic plan will address all three organizational elements:

structure, process, and culture. Some organizations are reluctant to commit to a written plan, as there is concern that this will lead to inflexibility and inability to adapt to change. In that case, at a minimum, organizations should engage in strategic thinking: considering where the organization is now, where it wants to be, and what it needs to do to move forward. In either case, change agents must be aware of how the change process functions.

> Planned organizational changes are often set up to fail by the very change methods used. The initial inputs to an organization change effort are unconscious biases about what the organizational effectiveness really means. These biases direct our choice of change methods to those that perpetuate the very values to be changed. For example, an organization wants to introduce process changes to improve effectiveness. Because of a strong belief in the importance of a proper structure, the change method chosen attacks the structure rather than the processes. Consequently, what starts as a process redesign ends as a structural redesign. The processes continue as ineffectively as before, although in new clothes. (Izumi & Taylor, 1998, p. 1)

During the preparation stage, intervention strategies should be identified and selected. For example, to support seclusion and restraint reduction, a structured staff-training curriculum might be implemented to enhance staff competencies. Also, during the preparation stage organizational leadership should have considered and planned for: (1) timeframes for realistically implementing interventions and programs, (2) resources needed to support change, (3) costs associated with the change process, (4) responsibility—who will lead the change effort (this might include committees, designated internal change agents, or champions), and (5) the impact change will have on organizational culture.

Implementation and Maintenance. Ultimately, observable and measurable activities are undertaken to implement change. During the implementation/ action stage, those responsible for change ensure that activities are carried out as planned and within designated timeframes, that resources are made available, and that there is constant evaluation of the process to ensure that it is being implemented as intended. Because this is where the rubber meets the road some members of the organization may fully commit to the concepts and activities, some may take a middle of the road, wait and see stance, while others may reject and even work against the process (Colton, 2003). Once again, management and the organization's change agents must be cognizant of the impact that change has on climate and culture. Even when employees have been brought into the process through open communication, participation in committees and work teams, and training, "during change initiatives situations of uncertainty, ambiguity, and stress abound" (Dooley, n.d., p. 6).

Finally, the organization commits its resources to sustain the change process and the activities it has implemented. For example, if the organization has been able to achieve a measurable decrease in seclusion use, a conscious effort is made to maintain the activities that led to that reduction. Although changes in key personnel can influence this process, these actions are so integrated into the organization's structure that they are self-sustaining. During this phase, the new structures, processes, and culture that have developed begin to 'refreeze' and as new members enter the organization they are inculcated to the treatment philosophy and work environment this creates.

Regarding seclusion and restraint reduction, in organizations that have undergone cultural change, a visitor might observe verbal interactions that are essentially free of external control language, staff that report feeling safer and more confident in their abilities and patients who report greater satisfaction in their inpatient experience and the outcomes of treatment (Kalogjera, Bedi, Watson, & Meyer, 1989). Continuous evaluation and improvement of processes should produce reductions in seclusion and restraint use (frequency and duration) that are *sustained* over time. This in turn should help solidify changes in the organizational culture.

Methodology and Facility Description

Eight mental health facilities serving children and adolescents were identified and invited to participate in this study. The invitation was made by e-mail and included a copy of the study protocol. Six organizations expressed interest and five participated (the sixth organization dropped out due to the key informant changing employment). The interviews averaged more than an hour in length and provided the investigator an opportunity to gain an understanding of what the organization was doing to reduce seclusion and restraint use and how those actions impacted on service providers. Informants readily provided supportive data (see Figures 8-1 through 8-5). On the other hand, due to resource constraints the interviews were conducted by telephone with just one informant within the organization.

While this provided an opportunity for examining multiple sites, it placed limitations on verifying the information, as the investigator could not make physical observations or talk to others within the organization. Nonetheless, respondent's willingness to share information about interpersonal dynamics within the organization suggests they were candid and that their recollections are valid perceptions of the change process.

Cases

This study is based on interviews of key informants working at five different inpatient/residential mental health facilities serving children and adolescents. All five facilities are located in the eastern part of the United States—from New England, through the Mid-Atlantic States, and into the upper South. Although the sites differ in size (such as bed capacity and average daily census) and program structure, they serve similar populations: heterogeneous groups of emotionally disturbed children or adolescents based on diagnosis and history. This is important because in this regard the study is comparing apples to apples; the actions taken to reduce seclusion and restraint should apply across settings.

For reference, the programs have simply been labeled A to E and pseudonyms have been given to the informants. Table 8-2 summarizes distinctive features of these organizations.

Program/Facility A: At the time the study was initiated, this organization was beginning the change process and during the course of the study had moved into an action stage. A number of activities occurred to raise the level of awareness of staff in regard to the topic of seclusion and restraint reduction and some actions were taken to support staff in this process. Most notably, the organization has recently contacted a consultant and is in the preparation stage for implementing a specific intervention strategy. There is growing evidence that this is a successful intervention that can be applied in institutional environments, as well as in home settings.

Figure 8-1 illustrates seclusion use at Facility A for the past 2.5 years (average is straight line in all graphs); month-to-month variation is indicative of an organization that has not yet taken a systematic approach to seclusion/restraint reduction.

> In quality improvement parlance, processes are out of control in this facility as there is considerable variation from month to month. This pattern is typically observed when seclusion is applied to a significant percentage of clients served (common cause variation) or when a few clients requiring high utilization of these interventions skew the data (special cause variation). When viewed over the short term, drops in use may create a false impression that usage is declining and treatment staff may be lolled into believing that their efforts to reduce seclusion and restraint are working. (Colton, 2004, p. 13)

TABLE 8–2: Cases

TYPE/LOCATION	DEMOGRAPHICS	INFORMANT
A. University affiliated unit in a children's hospital	15-bed unit serving children ages 5 to 13. Average daily census of 13 and median length of stay of one month.	Robert, MD: Clinical director of the unit.
B. University affiliated unit in a general hospital	13-bed unit serving children ages 3 to 12. Average daily census of 12.	Sheila, RN: Nurse manager with a Master's degree in health administration.
C. Nonprofit children's program operating a day school, outpatient service, and residential treatment center	96-bed residential program serving children ages 5 to 14. Average daily census of 90 and average length of stay of 8 months.	Denise, RN: Director of quality improvement with a Master's degree in nursing.
D. State funded acute care facility for children and adolescents	48-bed facility consisting of four 12 bed units, serving children ages 6 to 17. Average daily census of 30 and median length of stay of 14 days.	James, RN: Facility director.
E. University affiliated children's center operating a day school program, partial day treatment program, short-term acute evaluation unit, and residential treatment center	20-bed residential program serving children ages 6 to 14, with an average length of stay of one year. 10 bed evaluation unit serving children ages 6 to 12 with an average length of stay of 75 days.	Gary, PhD: Executive director of the center.

Program/Facility B: This organization implemented a specific intervention strategy several years ago and is actually a site that is being used to evaluate its effectiveness as an evidence-based practice (Figure 8-2). The program director is in the process of refining the structural, procedural, and cultural changes that occurred in order to sustain the gains that have been made.

In the ideal situation, a focused, comprehensive approach to seclusion/restraint reduction should result in sustained reduction in restrictive interventions; the hypothetical situation described in the following paragraph is exactly what we observe in the graph for this organization.

FIGURE 8–1: Facility A: Seclusion Use—January, 2002 to April, 2005

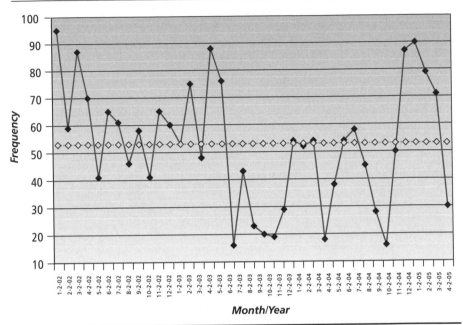

The...graph depicts an organization, which has been implementing a number of actions to reduce seclusion use. As
additional activities are initiated, the use of seclusion
decreases. In addition to a downward trend in utilization,
there is less variation from month-to-month. Similar trends
might be observed when the duration of restrictive interventions are charted, for example, the average amount of time
that clients are secluded or restrained should decrease as
well as the frequency of these events. (Colton, 2004, p. 13)

Program/Facility C: This organization has taken two approaches to restrictive intervention reduction. The rapid reduction in seclusion was accomplished by
initiating training with staff and by taking a number of seclusion rooms off-line
(Figure 8-3). Restraint reduction is currently being addressed as a quality
improvement initiative that encompasses creating a vision, studying the literature
to identify new approaches, developing an action plan, and involving consumers.

Program/Facility D: This facility has taken several actions to influence
seclusion restraint use, most notably implementing a process that monitors
and compares use against thresholds (Figure 8-4). This data is then used to

FIGURE 8–2: Facility B: Restrictive Interventions Reduction—September, 2000 to September, 2004

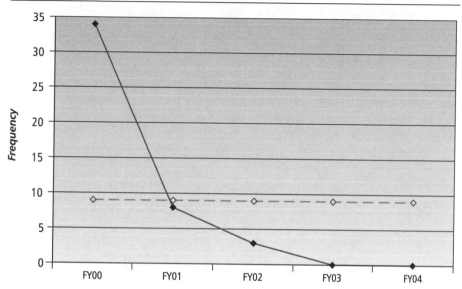

FIGURE 8–3: Facility C: Average Seclusions—FY00 to FY04

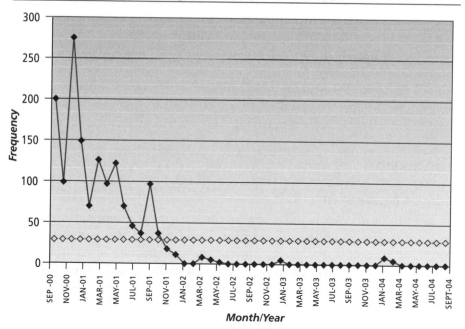

FIGURE 8–4: Facility D: Number of Seclusions from January, 2002 to April, 2005

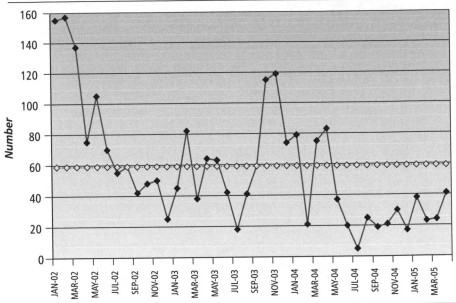

notify treatment teams when there is an outlier case that needs to be reviewed. The organization is still in the early phase of identifying intervention strategies and training staff to those approaches. Consequently, as the graph illustrates, although there has been a reduction in overall use, it has been an uneven process as there still are monthly fluctuations.

    Program/Facility E: As illustrated in Figure 8-5, there is a notable decline in seclusion usage during the past year, although some month-to-month variation is observed. This pattern is indicative of an organization that has implemented one or more interventions to reduce seclusion and restraint, but may need to initiate other actions to gain greater control of the process.

Discussion

Role of Leadership

Leadership Leads. When Sheila applied for her current position, her employers were candid about the situation she would inherit. It was the spring of 2001 and the unit was under scrutiny by the state because of its high use of restrictive interventions. Additionally, the unit had experienced massive staff turnover including clinicians, nurses, and milieu counselors. In fact, Sheila

FIGURE 8–5: Facility E: Seclusions Use from January, 2002 to March, 2004

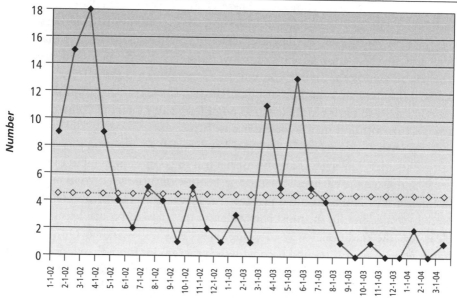

would be the fourth nurse manager in five years. It was also a frustrating work environment for those she supervised, as

> ...nobody was happy with the amount of assaults taking place on the unit and nobody was happy with the degree of restraining and secluding they were doing, but they couldn't imagine any other way, and the more people were assaulted, the more they were restraining and secluding, so they were caught in this unproductive dynamic.

Four years later, Sheila and her staff have virtually eliminated the use of seclusion and mechanical restraint and have significantly reduced the use of physical holds (Figure 8-2, Program B). Sheila's approach to leading this transformation is in some ways a textbook example. Structural changes were initiated including implementation of a specific treatment approach and redesign of the program to support the treatment model. New processes were developed to ensure that staff received ongoing training to implement the treatment model with consistency. To support a treatment philosophy based on empowerment, staff had to be empowered; therefore the nurses and milieu staff were given greater authority for decision-making such as the ability to make decisions about a child's treatment without getting the immediate approval of the entire treatment team (i.e., decisions that did not require the approval of a licensed clinician). These changes were carried out under an individual who provided focused, demonstrative, yet supportive leadership.

Has the culture on Sheila's unit changed? Sheila acknowledges that staff may still use the old vocabulary of providing safety, consistency, and structure but she also adds that what you will see is something quite different. When asked if the changes would be sustained if/when she leaves the program, Sheila responded: "I think it's in their blood now. They can't imagine doing the work any way than [how] they're doing it now."

The change process for Sheila as well as the other programs in this study was not without its challenges. Early on, Sheila had to confront a number of employees who resisted the changes. Fortunately, because of turnover, a good number of her milieu staff had been hired just the year before Sheila came on board. They were frustrated but for the most part willing to try a new approach because it was clear that the traditional way of doing things was not working. On the other hand, some of the nurses had been with the program for more than a decade and either covertly or overtly resisted the process. When it became evident that the hospital administration backed Sheila's efforts, these individuals chose to leave.

Peters and Waterman (1982) refer to the use of champions within the organization who become leaders in the change process and Sheila noted that there were indeed several individuals who helped move the change process forward. For example, one of the milieu counselors became, "a spokesman out on the milieu in terms of talking about these ideas and giving them credence in a way that was supportive to what I was saying in more formal fashions and meetings."

The influence that leadership has on reducing or eliminating seclusion and restraint cannot be underestimated. Both clinical and administrative leaders must communicate and support a philosophy based on minimal, appropriate use of seclusion and restraint and incorporate that conviction in the organization's vision, goals, and objectives; indeed, Schein (2004) notes that culture and leadership are two sides of the same coin. The Commission on Quality of Care Restraint and Seclusion Practices in New York State Psychiatric Facilities (1994) determined that leadership might be the *primary* determining factor for reducing the use of restrictive interventions.

Leadership Is Optimistic and Committed. Although there were differences in style and approach to leadership, there was also a common thread between the informants. All believe things can be different and better. In those organizations that have made the most progress, leadership was dogged, decisive, and committed to the change process. For example, Sheila described herself as someone who has strong opinions, who was not interested in managing a mediocre unit, and who was willing to push the envelope in order to challenge and motivate employees: "I wanted to work collaboratively with people, but my style was not the kind of 100% democracy where you spend four years getting consensus."

Conversely, Robert (Program A) had to take a patient and deliberate approach to change: "I saw right away that we overuse seclusion and restraints and when I started approaching this it became very clear that if I chose this as my number one objective that I would very quickly alienate the milieu." Changes in organizational structure and turnover of staff have provided Robert with a window of opportunity to begin the change process. With the hiring of a nurse/program director who is also interested in improving the quality of treatment and addressing the seclusion and restraint issue, Robert and his colleague have begun a process of educating staff to the possibilities of new approaches.

Leaders Communicate Clearly and Consistently. These leaders believed in themselves, although they experienced periods of doubt and had to occasionally reaffirm their dedication to the effort. Visibility, accessibility, and communication skills appear to be important components of leadership as informants spoke about the many meetings, both formal and informal, they held with staff to communicate the organization's vision, goals, and plans.

For James (Program D) the biggest challenge has been to convince the organization's clinicians that reducing seclusion and restraint is a desirable and doable goal. When he became director, it was evident that many of the facility's psychiatrists and psychologists believed that seclusion and restraint was a necessary evil and a part of doing business. Some even believed that these interventions had a therapeutic benefit.

> This process of discussion and pulling in data brought
> about a change in the clinical staff. It brought about a
> change in them examining their own values and beliefs
> toward seclusion and restraint and I think it has led to a
> uniform feeling that seclusion/restraint isn't a good thing.

James believes that the clinical staff have turned the corner and recognizes that seclusion and restraint are not therapeutic interventions, although in the process,

> ...it was necessary for one or two individuals to leave the
> organization. I don't think we have a single clinician here at
> this facility now that believes being placed in seclusion or
> restraints has a therapeutic benefit to the patient. It may be
> necessary but it's not therapeutic.

It was evident that James believes in the importance of changing the under-lying belief system in preparation for making structural and process changes and he acknowledges that there is still a way to go: "We're in a point in time on our continuum that we don't think it's a good thing but we're not to the point that we think it must be prevented at all cost."

This organization is a good example of how structural and process changes can occur at different rates. For example, the facility has established a treatment plan review process that is triggered when the number of restrictive interventions reaches a pre-established threshold. However, the organization has not made as much progress in developing a staff-training curriculum or modifying the pro-gram structure. Consequently, James acknowledges that systemic cultural change has not yet taken place.

Leadership Is Shared Throughout the Organization. Although the data suggest that leaders who are focused and determined can have a significant influence on the change process, Denise's description of how her organization is addressing seclusion and restraint reduction indicates that leadership does not have to be embodied in a single individual to be effective. Denise (Program C) noted that prior to becoming quality manager her organization already had a thriving qual-ity improvement program. The organization has adopted the PDSA (plan, do, study, act) cycle developed by Joseph Juran and obtained national recognition for their quality improvement activities (Colton, 2000). So it was a logical step to address seclusion and restraint reduction as a quality improvement initiative.

Denise related that a work group was formed in response to JCAHO (Joint Commission for the Accreditation of Healthcare Organizations) requirements to examine and address use of seclusion and restraint. The work group consisted of program managers and direct care staff who determined that to move the process forward, one of several actions to reduce seclusion was to take the seclusion rooms off-line. Although this decision was combined with staff training to facilitate structural and process changes, in retrospect Denise acknowledges,

> We didn't do it in a planful way as we've done the thera-
> peutic hold initiative and we moved fairly quickly and
> decided to get rid of the (seclusion) rooms, so I think we
> learned something; although it did turn out to be a good
> thing. But I think the way we did it we probably could've
> done it a little bit better.

In regard to the leadership that quality improvement committees provide, Denise highlighted the fact that there are family members and consumers on the quality council and a parent on the quality improvement team addressing restraint reduction. "She's right there with us and has an equal membership and partnership in this committee."

The Role of Program Change

If leadership is an essential component for guiding and sustaining change, there must also be a 'product' on which change is centered. For most organizations this is operationalized as reconceptualizing treatment philosophy, modifying the program structure, and providing staff with skills that change the process of patient/client-staff interactions. This study found considerable diversity as to how the organizations approach this process and even in the terminology used to describe the process.

When asked what the organization was doing to reduce seclusion and restraint, the informants indicated that staff were receiving training that would change the way they perceive and engage the child. Some referred to this as a *relational-based approach,* a *strengths-based model,* or a *nurturing environment,* and some did not have a specific term, describing it as providing staff with a toolbox of techniques.

There was general agreement that changing the approach and structure for treatment was vital for changing organizational culture as it provides staff with a different way of conceptualizing behaviors and their relationship with the child. For example, some organizations have adopted the concept of *trauma informed care* as articulated by the National Association of State Mental Health Program Directors (2005). That was the focus of staff education this past year at James' organization.

> If we took the patients and looked at them as a person who has experienced a lot of traumatic events in their life and is responding to trauma, then you start looking at that patient differently when they come through the door. They aren't just a bad person. They aren't just a patient that's there to hurt people and I found that the staff had more empathy.

Likewise, Sheila noted that 85% of children on psychiatric units in her state have been victims of trauma and that the process of implementing restrictive interventions also created traumatic situations for staff.

Sheila stated that she had attended a one-day conference where she heard a psychologist present an approach to working with children who appeared out-of-control and unresponsive to attempts to de-escalate them in a crisis. The psychologist, Ross Greene (2001), referred to them as explosive children and described his approach as collaborative problem solving. Shortly after being hired and recognizing that what they were doing was not effective she began to think about Greene's presentation.

I thought what a great leveling factor if we could find a model of care that fits with our children and was something here that nobody knew so that we would all be learning together. And I wanted a model that had a reasonable chance of success. And while I was thinking about that and trying to figure out what kind of models I would look for, I had this 'Ah-ha' moment and thought back to the collaborative problem-solving approach.

Sheila did more than think about it. She contacted Greene and asked him to consult with the program. Staff received training and also ongoing supervision that often took the form of open discussions about what worked and what did not. Sheila also notes that although they did not dissemble the existing program, which included a point and level system, eventually "staff were begging us to get rid of the level system because none of them were implementing it (as) it made absolutely no sense with our new approach."

A number of crisis management programs exist and the organizations that took part in this study are using different ones. Denise's organization had been using the program developed by the Crisis Prevention Institute (CPI) but has switched to Therapeutic Crisis Intervention (TCI) developed by the Family Life Development Center at Cornell University (2001). Gary's organization (Program E) had the benefit of being a recipient of a U.S. federal government SAMHSA (Substance Abuse, Mental Health Services Administration) technical assistance block grant to study approaches to reducing seclusion and restraint. The funding was used to enhance training and the organization adopted Satori Alternatives to Managing Aggression (SAMA). As a state agency, James' organization implements the crisis management curriculum selected for all state hospitals, which for years was MANDT (named for its founder, David Mandt). Several years ago the state created its own program it calls Therapeutic Options. Finally, Robert's organization is exploring alternatives and is considering use of collaborative problem solving. Although these programs share basic concepts, they differ in content and comprehensiveness, with some focusing on the crisis management aspect and others providing a broader approach to working with clients. Adoption of these programs demonstrates a change in organizational structure and process; however, most of these programs are just now being evaluated for effectiveness and may not be recognized as an evidence-based approach.

Improving the Overall System of Care

In regard to programmatic change there was also a consensus that these changes are being made not solely to reduce seclusion and restraint, but more broadly to create healthy and effective treatment settings. For example, Robert thought it important to point out the "distinction between milieu change as opposed to seclusion and restraint change" as an opportunity to improve the "day-to-day operations and the way we engage the kids, the way we problem solve with kids...that people are going to be very fired up about that." James also addressed the need to think in broader terms so that seclusion and restraint reductions become a by-product of improving the overall quality of care.

The informants viewed change as a multiyear process, with the most time spent in the preparation phase, and that change is not a linear process. In regard to preparation, informants described a number of structural changes that were necessary prior to even considering modifying programs and rethinking the treatment philosophy. For example, Robert had to work with the hospital and the university to work out clinical rotations for psychiatrists, psychologists, and nurses, which was a sticking point.

Sheila noted that staff were empowered to collaborate with the children and be creative in developing solutions without having to wait for the treatment team to approve the solution or wait to bring it to clinical rounds. Denise noted that even though they have selected TCI as their primary tool, they are still revising and honing the treatment philosophy and shared that, "we're more of one mind today than we might have been at the very beginning (of the change process)." James acknowledged that although they have turned the corner in regard to recognizing that seclusion and restraint are not therapeutic, there is still no consensus about a model of care or approach to be implemented. In that regard, James' organization is still very much in the preparatory stage with discussion and consideration of various models but no specific structural format to provide staff at this time. Gary spoke to changes in the external environment that have helped shape the agenda for change and move most organizations forward in their seclusion and restraint reduction efforts such as revisions to the JCAHO standards and in his case, state mandates.

The respondents noted that real, long-term cultural change is difficult to achieve and reflects commitment to a long-term process. Robert noted that employee behaviors might change in response to structural and process change, and attitudes might change in response to training, but an individual's values are much slower to change; thus true cultural transformation may not be visible for years after the change process has begun. Robert believes that the belief system on which staff base their interactions has been successfully transformed in his organization and that the culture has truly changed. He bases that observation in part to the mesh or fit between the organization and the employee. Those employees who take a hard line toward children do not stay with the organization, they are either fired or find that their behaviors are not tolerated by their coworkers and choose to leave.

Denise noted that you have to take an organization's history into consideration when thinking about cultural change; organizations should not be overly critical of themselves for past practices that may be viewed differently given current information. For example, her organization started as an orphanage with a highly structured behavioral system, so staff behaviors that were successful for that time and setting look different in light of contemporary theory and processes.

James observed that cultural change is difficult when individuals do not perceive the system is in need of fixing. "It's easier to get buy-in when something is broken and needs to be fixed, [but] harder to convince people that improvement should be done for improvement sake." In regard to seclusion and restraint reduction, James felt that underlying belief systems had to be challenged prior to attempting structural and process change. Conversely, he described making structural and process changes to the way clinical documentation is disseminated in his organization. In that situation, he believes that this changed the way that clinicians think about the documentation process and thus leads to a change in their behaviors, attitudes, and values; that is, cultural change. This suggests that the approach taken is situational and contextual.

Sheila agreed that core values need to be challenged as a first step but added that you cannot wait for everyone to get on board.

> I think you have a window of opportunity...in the first year. I know long-term changes take five years, but if you wait in this insidious gradual process you may never get there, because you have a window of opportunity when you have a group of excited people that are ready to make that leap. You are asking people to buy into something that they can imagine is going to be better, but you're asking (them) to make that leap before they have confidence or the skills in their ability to do it.

Sheila believes the culture has changed because direct care employees are willing to invest time working with children before, during, and after a crisis, whereas before they would have given "lip service to some rule and then start enforcing limits." A palpable measure has been a reduction in turnover of direct care employees. During the transition phase turnover increased, particularly among staff who could not or would not buy into the change process.

Today turnover is less then 20% a year, and that turnover is due to factors other than work conditions and job dissatisfaction.

Conclusion

The five cases profiled in this study provide a window into organizations at different stages in the change process and illustrate different approaches taken to reduce or eliminate use of seclusion and restraint in the provision of mental health treatment to children and adolescents.

In regard to the assumptions that provided direction to the study, it appears that tackling multiple factors moves the change process forward more decisively than addressing just one or two at a time. For example, Sheila's organization, which demonstrated the most systematic change and has been able to sustain outcomes, focused on redefining its vision as a treatment program, training and staff development, structural changes to the program, and empowering staff.

The study helps confirm the factors that influence seclusion and restraint reduction (Colton, 2004). For example, it is evident that leadership is a decisive factor in the process, as the findings suggest that the level of commitment to a vision and involvement in the process of change influences the ability of the organization to initiate and sustain organizational and cultural change. These leaders, whether as individuals or as a group take time to prepare employees by communicating their vision and goals, and by encouraging buy-in. Nonetheless, they do not wait for staff consensus to implement changes.

This last factor has significance for organizations in the early stages of change; how far do you go to get understanding, involvement, and commitment before you initiate change? Upon reflection, in part, this appears to be a question of timing. Although she met some opposition, many of the employees in Sheila's program were dissatisfied and willing to try a different approach and thus she found a tipping point early into her tenure as a program manager. In contrast, both Robert and James were working with organizations where staff, including clinicians, were comfortable with the status quo and did not question the appropriateness of seclusion and restraint. To have initiated major structural and process changes at this time would have lead to increased dissatisfaction and opposition. Consequently, the preparation phase had to be extended to support changes in belief systems, which has lengthened the time it has taken to move the organization to a point where it is ready for change.

Gladwell (2002) suggests that tipping points occur as the result of multiple factors coming together at a precipitous moment; leadership has little influence on the process. It appears that in the context of this study, however, leadership is indeed a critical factor. Metaphorically, a piece of music may include intermezzos and stirring crescendos. It would appear that like an orchestra conductor, effective leaders know when to adjust their style and actions to the music of events within the organization. For example, these leaders find opportune times to introduce new ideas and to implement change, are sensitive to staff reactions to the change process, and have thought through possible responses to support change efforts.

Because Sheila's organization is further along in the process and has had the most success as measured by total reduction in restrictive interventions, it has served as a benchmark when analyzing the data. To that end, it appears that operationalizing the vision by having a specific programmatic approach helps to further both organizational and cultural change, as staff have something concrete to work with. Nonetheless, although this study identified different programmatic approaches that these organizations have adopted, additional evidence is needed regarding the effectiveness of these interventions and whether outcomes can be replicated.

All of the informants appeared to have thought out the process strategically, though some more than others and it was not clear if any of these organizations had developed and articulated written strategic plans. Nonetheless, this suggests the benefit of strategic planning, for without it the change process could be like Ulysses' journey home from the Trojan Wars: the organization may have a broad goal in sight but the route is uncharted and the journey might get side-tracked and take longer to achieve.

It was evident that change was not a linear or static process. The organization does not unfreeze in order to make structural and process changes and then refreeze with a new and different culture intact. As the organization chisels away at the existing structure, a new structure will emerge. Ideally, changes in structure and process become so imbedded that the underlying culture ultimately is transformed.

The individuals that participated in this study represent organizations that are attempting to transform programmatic constructs and staff behaviors that are deeply ingrained. As one respondent noted, "We are dealing with years of history in what was thought to make a difference and help children and all of that is being turned on its head. It requires the organization to think through almost every process connected with the therapeutic milieu." Hopefully, this study acknowledges that effort and provides information that can be useful to other behavioral healthcare organizations attempting to improve quality of care by reducing or eliminating the use of restrictive interventions.

References

Antoinette, T., Iyengar, S., & Joaquim, P. A. (1990). Is locked seclusion necessary for children under the age of 14? *American Journal of Psychiatry, 147*(10), 1283–1289.

Burnes, B. (2005). Complexity theories and organizational change. *International Journal of Management Reviews 7*(2), 73–90.

Collins, J. (2001). *Good to great.* New York, NY: Harper Collins Publishers.

Colton, D. (2000). Quality improvement in health care: Conceptual and historical foundations. *Evaluation & the Health Professions, 23*(1), 7–42.

Colton, D. (2003, December/January). Overcoming resistance to performance measurement in behavioral healthcare organizations. *Measuring Up, 1*(5).

Colton, D. (2004). *Checklist for assessing your organization's readiness for reducing seclusion and restraint.* Available online at www.ccca.dmhmrsas.virginia.gov/content/SR%20Checklist.pdf. Staunton, VA: Commonwealth Center for Children & Adolescents.

Commission on Quality of Care Restraint and Seclusion Practices in New York State Psychiatric Facilities (1994). *Voice from the frontline: Patients' perspectives of restraint and seclusion use.* September. Available online at http://www.cqcapd.state.ny.us/publications/pubvoice.htm. New York: Author.

Dooley, J. (no date). *Cultural aspects of systematic change management.* Available online at www.well.com/user/dooley/culture.pdf. San Francisco: The WELL.

Duck, J. D. (2001). *The change monster: The human forces that fuel or foil corporate transformation and change.* New York, NY: Crown Business.

Family Life Development Center. (2001). *Therapeutic crisis intervention.* Ithaca, NY: Cornell University, The Residential Child Care Project.

Gladwell, M. (2002). *The tipping point: How little things can make a big difference.* New York, NY: Little, Brown & Company.

Gordon, J. R. (1999). *Organizational behavior: A diagnostic approach.* Upper Saddle River, NJ: Prentice Hall.

Greene, R. W. (2001). *The explosive child: A new approach for understanding and parenting easily frustrated, chronically inflexible children.* New York, NY: Harper-Collins Publishers.

Izumi, H., & Taylor, D. M. (1998). Planned organizational change as cultural revolution. *Management Development Forum, 1*(1). Available online at www.esc.edu/MDF.

Joint Commission on Accreditation of Healthcare Organizations. (2004). *Millcreek Behavioral Health Services Earns Joint Commission's 2003 Ernest A. Codman Award.* Available online at www.jointcommission.org/Codman/03_millcreek.htm. Oakbrook Terrace, IL: Author

Kalogjera, I. J., Bedi, A., Watson, W. N., & Meyer, A. D. (1989). Impact of therapeutic management on use of seclusion and restraint with disruptive adolescent inpatients. *Hospital and Community Psychiatry, 40*(3), 280–285.

Kotter, J. P. (1996). *Leading change.* Cambridge, MA: Harvard Business School Press.

Mohr, W. K., & Anderson, J. A. (2001, November). Faulty assumptions associated with the use of restraints with children. *Journal of Child and Adolescent Psychiatric Nursing*. 26.

National Association of State Mental Health Program Directors. (2005, January). *NASMHPD Position statement on services and supports to trauma survivors*. Washington, DC: Author.

Peters, T., & Waterman, R. (1982). *In search of excellence*. New York, NY: Harper & Row.

Prochaska, J. O., & DiClemente, C. C. (1984). *The transtheoretical approach: Crossing traditional boundaries of therapy*. Homewood, IL: Dow Jones-Irwin.

Schein, E. H. (2004). *Organizational culture and leadership*. San Francisco, CA: Jossey-Bass.

Troutment, B., Myers, K., Borchardt, C., Kowalski, R., & Bubrick, J. (1998). Case study: when restraints are the least restrictive alternative for managing aggression. *Journal of the American Academy of Child and Adolescent Psychiatry, 37*, 554–558.

CHAPTER 9

A Case Study of an Organizational Intervention to Reduce Physical Interventions

Creating Effective, Harm-Free Environments

Ronald W. Thompson,
Jonathan C. Huefner,
Dennis G. Vollmer,
Jerry L. Davis, and
Daniel L. Daly

Introduction

Safety of staff and youth in out-of-home care and treatment settings has become a topic of national concern. Injuries, and in rare cases, even deaths have occurred when youth have been restrained in out-of-home care settings (Nunno, Holden, & Tollar, 2006). Reports in the literature have also included physical abuse of youth in care and exacerbation of trauma with youth who have been traumatized in the past as a result of the application of physical restraints (Acoca & Dedel, 1998; Ryan & Peterson, 2004). In response, there have been a number of reports in the literature about initiatives directed to improve the safety of youth who are placed in residential care and treatment facilities. A commonly reported dependent measure is the frequency of using restraint, and the goal is to reduce or eliminate these events (e.g., Donovan, Siegel, Zera, Plant, & Martin, 2003; McCue, Urcuyo, Lilu, Tobias, & Chambers, 2004). National associations and federal agencies have affirmed their commitment to reducing or eliminating the use of restraints in treatment facilities (APNA Seclusion and Restraint Task Force, 2001; Child Welfare League of America, 2004; Curie, 2005; Glover, 2005; Herzog et al., 2003).

Staff training in a systematic crisis intervention system has been shown to be an effective method to reduce the use of restraints (Nunno, Holden, & Leidy, 2003). Reliance on training alone, however, may not produce sustained effects over time, and it can lead to undesirable secondary effects like increased injuries

---

Author Note: We wish to acknowledge Jim Nardini and Beth Chmelka who provided invaluable assistance in organizing and analyzing the data.

to youth and staff (Khadivi, Patel, Atkinson, & Levine, 2004). The National Technical Assistance Center for State Mental Health Planning has suggested six core strategies to make broad changes in the culture of treatment programs to produce lasting reductions in the use of restraint necessary to improve safety (Huckshorn, 2005). These categories include: effective leadership, using data to inform practice, workforce development, using assessment and prevention tools, consumer input, and use of debriefing techniques.

In this chapter we argue that producing a sustained reduction of the use of high-risk restraint interventions is, in fact, a complex process requiring a transformation of the culture of the treatment program or organization. We summarize our definition of a culture of safety for treatment programs, elements of which have been previously reported by Daly and Dowd (1992). We also describe a case study of an organizational intervention based on quality improvement and applied in a therapeutic group home program using the teaching family model. Finally, we will report the results of evaluation data that support the utility of this approach and discuss issues related to making residential treatment settings safer for youth.

Components of a Harm-Free Environment

Our basic premise is that a safe treatment environment is one that is both effective and harm-free. This requires paying close attention to youth rights and offering youth an opportunity to develop in spiritual, emotional, intellectual, and physical domains. It also requires a systemic commitment to quality assurance from the governing board to the direct care staff (Evans, Faulkner, Hodo, Mahrer, & Bevilacqua, 1992). Effective, harm-free environments are the product of a well-integrated system of caregiver support, a clearly defined model of care, a focus on teaching positive behavior, a consumer orientation, comprehensive ongoing staff training, program and staff evaluation, facilitative leadership, and an independent internal program audit. Each of these components will be described in the paragraphs that follow.

Caregiver Support

The first component in an effective, harm-free treatment environment is support of the direct caregivers. This includes adequate compensation and time off, lower adult-child ratios, a responsive supervision system, and caregiver responsibility and accountability for making treatment decisions. Studies of employee satisfaction have concluded that compensation is not the most important factor, but inadequate compensation can be a factor in frequent employee turnover that requires a need for constant training and careful supervision of new staff (Petty, Brewer, & Brown, 2005). High adult-child ratios are not uncommon in treatment facilities, but they can result in caregiver burnout and excess use of control techniques such as early bedtimes, compulsory naps, and unnecessary use of medication, time-out, seclusion, and restraint (Maslach, 2003).

The practice standard in our family-style group care is an adult-child ratio of no more than four to one and no more than eight children in each family-style living unit. This standard can vary depending on characteristics of youth, staffing patterns, and building designs, but in some of our research on adult-child ratios, we found a direct relationship between them and the frequency of critical incident reports (Friman, Jones, Smith, Daly, & Larzelere, 1997). These findings caused a reduction of these adult-child ratios even further with the most challenging youth. Caregivers who are married couples are provided with a full-time assistant and they receive two nights off per week, one weekend off per month, and a minimum of 10 vacation days per year.

A responsive supervision system requires that supervisors have expert knowledge and experience with the model of care and direct caregivers have decision-making authority, accountability, and status (Dangel, 1986). Caregivers should be involved in the decision-making process, and have the authority to make important decisions themselves, because they are the ones closest to the children. In too many cases the caregiver is the last person in the decision-making hierarchy. When caregivers depend too much on supervisors and bureaucratic policies and procedures for making treatment decisions, the system will reflect poor responsiveness to the needs of the children.

A Clearly Defined Model of Care

The second component in an effective, harm-free environment is a clearly defined model of care that includes a set of safe and effective practices that are employed in fundamentally the same fashion across youth and situations. The development of this type of model requires an ongoing applied research-to-practice feedback loop, and even though it includes carefully defined treatment methods it is not inconsistent with individualized treatment plans. Our program model elements that have been shown to be effective are proactive teaching that prevents problems before they occur, a focus on positive behavior and consequences, nonaversive consequences for negative behavior, teaching self-control strategies, and tested methods for crisis intervention.

A clearly defined model reduces the ambiguity for direct caregivers that can lead to erratic, inappropriate, and excessively negative caregiver behavior. This consistency also provides children the predictability they need in interpersonal interactions. Finally, it enables an organization to evaluate the fidelity of model implementation and what works and what does not work for each individual and for groups of individuals enrolled in specific programs.

Focus on Positive Behavior

The focus on positive behavior is at the core of our definition of an effective, harm-free environment. Caregivers need to be trained to constantly redirect interactions with youth to what children are doing right, and to proactively teach new skills to children in order to promote their success within the program. Children in out-of-home care often benefit from a curriculum of basic life skills (e.g., social, independent living, academic) in addition to treatment for their referral behaviors. We use another practice standard called the four to one rule. This involves praising a minimum of four desired behaviors for every behavior we correct. We have also found that for children with more severe behavior problems, it is often necessary to increase that ratio to 8 or 10 to 1 to have positive treatment outcomes (Friman et al., 1997). Finally, in addition to contingency management, we use tested methods of crisis intervention and teach youth self-control strategies to promote generalization to new situations.

Consumer Orientation

Effective, harm-free environments are scrutinized by persons outside the provider staff. Parents, teachers, coaches, neighbors, clergy, and the children themselves can be members of the treatment team and provide helpful feedback on the quality of care. Consumers should be routinely asked about both safety and treatment quality. These data can be used proactively to modify treatment plans, evaluate staff, and improve programs in a way that increases the safety and effectiveness of the program.

Staff Training and Supervision

Another critical component of an effective, harm-free environment is a comprehensive staff training and development program. This is also a basic ingredient to implementation of a model of care with fidelity. Preservice training can assure that all staff receive training in the basic principles and practices of residential care. Advanced training and supervision needs to be tailored to address individual performance and some of the more subtle and difficult aspects of program implementation. Only when caregiver skills have been adequately developed can the environment be effective and harm-free. Skilled caregivers feel in control and are less likely to react inappropriately or abusively. Most of the caregiver training needs to be managed by the organization itself, even if the content was developed elsewhere. Outside experts, although sometimes useful, are going to be less familiar with the organization's policies and practices, and not available for ongoing performance feedback.

Program and Staff Evaluation

Evaluation data allow an organization to make fact-based decisions about the effectiveness and safety of caregivers, training, and program elements. Real consequences, such as pay raises, promotions, and continued employment, need to be made contingent upon meeting objective evaluation criteria. Our evaluation data include measures of program implementation, progress of youth during treatment, and both short- and long-term follow-up youth outcomes. One type of data found to be very useful is critical incident reporting. The critical incident report consists of 40 distinct classes of clinically relevant problem behavior that clinical supervisors use to document observed instances of every youth's behavior on a daily basis. If this can be done reliably, the data provide a good reflection of caregiver skill and youth behavior, progress, and safety. These types of data can also be used to evaluate organizational interventions like the one described in this chapter.

Facilitative Leadership

Organizational leaders need to be knowledgeable and experienced in what this type of environment looks like and how it works. Quality components focused on both safety and effectiveness need to be central to organizational decisions that occur on a day-to-day basis, as well as those that are more strategic in nature. These components should also drive administrative functions such as staff recruitment, selection, promotion, and termination. Communication among youth served, direct caregivers, immediate supervisors, and organization leaders must be frequent and allow for prompt actions to promote safety and effectiveness and eliminate unsafe or ineffective practices. A flexible clinical management information system is a critical tool in this process. In our system for example, narratives about critical incidents are summarized and reviewed by clinical administrators every day, and quantitative data reports are reviewed at least monthly and more often if needed.

Internal Program Audit

The last, but equally important, component of an effective, harm-free environment is an independent system to detect abusive or neglectful practices and respond to and correct these problems immediately. It is important to detect and correct inappropriate practices before they become abuse or neglect. This requires reporting and investigation systems for even minor incidents that may compromise youth safety. Our system includes confidential, periodic interviews with children by a person not responsible for their care. During the interview children are asked questions about any inappropriate verbal, physical, sexual, or coercive behavior committed by adults or other children. The system also includes an independent investigation team who reports to a Board committee and follows up all alleged harmful practices with a complete investigation that is reported back to program administrators for any necessary administrative actions. Finally, the system includes a toll-free, confidential call-in center for either staff or youth to report any harmful or abusive practice or incident.

It is our experience an observer would see a number of concrete differences in safe and unsafe treatment environments. Examples are listed in Table 9-1. Even when these components of safe environments are present, however, they still require ongoing monitoring and periodic refinement and adjustment. The case study reported here involves a refinement and adjustment of some of these components following a program leadership change. The following sections include a brief description of the participants, program, restraint protocol, measures, setting, organizational intervention, and evaluation findings. Our position is that even a more subtle transformation of the treatment program's culture can produce a sustained reduction of the use in high-risk restraint interventions, and the case study provides a practical evaluation of an organizational intervention based on this premise.

Method

Participants

Data from January 2001 to June 2006 for 561 youth in a treatment group home program were extracted from the clinical information system with IRB approval. The data used in this study were collected for administrative and case management purposes, and they were stripped of all identifying information in order to guarantee anonymity. The first year and a half was a Baseline period prior to the leadership change, with the last four years being the Intervention period. The youth were 64% male and 68% Caucasian. Their average age was 14 years, and the mean Global Assessment of Functioning (GAF) score was 45. At admission, youth were either stepping down from a psychiatric hospital or intensive residential treatment setting or not successful in a more family-style group home. All youth had a diagnosed psychiatric disorder. The most common Axis I diagnoses were either oppositional defiant disorder (ODD) or attention deficit hyperactivity disorder (ADHD).

Program Description

The intervention occurred in a therapeutic group home program that is staffed 24 hours a day, seven days a week with a four to one adult-child ratio. The program addresses the needs of these youth with a bio-psycho-social model of

Table 9–1: What You Would See in Safe and Unsafe Treatment Environments

CATEGORY	SAFE CULTURE	UNSAFE CULTURE
Atmosphere	Professional language Mission-oriented philosophy Youth involved in treatment Family-like atmosphere	Street language Staff doing a job Staff responsible for treatment Institutional atmosphere
Approach	Focus on positive behavior Proactive skill development Staff model skills and values Safety protected by people	Focus on problem behavior Reactive response to behavior Staff take a "do as I say" approach Safety protected by policy
Reporting	QA data collected and used Internal and external monitoring Overreporting safety concerns Protection for the whistleblower	QA data not used External monitoring only Code of silence Report at your own risk
Other	Professional boundaries for staff Program uses consumer input	Porous personal boundaries for staff Consumer input not solicited

treatment. The average length of stay is five months. The program is focused on teaching skills and building relationships. The overall goal is to help youth progress to a less restrictive level of care as quickly and effectively as possible. The program uses a structured treatment approach that:

- provides a safe, secure residential environment necessary for psychiatric, behavioral, and cognitive treatment;
- develops individualized, ongoing treatment designed specifically for each youth's particular needs;
- identifies and builds upon family and individual strengths;
- actively engages youth and family members in intense family therapy;
- provides skill development to enhance academic, family and social functioning; and
- assists professionals in the youth's home community to ensure a successful transition to a less restrictive level of care.

Individual homes are separated by gender with up to 27 boys in two homes and 14 girls in another home at any given time. Specific requirements for admission include a psychiatric diagnosis and a statement of medical necessity from a referring physician, psychologist, or psychiatrist. The target population is youth with behavioral and emotional disturbances. The program is not designed to meet the treatment needs of youth who are actively chemically dependent, have a history of sexual perpetration, are active fire setters, actively suicidal, or whose cognitive functioning falls below borderline range.

Each youth's family is involved in the treatment process, beginning at admission to the program. Improving the relationship between the children and their parents or legal guardians is a key program objective. This usually means something different though for each family. This process involves defining the roles and expectations for each family member and producing a signed contract specifying the nature of the family's participation in the treatment services. Parents or guardians are involved in ongoing treatment plan development, review, and modification.

Restraint Protocol

Formal protocol stated that restraints were never the treatment of choice and were only to be used when two conditions had been met. The first was that less restrictive interventions had to have been attempted and failed, and the second was that restraints were only to be used in situations of clear and imminent danger to the physical safety of the youth or others.

All staff from directors to direct-care staff were trained in crisis prevention, crisis intervention, and restraint techniques. Additionally, all staff underwent the Crisis Prevention Institute's annual Nonviolent Crisis Intervention (NCI) training throughout their employment. NCI techniques employed included the team control position, transport technique, and child control position for younger residents. Restraints were called safety holds to emphasize that their purpose was safety not discipline.

The program director was expected to provide guidance and oversight during restraint incidents, and if applicable, staff involved in the restraint were required to contact their supervisor every 10 minutes for continued approval of the restraint. If the restraint incident was serious enough, police intervention was utilized. Additionally, there was a safety and ethics line available to youth 24 hours a day. All restraints were verbally reported to program directors, recorded as a critical incident report, and tracked with the organization's clinical information system.

Measures

The dependent measures were taken from the Treatment Progress Checklist (TPC) system (Larzelere, Chmelka, Schmidt, & Jones, 2002). The TPC is used for treatment planning and tracking progress and includes a count of the number of specific behaviors collected at the end of each of the three shifts. The daily totals are entered into the organization's database and reported out to clinical administrators. Restraints, physical assaults toward adults and peers, and physical aggression were the key dependent measure of interest, but property damage, Town Hall interventions (described later in this chapter), and police contacts were also included. We wanted to make sure that as the program reduced the use of restraints, there was not a concomitant increase in assaultive or aggressive behavior. The definitions of each of the dependent measures are as follows:

- *Physical restraint:* A staff member or other adult therapeutically holds a youth to keep him from harming self or others.

- *Physical assault on adults:* Youth assaults an adult. Injury may or may not have resulted, but intentional aggressive physical contact occurred (e.g., biting, choking, kicking, punching, scratching, pushing, jumping on, spitting at, throwing objects at, head-butting).

- *Physical assault on peers:* Youth assaults a peer or sibling. Injury may or may not have resulted, but intentional aggressive physical contact occurred (e.g., biting, choking, kicking, punching, scratching, pushing, jumping on, spitting at, throwing objects at, head-butting).

- *Physical aggression (toward objects):* Youth displays an outburst of anger involving physical behavior directed at objects (e.g., throwing or kicking objects, slamming doors, overturning furniture, slamming books or fists, or tearing up point cards). There may be an attempt at intimidation but there is no physical contact between people.

- *Property damage:* Youth intentionally damages property (e.g., chipping paint off wall, breaking ceiling tiles, tearing clothes, putting holes in walls, breaking furniture).

- *Town Hall:* Youth goes to Town Hall to work on self-control strategies.

- *Police contact:* Youth has been arrested, ticketed, reprimanded, detained, or questioned by an officer of the law about involvement in illegal acts. Includes any negative contact involving the police (e.g., runaway, shoplifting, drug search, assault, or domestic disturbance). Includes when police are contacted to assist in Town Hall interventions.

The Setting

At the time of the organizational intervention, the program had just undergone a change in leadership. While elements of an effective, harm-free environment described above were generally in place and the restraint protocol was being followed, observation on the living units and an analysis of program data suggested that the unit culture was in need of some adjustment. There were several troubling trends, e.g., caregiver teaching had become reactive rather than proactive, behavioral tolerances were high, and restraints were not limited to safety.

The most troubling issue dealt with how restraints were being used and how restraint debriefings were being conducted. It was fairly clear that, to an extent, restraints had become punitive rather than safety focused. This was evident in situations where restraints were occurring when youth were just being disruptive, with no safety threat to themselves or others. This shift in focus from safety to punishment was supported by restraint reviews and debriefings being entirely internal. Consistent with procedure, another person within the program staff would conduct the debriefing, but there was a sense that staff were "watching each other's back." This created a situation that supported the need for a cultural shift that included justifying and reinforcing new restraint practice standards.

The Intervention

The first step of the intervention was to review preservice training material with all staff to ensure that caregivers at least had an understanding of all model of care components. This was to reemphasize proactive, positive teaching, nonviolent de-escalation of crisis situations, and self-control strategies. In practice this meant more teaching to both positive *and* negative behaviors by caregivers, maintaining at least a four positive to one negative ratio. Retraining and meeting criteria also resulted in the termination of one staff member who had been involved in an unusually high number of restraints.

This laid the necessary foundation for implementing a lowered tolerance for negative behavior, which often escalates into physical aggression and property damage. A key practice in lowering tolerances was an emphasis on using the Town Hall intervention earlier in out-of-control situations. The treatment program occupies land that is an independent township, and the Town Hall is where the administrative offices and police department for the town reside. Town Hall was a room next to the police offices with four cubicles and a conference table.

The goal of Town Hall was to remove youth from the home and contact with peers, require the youth to come under control by using her self-control strategies, review the causes of the problem, and encourage the youth to take responsibility for the situation. Only then is the youth returned to the home. Staff initiated Town Hall interventions by asking the youth to voluntarily get into a car to be taken to the room next to the police station. If the youth refused, the police department would be called in to help move the youth. During the

Town Hall intervention a member of the home's staff remained and worked with the youth, and these sessions might last between a half hour and several hours. In cases where the youth's misbehavior involved breaking the law (e.g., property damage, disturbing the peace, assault), the youth was removed from the home and placed in police custody. Because of our independent township status, however, youth who did not actually break the law did not have incidents recorded in a criminal record, as they would be in most community settings.

Supervision focused on positive teaching interactions, relationship building, and restraints being used only as a last resort. For the first time, the independent audit department was also used to review every occasion in which a restraint was used. The audit department determined if further investigation was warranted. Every restraint was thoroughly documented and used as a learning experience within the program.

Results

Table 9-2 summarizes the overall results of the intervention. There were significant reductions in the key dependent measures: use of restraints, physical assaults on staff and peers, physical aggression, and property damage from Baseline to Intervention periods. There was an 80.2% reduction in the mean frequency of restraint use from Baseline (January 2001 to June 2002) to Intervention (July 2002 to June 2006) periods. Paradoxically, both the use of the campus police and occasions spent in Town Hall also decreased, although not significantly so. This was noteworthy given the intervention's focus on a lower tolerance for misbehavior and using Town Hall as part of the intervention.

In Figure 9-1, mean monthly per youth rates for restraints, physical assaults on adults and peers, and aggression for six-month intervals and trend lines are graphed to show data trends over time for indicators of primary interest from Baseline to Intervention periods. The data do suggest a slight increase in these dependent measures during the final year of the Intervention period. This has been brought to the attention of program administrators, and the trend will continue to be monitored to make sure that there are not further adjustments needed to sustain these improvements in the future.

Discussion

These results support the notion that the refinement and adjustment of the components of an effective, harm-free environment that occurred after the leadership change resulted in a dramatic impact on both the use of restraints by staff and physical aggression by youth. It is difficult to determine specifically which parts of the intervention created the outcomes in this type of analysis,

TABLE 9–2: Mean Critical Incident Rates During Baseline and Intervention Periods

VARIABLE	BASELINE MEAN (SD)	INTERVENTION MEAN (SD)	F	EFFECT SIZE d
Restraint	0.41 (2.33)	0.08 (0.97)	31.13**	.472
Physical Assault—Staff	0.99 (3.39)	0.47 (2.36)	22.45**	.400
Physical Assault—Peer	1.28 (3.26)	0.75 (2.09)	27.84**	.446
Physical Aggression	7.60 (14.00)	6.50 (11.83)	4.56*	.181
Property Damage	0.57 (1.68)	0.43 (1.65)	4.40*	.177
Town Hall Interventions	2.60 (4.51)	2.37 (4.20)	1.67	.109
Police Contact	0.73 (2.39)	0.73 (2.16)	0.002	.004

*$p < .05$; **$p < .001$.

but results indicate a sustained, safer treatment environment for both youth and adults over an extended period of time (4 years). It is important to note that the significant decrease in restraints was not offset by increases in other undesirable events. In fact, parallel significant reductions in physical assaults on staff and peers and aggression, may indicate a cycle of reciprocity among staff and youth aggression. The practical implication of this is that restraints, rather than being a disincentive, may in fact reinforce a culture of aggression.

We have also found that this type of effective, harm-free environment can be successfully implemented in other types of treatment settings with different models of care (Hurley, Ingram, Czyz, Julian, & Wilson, 2005). Obviously, the implementation of the components will vary according to the size of living units, staffing patterns, and client characteristics. Systems that adequately address caregiver support, a clearly defined model of care, a focus on teaching positive behavior, a consumer orientation, comprehensive ongoing staff training, program and staff evaluation, facilitative leadership, and an independent internal program audit can provide youth with a safe environment in which to develop.

We argue that safety is a systemic issue that is best addressed with a comprehensive cultural assessment and intervention. Such organizational interventions are imprecise endeavors. Unlike more controlled research, it is impossible to rule out threats to internal validity such as monitoring, external events, passage of time, and maturation. With this example in the therapeutic group homes, the leadership change, focus on proactive teaching, and lowered tolerances for misbehavior were somewhat less susceptible to outside influences due to greater organizational control over the environment. We call this definition of an effective, harm-free environment a practice-based theory. It was developed over time by testing methods formally and informally. Informal testing occurred as practitioners used trial and error methods to establish preferred practices. Formal testing included more controlled studies that involved hypothesis testing, more

FIGURE 9–1: Therapeutic Group Home Average Montly Per Youth Incidents for Restraint, Physical Assault on Adults and Peers, and Aggression for Six-Month Intervals with Trend Line for Baseline and Intervention Periods.

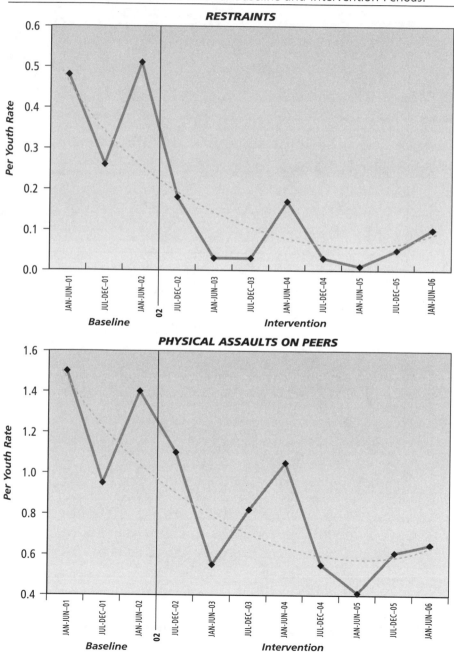

FIGURE 9-1 continued

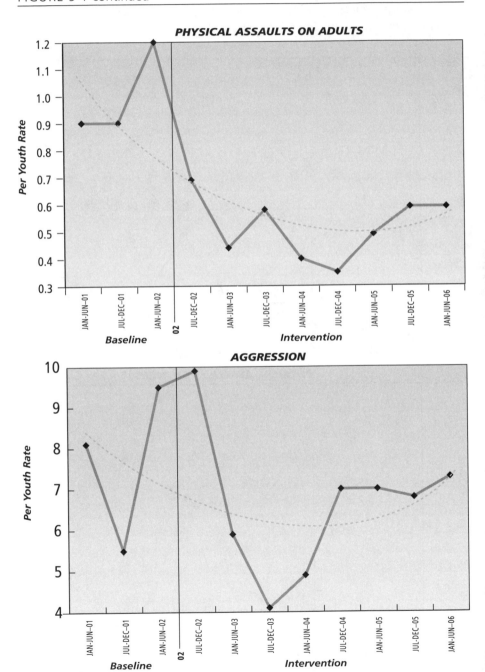

intense data collection, and tests of statistical and practical significance. Some of these have been reported in the literature (e.g., Friman, 1999).

The organizational intervention reported in this chapter, on the other hand, was designed to test the entire approach. Organizational interventions, if done carefully, are one approach that can help build a knowledge base about safety of high-risk interventions for children in situations where more formal randomized group trials or quasi-experimental studies might not be possible.

Organizational interventions require accurate and frequent reports of clinical management information. To help do this, we have defined a set of critical success factors that have strong social validity and are closely aligned to our model of care. Indicators include administrative data such as staff turnover and certification (meeting their practice standards), direct caregiver data such as positive to negative teaching ratios and use of restraint, and client data such as progress toward treatment goals and aggressive behavior. To keep our focus on client outcomes, we also developed a series of behavioral indices that can be calculated from reports of critical incidents and monitored over time. The behavioral domains in the Treatment Progress Checklist include lethality/self harm, aggression, sexual behavior, school behavior, substance abuse, avoidance, and other problem behaviors. Each behavioral domain score is the product of multiple incident codes weighted on severity. We found that the reports of these indicators provide reliable and valid indicators of treatment progress for youth with a wide variety of presenting problems.

In addition to providing a picture of the organization's vital signs, the ongoing measurement of critical success factors empowers an organization to pinpoint areas that need adjustment and identify effective practices in both management and client services. Our system includes daily narrative reports of critical incidents, monthly data reports of critical success factors, and a variety of easy-to-run clinical data reports for use by clinical administrators. Finally, organizations can use this type of system to formally assess the impact of interventions such as the one outlined in this chapter. We feel it is vital that youth care organizations be proactive in the process of using accurate staff and youth information to make their programs safer and more effective for the children they serve.

References

Acoca, L., & Dedel, K. (1998). *No place to hide: Understanding and meeting the needs of girls in the California juvenile justice system.* San Francisco, CA: National Council on Crime and Delinquency.

APNA Seclusion and Restraint Task Force. (2001). American Psychiatric Nurses Association position statement on the use of seclusion and restraint. *Journal of the American Psychiatric Nurses Association, 7,* 130–133.

Child Welfare League of America. (2004). *CWLA best practice guidelines for behavior support and intervention training.* Washington, DC: Author.

Curie, C. G. (2005). SAMHSA's commitment to eliminating the use of seclusion and restraint. *Psychiatric Services, 56,* 1139–1140.

Daly, D. L., & Dowd, T. P. (1992). Characteristics of effective, harm-free environments for children in out-of-home care. *Child Welfare, 71,* 487–496.

Dangel, R. F. (1986, September). *Year 2000: Will you still be there?* Keynote address of the Twelfth Annual Conference of the National Association of Homes for Children, Denver, CO.

Donovan, A., Siegel, L., Zera, G., Plant, R., & Martin, A. (2003). Seclusion and restraint reform: An initiative by a child and adolescent psychiatric hospital. *Psychiatric Services, 54,* 958–959.

Evans, O. N., Faulkner, L. R., Hodo, G. L., Mahrer, D. L., & Bevilacqua, J. J. (1992). A quality improvement process for state mental health systems. *Hospital & Community Psychiatry, 43,* 465–469.

Friman, P. C. (1999). *Family-style residential care really works: Scientific findings demonstrating multiple benefits for troubled adolescents.* Boys Town, NE: Boys Town Press.

Friman, P. C., Jones, M., Smith, G. L., Daly, D. L., & Larzelere, R. E. (1997). Decreasing disruptive behavior by adolescent boys in residential care by increasing their positive to negative interaction ratios. *Behavior Modification, 21,* 470–486.

Glover, R. W. (2005). Reducing the use of seclusion and restraint: A NASMHPD priority. *Psychiatric Services, 56,* 1141–1142.

Herzog, A., Shore, M. F., Beale, R. R., Padrino, S. L., Vogel, A. V., Freshman, M., & Hart, C. (2003). *Patient safety and psychiatry: Recommendations to the Board of Trustees of the American Psychiatric Association* Arlington, VA: American Psychiatric Association.

Huckshorn, K. A. (2005). *A snapshot of six core strategies for the reduction of S/R.* Alexandria, VA: National Technical Assistance Center.

Hurley, K. D., Ingram, S., Czyz, J. D., Juliano, N., & Wilson, E. (2005). Treatment for youth in short-term care facilities: The impact of a comprehensive behavior management intervention. *Journal of Child & Family Studies,15*(5), 617–632.

Khadivi, A. N., Patel, R. C., Atkinson, A. R., & Levine, J. M. (2004). Association between seclusion and restraint and patient-related violence. *Psychiatric Services, 55,* 1311–1312.

Larzelere, B., Chmelka, B., Schmidt, M. D., & Jones, M. (2002). The treatment progress checklist: Psychometric development of a daily symptom checklist. In C. Newman, C. J. Liberton, K. Kutash, & R. M. Friedman (Eds.), *Proceedings of the 14th Annual Florida Mental Health Institute Conference. A system of care for children's mental health: Expanding the research base.* (pp. 359–362). Tampa, FL: University of South Florida.

Maslach, C. (2003). *Burnout: The cost of caring.* Cambridge, MA: Malor Books.

McCue, R. E., Urcuyo, L., Lilu, Y., Tobias, T., & Chambers, M. J. (2004). Reducing restraint use in a public psychiatric inpatient service. *Journal of Behavioral Health Services & Research, 31,* 217–224.

Nunno, M. A., Holden, M. J., & Leidy, B. (2003). Evaluating and monitoring the impact of a crisis intervention system on a residential child care facility. *Children & Youth Services Review, 25,* 295–315.

Nunno, M. A., Holden, M. J., & Tollar, A. (2006). Learning from tragedy: A survey of child and adolescent restraint fatalities. *Child Abuse & Neglect: The International Journal, 30*(12), 1333–1342.

Petty, G. C., Brewer, E. W., & Brown, B. (2005). Job satisfaction among employees of a youth development organization. *Child and Youth Care Forum, 34,* 57–73.

Ryan, J. B., & Peterson, R. L. (2004). Physical restraint in school. *Behavioral Disorders, 29,* 154–168.

CHAPTER 10

Beyond a Crisis Management Program

How We Reduced Our Restraints by Half in One Year

Jeff Carter,
Judy Jones, and
Kim Stevens

Introduction

The government of Ontario (Canada) has identified the practice of staff holding clients to control violent behavior in children's mental health settings (i.e., physical restraints) as a significant problem. Physical restraints are potentially dangerous, even deadly (e.g., *The Killing of Stephanie*, 2002). The experience at Madame Vanier Children's Services demonstrates that deescalating and defusing potentially violent situations and managing aggression when it occurs is not enough—we needed an agencywide, systematic, and systemic effort to reduce the number of physical restraints. Several major themes emerged from our efforts: each person is unique, every restraint is important, agency culture affects restraints, a data-driven approach is needed, and therapeutic relationships are critical.

Vanier is a children's mental health agency in London, Ontario, Canada. In 1968, Vanier was the first private treatment center licensed in the province of Ontario. In 2004, Vanier served about 1,350 children between the ages of 0 and 14 years. Of that number, two residential units (9 beds each, both units on the main campus) served a total of 52 children; 66 children, primarily those in residential treatment, were served by four on-campus day treatment classrooms; and 41 children were served by three off-site day treatment programs, comprising four classrooms of six to eight desks.

The crisis management system currently in place at Vanier is the Prevention and Management of Aggressive Behaviour (PMAB) (Prevention and Management of Aggressive Behaviour, 2004). Preventing aggressive behavior is a strength of the PMAB system (Garbe, 2000, pp. 12–17). At Vanier, we have on staff one PMAB Instructor responsible for training PMAB Trainers, of which Vanier has three on staff, who provide the initial training and annual recertification for staff.

No consensus in the literature has been reached regarding the meaning of the word *restraint*. For the purposes of this chapter, the word will be used in a manner consistent with provincial regulations. Any contact with a child against the child's will with the intention of modifying or controlling the child's behavior constitutes a restraint (see Intersectoral/ Interministerial Steering Committee on Behavioural Management Interventions for Children and Youth in Residential and Hospital Settings, 2001, p. 2). Vanier has no secure isolation or seclusion rooms, and Vanier does not use mechanical restraints.

Informal examination of Vanier's data on restraints revealed a few trends. First, as shown in Figure 10–1, physical restraints have been a growing problem at Vanier for several years. The average number of restraint incidents per year from 2000 through 2003 was 600.5. Second, a small number of children account for a disproportionately large number of restraints (see Figure 10–2). Third, seasonal variations recur, with the most restraints in the fall (September through November), a smaller peak in the spring (around March), and the fewest restraints in the summer (July and August) (See Figure 10–3).

The importance of each restraint was highlighted when provincial regulations in Ontario regarding restraints became more stringent in April 2003. All restraints of children in residential treatment facilities became Serious Occurrences that must be reported to the Ministry governing the treatment center. For these children, restraints are permitted only when the child is at immediate risk of causing serious physical harm to themselves or others. In custody settings—but not in treatment centers like Vanier—children may be restrained if they are escaping or engaging in serious property damage (i.e., riots). The regulations also require separate debriefing sessions with the child who was restrained and with the staff involved in the restraint.

As shown in Figure 10–3, the new provincial legislation failed to have an immediate effect of reducing the number of restraints. The small drop during the summer months is consistent with previous years, but the peak in the fall is greater than previous years. Also as shown in Figure 10–3, in the fall of 2003, senior management at Vanier decided to restructure the residential units, so that children referred by the child welfare system and children referred from the community were no longer segregated. This restructuring

FIGURE 10–1: Number of Physical Restraints, 2000 to 2003

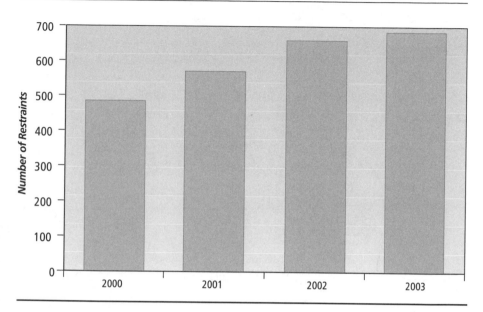

FIGURE 10–2: Number of Restraints, for All Clients in Intensive Services at
Vanier Between January 31, 1999, and January 31, 2002 (Carter, 2002)

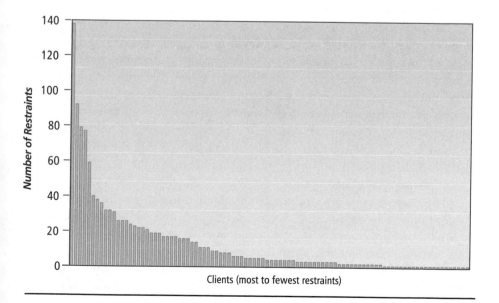

FIGURE 10–3: Number of Restraints and Selected Events from January 2003 to March 2005

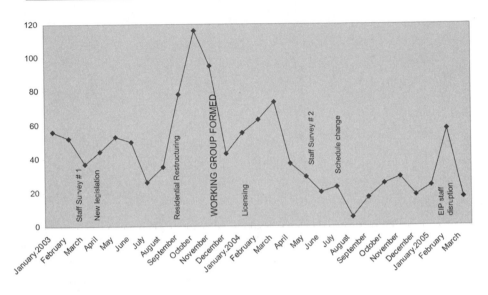

was motivated, in part, because of concerns about the large number of restraints occurring with the child welfare system children.

No clear explanation is available to explain the trend toward increasing numbers of restraints, but anecdotal evidence suggests two possibilities that may interact with each other. First, in the past several years, clients in residential treatment seem to have increasingly severe psychopathology, which may contribute to more restraints. Second, contagion effects may play a role, in that as children act aggressively and are restrained, a climate of violence may develop that encourages further acts of aggression, leading to more restraints. One hope for restructuring was that dispersing the more severely disturbed clients across two programs instead of one would decrease the number of restraint incidents.

The need to reduce restraints was becoming urgent because the number of restraints was approaching record levels and multiple staff were being injured. For a time, one of the two residential treatment units was closed to new admissions so that staff from that unit could provide support in the other unit. Around this same time, several different staff members were each independently engaged in other activities that converged on the need to reduce the number of restraints. These activities included attending a conference on trauma and preparing a literature review on restraints.

Theoretical Background

Trauma. In the spring of 2003, a workshop regarding trauma by Dr. Bruce Perry greatly influenced clinical thinking at Vanier. Important ideas from Perry's presentation involved the effects of trauma on children's development (Perry, 2001). Children may have noncognitive, preverbal memories of trauma that may be triggered in a host of unexpected ways. Further, trauma can result in physiological changes to the brain and disrupt emotional, behavioral, and cognitive development.

Another major theme of that workshop was attachment (Perry, 2001). Children who have been abused or neglected in early childhood have a greater risk than other children for developing avoidant, ambivalent, or resistant attachment. Children with attachment problems develop other significant problems, including lack of empathy and poor impulse control, which, in turn, contribute to aggressive behavior. Perry (2002) recommended nurturing and trying to understand these children. He also recommended caregiving based on emotional age, being consistent, predictable, and repetitive, modeling and teaching appropriate social behaviors, and having realistic expectations for the children and ourselves.

Several themes emerged from discussions among staff subsequent to the Perry conference. One was the importance of knowing the internal state of the child, especially regarding the child's level of arousal. A second theme was the importance of the social network around the child, with an emphasis on enlarging this network and involving children in positive community activities. A third theme was the need to recognize the unique trauma histories of our clients through thorough assessments so that we can predict the triggers that increase arousal for individual children. A related idea included the need to consider the emotional age of each individual child and adjust our expectations. The final theme was the need for a secure base, which is developed in the therapeutic milieu through consistency, routine, and structure, and through solid therapeutic relationships.

Literature Review. Turning to the literature regarding physical restraints, several themes emerge. A few authors emphasized the value of building relationships with clients to manage violent and aggressive behavior more effectively (Bailey, Mrock, & Davis, n.d.; Intersectoral/Interministerial Steering Committee on Behavioural Management Interventions for Children and Youth in Residential and Hospital Settings, 2001; Masker & Steele, 2004). A related issue was to emphasize to clients and staff on a personal level the effect of the experience of being restrained (e.g., Fox, 2004; Kirkwood, 2003). Other related themes were the need for individual treatment plans (American Psychological Association, American Psychiatric Nurses Association, & National Association of Psychiatric Health Systems, n.d., Chapter 5; Intersectoral/Interministerial Steering Committee, 2001; Knight, 2002) and a critical shift in agency culture moving away from a treatment model that punishes misbehavior to one that builds on children's strengths (Day, 2000). The importance of staff training, education, and ongoing supervision in achieving these changes was often emphasized (APA et al., n.d., Chapter 3; Bailey et al., n.d.; Intersectoral/Interministerial Steering Committee, 2001; Knight, 2002). Accurate data management regarding restraints was called for, including specific recommendations for improved documentation (APA et al., n.d.) and quality assurance reviews (Day, 2000).

Role of Management. The literature also stresses the importance of involving senior management in efforts to reduce restraints (e.g., APA et al., n.d., Chapter 2; Colton, Chapter 7 of this volume; Gupta, 2004). This involvement needs to fit with agency culture. Our experience illustrates that senior management can support the process while still encouraging the autonomy of staff. Management at Vanier has been strongly influenced by chaos theory. Chaos theory as applied to management views an agency as a self-organizing system (e.g., Wheatley, 1994). In this way of thinking, managers need to create a space or field in which creative solutions emerge. This approach contrasts with a more traditional approach that requires managers to direct change. The management approach taken at Vanier to reducing restraints was consistent with recommendations by Nickols (2004) for senior managers trying to effect change: build a team, give them resources, and stay out of the way of the team leader.

Steps Taken to Reduce Restraints

The first step was to create the Reduce Restraints Working Group. This group is accountable to Vanier's Value Team. The Value Team is a multidisciplinary committee that includes representatives from each clinical team, as well as representatives of various disciplines (such as child and youth counsellors [CYCs], child and family therapists, and psychologists), and levels of management. The Value Team is responsible for program evaluation and research, and it approved interventions and evaluations conducted by the Working Group. The Working Group is larger and less formal than the Value Team. It consists of about 20 members from various disciplines and levels of management, and we made a particular effort to include as many CYCs as possible.

Because of the literature on organizational change (e.g., Wheatley, 2001) and our recent experience with a major change (restructuring the residential programs), we knew that we needed to involve everybody in the agency to make the fundamental change in agency culture required to reduce the number of restraints. We required a broad base of interested staff directly and actively involved in the Working Group. All of the Working Group activities are focused on the specific goal of reducing the number of restraints at Vanier, and it coordinated and implemented plans to achieve that goal.

We needed a clear objective. In November 2003, the Reduce Restraints Working Group discussed options and reached a consensus to reduce the number of restraints in half compared to the previous year. We considered the goal of completely eliminating restraints. We questioned whether it would be possible to have no restraints, given our population of highly aggressive children. We decided that trying to reduce restraints by half in one year was ambitious enough.

Barriers. One of the first tasks of the Working Group was to identify the barriers to reducing restraints. One of the most prominent barriers is the client profile that Vanier serves. Standardized assessment measures taken at intake (Cunningham, Pettingill, & Boyle, 2003; Hodges, 2000) indicate that Vanier clients have more severe symptoms and a lower level of adaptive functioning in almost all areas than the average scores on these measures for other children's mental health centers across the region (Carter, 2005).

Clients typically present with a combination of clinically significant internalizing (e.g., mood and anxiety) and externalizing (e.g., rule-breaking and aggressive behaviors) problems, often compounded by family issues. Many clients have diagnosed learning disabilities or other cognitive problems, but clients with overall intellectual functioning below the second percentile are usually (but not always) treated elsewhere. At least 30% of the children served by Vanier have aggression identified by the referral source as a presenting problem (at least 70% for the residential programs). In almost all cases, less intrusive forms of treatment have been attempted and not been successful before a referral is made to an intensive service (such as day treatment or residence).

Other barriers included limited time, money, staff, and space. Agendas for team meetings are often full, leaving little time for collective problem solving. Learning to do things differently takes time. A related barrier is limited money. The monetary cost of increasing the number of staff is relatively easy to calculate, but the costs involved in additional training or learning new treatment models could well be greater. Limited staff resources also constitute a barrier, in the form of less than perfect staff ratios to implement preventative strategies or cope with crises.

In addition to the costs for new training in terms of time and money, another barrier is the inevitable resistance to change (Barwick, Boydell, Stasiulis, Ferguson, Blasé, & Fixsen, 2005). Individual differences among staff also play a role. People can be categorized as Innovators (who may be viewed as incautious), Early Adopters (who tend to be opinion leaders), Early Majority (who seem to learn from watching Early Adopters), Late Majority (who typically adopt change only when it appears to be the new standard of practice), or Laggards (who persist in traditional approaches to care) (pp. 31–32). These categories are somewhat arbitrary, but they may still be helpful in developing a strategy for implementing change. For example, targeting the roughly 15% of the population who are Laggards may not be effective. In keeping with the strength-based agency culture at Vanier, our hope was that the Reduce Restraints Working Group would attract people who would lead by example (i.e., Early Adopters).

Another set of barriers to reducing restraints is related to the physical space of the agency. Due to its location and physical structure, Vanier has limited space for clients to go when they are upset. Concerns were raised among the Working Group about contagion effects, the response from neighbors, and the safety of the neighborhood if aggressive behaviors were not prevented by the use of restraints.

Data-Driven Practice. For several years, Vanier's Value Team had been reporting on the number of restraints each quarter, and an electronic clinical database that includes each restraint incident has facilitated this reporting since 1999. We were able to build on this existing structure to report regularly on our progress. In addition, when the residences were restructured (in 2003, shortly before the Working Group was formed, see Figure 10–3), a new CYC position was developed. The high number of restraints was a concern at that time. One of the responsibilities of this person is to process all of the Serious Occurrence Reports related to restraints, placing this person in an ideal position to watch for trends in restraints. Another way of monitoring progress was to add a new section, Significant Events, to the template for the monthly review of treatment plans for children in residence. This section is intended to include events such as restraints and leaving the program without permission. Education was needed for many CYCs to consider restraint incidents as an event that is significant enough to mention in the monthly report.

Part of our data-driven practice is to provide feedback to staff. One mechanism was through the well-established quarterly reports on the number of restraints. Another was through the agency's staff newsletter. In the spring of 2004, the Reduce Restraints Working Group published a summary of our work to that point. The results of staff surveys were shared through written summaries sent by e-mail to all staff, and these summaries were discussed at staff meetings.

Face-to-face contact with staff in presenting results has been helpful, not only to ensure that information is communicated clearly, but also to provide an opportunity for staff comments to stimulate the next round of discussion.

Agency Culture. Staff attitudes towards restraints are an important component of agency culture. A survey was conducted in May 2003; out of about 100 surveys distributed, 33 completed forms were returned. The results showed agreement across the agency on the beliefs about the factors that contribute to restraints and injuries. About three-quarters of all respondents indicated that child characteristics were a factor in the number of restraints and injuries, that staff experience was a factor in the number of restraints, and that the number of staff on shift was a factor in the number of injuries. The survey also revealed some areas where people in different roles have varying perceptions that could be expected to increase conflict between staff groups. For example, almost all of the CYCs—but almost nobody from other staff groups—indicated that agency policies on restraints limit staff judgment too much.

We measured changes in staff attitudes by repeating the staff survey one year later in May 2004. The number of people responding increased to 47, again, out of about 100 surveys distributed. One of the more disturbing findings of the second survey was that some staff indicated that the frequency of restraints was too low. Another issue on the second survey related to the number of staff per shift. People at all levels of experience and in all positions called for more staff overall. One of the conclusions from the second staff survey was the need for discussions of staffing needs for every shift because simplistic assertions based only on staff-client ratios were not sufficient.

Several respondents on the second survey called for a time-out or secure isolation room. Vanier has no such facilities. The licensing requirements to maintain such a room are seen as prohibitive. Further, there are practical concerns about how to transport a child to such a room and clinical concerns for children with trauma experiences and attachment diffficulties. Some of the suggestions, however, are consistent with a shift in agency culture towards a supportive environment. A time-out room does not necessarily need to resemble a locked cell (see Masters, Chapter 3, this volume). What may be needed for many children are (as one respondent put it), "Safe places for kids to vent and spin." Efforts were made to create such places in the day treatment and cottage milieus. One particular child responded very well to having a space with reduced stimulation in the form of a small tent set up in a classroom.

A second method to understand agency culture better was a detailed interview. Full time CYC staff who had been hired within 6 to 12 months were interviewed in the fall of 2004. Similar interviews were conducted and the plan is to repeat them regularly. One of the major themes from the initial set of interviews was the need for more emphasis on de-escalation techniques and how to avoid power struggles. Other suggestions included debriefing clients who are stressed, even if they were not actually involved in a restraint. Another theme was that even when a child's behavior met the criteria for a restraint (i.e., imminent danger to himself or others) other interventions might be more appropriate. One respondent pointed out that putting one staff on a one-to-one with a child during a critical time is better than needing two staff to restrain that child—and less paperwork!

Staff suggested more emphasis be placed on de-escalation techniques and that orientation be improved. The specific recommendations outlined that, at the time of children's admissions to any of our intensive services, workers speak to parents about the specific mandatory training of each staff member in crisis management. Orientation for new staff and CYC students now includes a detailed review of our agency policies and procedures as they relate to crisis management implementation.

Restraints were discussed in supervision with staff who were involved in a lot of restraints. The factors contributing to those restraints were explored. Some staff were surprised to learn that they were involved in more restraints than their coworkers, and this information alone helped them to reevaluate their practices. Team dynamics and the past experiences and individual personalities of staff also contributed to some staff being more likely to restraint than others.

Changing Agency Culture Through Training. The information from staff surveys and interviews facilitated changes in staff training and supervision. PMAB certification needs to be repeated annually. The recertification course was modified in response to staff attitudes—stronger emphasis was placed on verbal and nonverbal de-escalation techniques, including time for role-playing. The results of the staff survey were shared and discussed during the training. The importance of providing feedback among the staff during and after restraints was stressed.

Additional training was provided in response to specific issues. The PMAB Instructor reviewed every instance of a staff injury with the staff involved. They talked about what had happened, and if there had been alternative choices that could have been made. The PMAB Instructor consulted regarding specific clients. Issues included diffusion and de-escalation techniques for a particular client, alternative interventions, and selecting the most appropriate physical intervention when one is needed. Predictors of the risk of restraint, indicators of client anxiety, and the need to develop crisis plans were addressed. The PMAB Instructor also reviewed specific restraint techniques with individual staff and with teams.

One-on-one, face-to-face relationships are crucial to teaching new skills successfully (Barwick et al., 2005). Face-to-face exchanges allow for subtle nuances to be communicated, and for dialogue. They also promote the building of trusting relationships and the sharing of tacit knowledge (what we know from experience, but have difficulty explaining explicitly). For these reasons, individual supervision of front-line staff is an essential part of reducing the number of restraints. To this end, we assigned a highly experienced Intensive Services Supervisor, who is also a PMAB Trainer, to provide ongoing and immediate feedback to new staff as they are oriented to residential programs at Vanier.

Individual Treatment Planning. One of the most significant strategies in reducing the number of restraints is making changes related to treatment plans for individual clients. The Physical Restraint Template asks for detailed information for each child. This checklist includes whether the child has a history pertinent to physical restraints. Specific items include whether the child has been physically or sexually abused (and if so, the number and gender of perpetrators). The form asks whether the child has been neglected or witnessed woman abuse. Other items include substance abuse by the child and history of police involvement. The checklist has several items related to physical health risks. After asking about general health concerns, the form specifically asks about respiratory problems, obesity, and prescription medications. The file of any child taking Lithium must be red-flagged because of the association of this drug with a potentially lethal medical condition known as excited delirium. Developmental concerns (such as cognitive, verbal, and emotional functioning, awareness of safety and risk, and level of supervision required) are also noted on the form.

The last section of the form addresses physical restraints. Physical restraints must be discussed with the child's legal guardian and approved by the treatment team. The specific circumstances when restraints may be used must be listed on the Physical Restraint Template, as well as alternative intervention strategies. The most appropriate types of physical restraints for that individual child are listed on the form. More recently, we have developed a Behaviour Management Template for children who are involved in three or more restraints. This working document lists strategies that have been successful (or not) for that individual child at various points in the cycle of aggression (i.e., before, during, and after a crisis).

We also looked at the function of aggressive behavior for individual children, with a view to meeting their needs without aggression. The case examples that we published in the agency's staff newsletter illustrate the kinds of interventions that were implemented (Reduce Restraint Working Group, 2004, p. 2):

Scenario 1

> P. was restrained 28 times in less than 3 months, often for more than half an hour at a time. We looked at the restraints for patterns and found that her agitation increased over several days, and that she had the most

restraints at unstructured times of the day. Most of her restraints occurred after she became aggressive with staff who tried to intervene when she had problems with peers. At first, we thought that her restraints lasted longer when no male staff were involved, but when we looked more closely, we found that, in fact, she de-escalated more quickly when limits were set in a firm and matter-of-fact manner. We also learned that eye contact was also helpful in reducing her agitation. We identified that her behaviour tended to escalate quickly. This information was shared with staff, who changed how they interacted with her, such as being firmer with her and temporarily giving her recess at a different time from other children. For the 3 months after these changes were put into place, she was restrained only 13 times, and never for more than 20 minutes.

This case provides an example of how a detailed analysis of restraint incidents provided clues for how to modify an individual child's program. One technique was to plot the number of restraints by time of day (see Figure 10–4). This child had the most restraints during unstructured times with other children (i.e., morning and afternoon recess, and during the break after eating lunch). Another technique used was to plot the duration of restraints, divided by hypothesized situational variables. Figure 10–5 shows the duration of restraints for this child and whether male staff were involved in the restraint. This example illustrates the limitations of a purely actuarial approach and the value of an agency culture in which staff from different perspectives work collaboratively. Discussions with CYCs who were involved in restraints with this child revealed that the differences in duration seemed to be related more to staff's approach and mannerisms than to gender. When all staff began to interact in a particular style (more stereotypically masculine), the duration of restraints decreased.

The second case that we shared in the newsletter (Reduce Restraint Working Group, 2004, pp. 2–3) highlights the value of a program that targeted specific behaviors.

Scenario 2

A child from the day treatment program was being restrained on many occasions and these were of great concern to the program and to this child's parents. I began by listing these restraints, looking for any patterns as to the time of day, days of the week, and/or precipitating factors of the restraints. One factor began to stand out very clearly in almost every restraint that took place. This child would begin throwing objects whenever she got a response she did not like and it was this behaviour, which then often led to the restraints. With this information, I approached the day treatment worker with the suggestion that the reduction of her throwing behaviour be targeted. The worker then met with the child, reviewed this observation and a specific goal that focused on reducing her

FIGURE 10–4: Restraints by Time of Day for an Individual Client

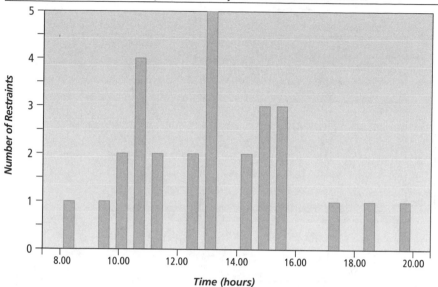

throwing behaviour was established. As part of this plan, I also met with this child's parents and reviewed the findings. I inquired about their experiences in the home and sought their assistance. They too acknowledged that this child's behaviour was problematic within the home. Parents were then asked to focus on assisting their child by helping her practice addressing her anger. I suggested that it would be very helpful to practice saying no, and then assisting their child in managing her disappointment in ways that did not involve throwing objects.

The results: From the beginning of the school year until November 25, 2003 this child had 23 restraints (approx 40 days). The following day a specific goal was implemented with this child that targeted the throwing behaviour. The goal was reviewed at the end of each quarter of the school day; so at a.m. recess, lunch, p.m. recess, and home time earning stickers whenever she was successful. From that day forward until her discharge from the program this child had no further incidence of physical restraint. An additional factor that certainly was felt to be of significance to this child's ability to make such significant changes quickly was that she began a stimulant medication. It must further be stated however that it was the feeling of the classroom staff that she had not always received this medication prior to coming to school and although she continued to struggle with impulsivity at these times she did not require physical intervention.

FIGURE 10–5: Duration of Restraints by Staff Involvement for an Individual Client

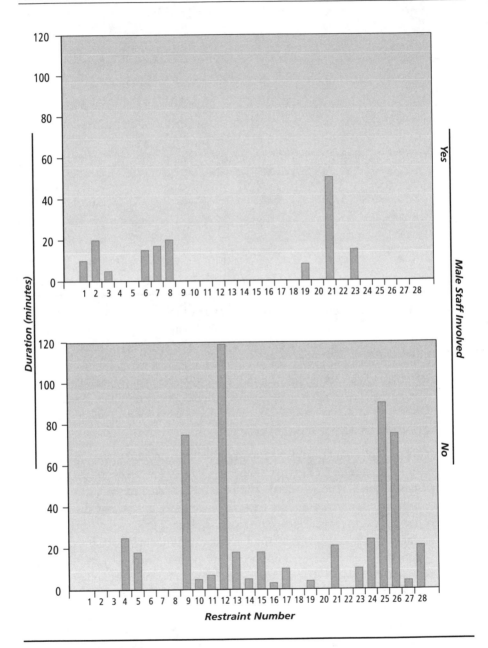

Agencywide Trends. After looking for trends among individual clients became our usual practice, we began to look for and address agencywide trends. Restraints were most common in the following order of frequency: immediately after lunch, on Mondays, Sunday nights, and Tuesdays. The staff schedule in the residences was changed so that more staff would be available during peak periods.

What Worked .

As shown on Figure 10–6, we achieved our goal of reducing the number of restraints by half in one year. The ongoing program evaluation does not allow for strong conclusions about causality, so it is difficult to tease out which of our interventions contributed most.

Each Person Is Unique. Individual treatment planning was a central feature of our efforts to reduce restraints. Individual staff needs were also addressed through individual supervision and consideration of each person's response to change.

Every Restraint Is Important. One of the factors we believe was critical was simply highlighting the importance of each restraint. We made restraints more salient through feedback on the number of restraints, the staff survey, including restraints incidents on the templates of regular reports, debriefing after restraint incidents, and many informal discussions about restraints.

Agency Culture. Another important factor in decreasing the number of restraints was to address the culture of the agency. Support from the highest levels of management was needed. Other aspects included involving everybody in the agency in the efforts to reduce restraints, and addressing through training and clinical supervision the issues raised in the staff surveys and interviews. Improved communication and feedback among staff during crisis situations and a collaborative multidisciplinary approach also seem to be elements of an agency culture that contribute to fewer restraints.

Data-Driven Approaches. Another factor was making adjustments in response to data. This data-driven approach maximized our flexibility. Examples of changes in response to data included many changes to the treatment plans of individual clients, changes in training and supervision, and a schedule change.

Therapeutic Relationships. Perhaps the most important factor in reducing restraints was the emphasis on therapeutic relationships. For example, as shown on Figure 10–3, our greatest setback occurred in February 2005. Most of the restraints in that time were with clients in the Early Intervention Program (day treatment for kindergarten-age students). During that time period, the teacher and classroom CYC were both not at work, for reasons completely

FIGURE 10–6: Restraints by Month: April 2003 to March 2005

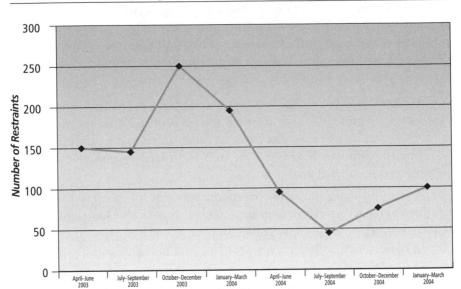

unrelated to the program. Without the consistency of the regular staff, the program experienced a crisis and an increased number of restraints.

Recent Developments and Future Directions

We recognize that reducing the number of physical restraints in an agency such as Vanier is a long-term project. We have several initiatives underway. One is that we have established a regional group that has met quarterly to network with similar agencies to compare our experiences in reducing the number of restraints. Another area we are exploring further is restraints with clients under the age of seven years. We are looking at how physical interventions are applied, current practices, and the special needs of this population. We are especially interested in less intrusive interventions.

Another initiative is to help us to understand better how staff use the terms *escort* (which is considered a physical restraint) and *gently guide* (which is not). To understand these terms better, we have developed a video for all staff to comment on various scenarios. Since the video and staff responses were incorporated into training, our number of restraints dropped by about one-third. We are also looking at staff training in related areas, such as vicarious trauma, cognitive-behavioral therapy, and attachment theory.

Another ongoing project is to create a debriefing model for staff to use after restraints. The plan is for this model to be Solution-Focused, and also to reflect aspects of cognitive development. Another project is to develop mandatory PMAB practice times for teams. Up to now, optional practice times have been well attended only when they have focused on specific concerns of high salience at the time.

We have explored the technical issue of how to take over from and end restraints safely. On a related note, we have introduced an approach similar to the "Two-Minute Restraint" approach developed at the Shiloh Treatment Center in Manvel, Texas (Mullen & Pitts, n.d.). In response to client deaths, that center introduced an arbitrary time limit on the duration of restraints. We are involved in another initiative involving a multisite research study that looks at children's residential experiences with regards to physical restraints.

Finally, through a special program evaluation initiative (Carter, 2006), we have improved our ability to summarize restraint incidents and to predict which clients are at the greatest risk for restraint from information available at intake. The same initiative allowed us to repeat the staff survey a third time, conduct interviews with staff, and evaluate the training video on escort versus gently guiding.

Having achieved our goal of reducing the number of restraints by half in one year, we are looking toward the future. During the course of the current year, we hope to reduce the number of restraint incidents by another 10% and to reduce the total duration of restraint incidents by half.

References

American Psychiatric Association, American Psychiatric Nurses Association, & National Association of Psychiatric Health Systems. (no date). *Learning from each other: Success stories and ideas for reducing restraints/seclusion in behavioral health.* Arlington, VA: Author

Bailey, K. A., Mrock, G., & Davis, F. (no date). *Changing the culture of care: From restraints to relationship.* Holson United Methodist Home for Children: Greeneville, TN.

Barwick, M. A., Boydell, K. M., Stasiulis, E., Ferguson, H. B., Blasé, K., & Fixsen, D. (2005). *Knowledge transfer and implementation of evidence-based practices in children's mental health.* Available at http://www.kidsmentalhealth.ca/documents/KT_full_report.pdf. Toronto, ON: Children's Mental Health Ontario

Carter, J. R. (2002). *Client factors in physical restraint: Preliminary report.* London, ON: Vanier Children's Services.

Carter, J. R. (2005). Effectiveness of innovations in time-limited intensive services. In C. Newman, C.. Liberton, K. Kutash, & R.M. Friedman (Eds.), *The 17th Annual Research Conference Proceedings: A System of Care for Children's Mental Health: Expanding the Research Base* (pp. 123–126). Tampa, FL: University of South Florida, Louis de la Parte Florida Mental Health Institute, Research and Training Center for Children's Mental Health.

Carter, J. R. (2006). *Monitoring of reducing restraints initiatives in intensive services: Final report.* London, ON: Vanier Children's Services. Funded by The Provincial Centre of Excellence for Child and Youth Mental Health at CHEO, Program Evaluation Grant # PEG 162606-042.

Cunningham, C. E., Pettingill, P., & Boyle, M. (2003). *The brief child and family phone interview* (BCFPI-3). Hamilton, ON: Canadian Centre for the Study of Children at Risk, Hamilton Health Sciences.

Day, D. M. (2000). *A review of the literature on restraints and seclusion with children and youth: Toward the development of a perspective in practice.* Report to the Intersectoral/Interministerial Steering Committee on Behaviour Management Interventions for Children and Youth in Residential and Hospital Settings, Toronto, Ontario.

Fox, L. E. (2004). The impact of restraint on sexually abused children and youth. *Residential Group Care Quarterly, 4,* 1–5.

Garbe, D. (2000). *A review of behaviour management intervention training.* Report to the Intersectoral/ Interministerial Steering Committee on Behaviour Management Interventions for Children and Youth in Residential and Hospital Settings, Toronto, Ontario.

Gupta, N. (2004). Reducing the uses of restraint and seclusion: Promising practices and successful strategies. *Residential Group Care Quarterly, 4,* 8.

Hodges, K. (2000). *Child and adolescent functional assessment scale.* Ann Arbor, MI: Functional Assessment Systems.

Intersectoral/Interministerial Steering Committee on Behavioural Management Interventions for Children and Youth in Residential and Hospital Settings. (2001). *Report of the Intersectoral/Interministerial Steering Committee on Behavioural Management Intervention for Children and Youth in Residential and Hospital Setting.* Toronto, ON: Children's Mental Health Ontario.

The killing of Stephanie. (2002, February 3). *The Globe and Mail,* F1, F8.

Kirkwood, S. (2003, September/October). Practicing restraint. *Children's Voice,* 14–19.

Knight, C. (2002). *A closer look: How they did it: A review of how six children's residential mental health facilities are attempting to reduce or eliminate the use of seclusion and restraint.* Columbus, OH: Ohio Legal Rights Service.

Masker, A. S., & Steele, J. (2004). Reducing physical management and time-out: A five-year update on one agency's experience. *Residential Group Care Quarterly, 4,* 6–7.

Mullen, J., & Pitts, K. (no date). *Restraint duration quicksand: One agency's outcome experience with physical intervention time limits.* Manvel, TX: Shiloh Treatment Center.

Nickols, F. (2004). *Change management 101: A primer.* Available online at http://home.att.net/~nickols/change.htm.

Perry, B. (2001). *Bonding and attachment in maltreated children: Consequences of emotional neglect in childhood.* Houston, TX: ChildTrauma Academy.

Perry, B. (2002). *Helping traumatized children: A brief overview for caregivers.* Houston, TX: ChildTrauma Academy.

Prevention and Management of Aggressive Behaviour. (2004). *A program for the prevention and management of aggressive behaviour among young offenders in a custody setting.* (2nd Ed.). Toronto, ON: Queen's Printer for Ontario.

Reduce Restraint Working Group. (2004, May). 'Reducing Restraints' Working Group. *Valuable Voices, 17,* 1–3. London, ON: Vanier Children's Services.

Wheatley, M. J. (1994). *Leadership and the new science: Learning about organization from an orderly universe.* San Francisco, CA: Berrett-Koehler.

Wheatley, M. J. (2001). Innovation means relying on everyone's creativity. *Leader to Leader, 20,* 14–20.

CHAPTER 11

Reducing the Use of Seclusion and Restraint in a Day School Program

Joseph B. Ryan,
Reece L. Peterson,
George Tetreault, and
Emily van der Hagen

THE USE OF SECLUSION AND RESTRAINT (S/R) has a long history of use within hospital, residential, and clinical settings. Recently however, there has been a concern that these procedures are being used increasingly more frequently in educational settings (Ryan & Peterson, 2004). These interventions are being employed in special education settings, particularly in those classrooms that serve students with emotional or behavioral disorders (EBD; diagnosis based on special education criteria), although they may also be used in programs for students with cognitive disabilities, autism, or other developmental disabilities. Forms of physical restraint and seclusion seem to also be becoming more widely used in general education schools and settings related to school violence reduction efforts. Despite these trends, there is very little information and virtually no formal research currently available about the extent or circumstances of the use of these procedures in educational settings.

History and Types of Restraint Used in Education

Although physical restraint has been used for several centuries within hospitals and psychiatry, particularly in the clinical treatment of violent persons (Romoff, 1985), its use in educational settings is relatively recent. One of the first times restraint was mentioned in educational literature dates back to the 1950s, when Redl and Wineman (1952) discussed restraint as one of the "techniques for the antiseptic manipulation of surface behavior" for students with EBD. In their description of restraint, they were very explicit that physical restraint should not be used as, nor associated with, physical punishment, and that the child losing control of his behavior should be viewed as an emergency situation where the educator or clinician should either remove the child from the scene, or prevent the student from doing physical damage to himself or others. The person performing the restraint should remain calm, friendly, and affectionate, and as a result maintain a potential relationship with the child, and thereby permit the opportunity for therapeutic progress once the child's crisis had subsided.

This "surface management" of behavior would then provide a bridge to opportunities for other intervention and therapy. Later literature mentioned physical restraint as an intervention technique for use by all teachers as a part of an armamentarium of classroom management strategies (Long, Morse, & Newman, 1996). While surface management of behavior has remained a commonly taught and used strategy for special education teachers, there is little evidence of how often or under what circumstances physical restraint is used for this purpose.

There are three types of restraint—physical, mechanical, and chemical. Physical, or manual restraint, is the most common form of restraint used in schools today. In physical restraint, one or more persons (staff) use their bodies to hold or limit the movement of another individual (student). The second type of restraint is called mechanical, and uses objects (e.g., straps) or other devices (e.g., standing chairs) to control an individual's body movement. While mechanical restraints have also been employed in schools for some students with physical or emotional disabilities, their use has been very limited by either policy or court decisions. The last type of restraint is chemical, in which medication is used to control a person's behavior. This type of restraint is virtually never employed directly by schools, although some have argued that drugs such as methylphenidate (Ritalin) prescribed by outside physicians may indirectly serve this type of purpose for schools. This chapter focuses solely on only on the use of physical or manual restraints used in schools which serve students with EBD and eligible for special education in this category of disability.

History and Types of Time-Out Used in Education

The use of time-out procedures in education has a much longer history. Since before the time of required mandatory school attendance, being sent home (suspended) from school was developed as a way to deal with unacceptable behavior or performance (Peterson, 2006). Most people are still familiar with the use of the "dunce cap" and "dunce chair" where a youngster was sent (usually in the corner of a room) for some misdeed, lack of adequate academic performance, or inappropriate behavior. For centuries, schools have used some version of what is now commonly referred to as time-out.

The growth of the behaviorist movement in the 1960s and 1970s led to the development of various time-out alternatives, which were supposed to provide "time-out *from positive reinforcement*." As the concept of time-out developed, three types of time-out in school were identified—inclusion, exclusion and seclusion. For the first type, there was an effort to withdraw the student's access to reinforcement while the student remained in the classroom. Examples of this might include a "time-out necklace" or "time-out chair" designating that the teacher and other students were not to provide any possible reinforcement (such as attention or comments) to a student while he wears the necklace or sits in a designated chair. This type of time-out is called inclusionary because the student can still see and hear the activities going on in the classroom.

The second type of time-out is exclusion, where the student was sent out of the classroom to some other location, with the assumption that the student would be thus be removed from the positively reinforcing environment in the classroom. Students might have been sent out into the hallway, to the Principal's office, or to some other location. The difficulty with exclusion time-out is that these alternative environments may inadvertently provide a wide variety of positive reinforcement for the student thus negating the intended purpose of this procedure—denying access to classroom reinforcement.

The final type of time-out is seclusion, where a youth is sent to a location isolated from her peers, and also from adults. The most common form of seclusion time-out was to place the student in a nearby empty room or a closet, although everything from cardboard refrigerator boxes to commercially constructed time-out booths have been used. These types of time-out rooms became common in special education settings during the 1970s and early 1980s, although problems with injuries and even suicides in these environments led to suggested guidelines for their use (Gast & Nelson, 1977). It was not long before a controversy surrounding the appropriateness of using this type of interventions in schools and for specific populations of students arose (Rothschild, 2004).

Schools personnel today may send students to time-out environments for many reasons other than removal from reinforcement. These may include providing a time to engage in personal reflection or problem solving, a time and location to cool down "hot" emotions, or to remove a disruption for other students or the teacher. Nevertheless these three types of time-out options (inclusionary, exclusionary, and seclusionary) exist regardless of the intended rational or theory proposed for their use.

This chapter focuses solely on the use of seclusion time-outs in schools that serve students with EBD, and specifically focuses on the use of seclusion at one particular day school program for EBD students.

Policies for Use of S/R in Education

The potential dangers associated with the use of S/R among our nation's youth garnered national attention following a series of articles run by the *Hartford Courant* newspaper (Weiss, Altimari, Blint, & Megan, 1998). After the series reported a staggering 142 restraint-related deaths across the United States during a 10-year period, 33% of which were caused by asphyxia, the use of these procedures quickly warranted investigation at both the state and federal level. It was not long before policies and guidelines were either created or amended in response to the national furor. Often these standards include accreditation requirements from governing bodies such as the Joint Commission on Accreditation of Healthcare Organizations or other agencies such as the National Association of Psychiatric Treatment Centers for Children (Cribari, 1996) and the American Academy of Pediatrics (American Academy of Pediatrics, Committee on Pediatric Emergency Medicine, 1997). These requirements have resulted in widespread training and certification for staff in these programs. In addition, the passage of the Children's Health Act of 2000, established national standards regarding the use of physical restraint with children in psychiatric facilities.

Unfortunately, neither the accreditation requirements nor federal legislation mentioned applies to public schools nor many privately operated schools. The lack of these commonly accepted guidelines or accreditation standards in schools might make these more susceptible to misunderstanding, improper implementation, or even abuse of these interventions. To make matters worse, school staff may lack training regarding effective behavioral interventions necessary for the prevention of emotional outbursts, typically associated with children who have severe behavioral problems (Moses, 2000). Such interventions are critical in preventing student behavior from escalating to potentially dangerous levels, where restraint or seclusion may be needed.

Given these circumstances, there is a strong need to better understand the use of S/R procedures in the field of education. Information is needed concerning how often these procedures are used, and under what circumstances, as well as the environmental circumstances that may be affecting their use. Information is also needed about what factors (such as training of staff) might influence the frequency with which these procedures are used, and about the outcomes for the use of these procedures. The purpose of this pilot study was to: (a) identify the current use of S/R procedures in a special day school for students with EBD, and (b) determine if staff training in de-escalation procedures would reduce the use of S/R procedures. The pilot study also served as a test for data gathering procedures that will be used for a larger study in the future.

Methods

Subjects

This pilot study was conducted in a public special day school for students with EBD in a medium-sized city in Minnesota (population approximately 12,500). Students were placed in the school from the surrounding public school districts and a nearby residential facility on both a short- and long-term basis due to inappropriate behaviors. The school had an average daily enrollment of 90 students during the course of the study, but provided educational services for a total of 316 different students throughout the school's 171-day academic calendar year. Participants for this study were 42 students who attended at least 75 school days during both the 2002–2003 and 2003–2004 academic school years. There were 40 males and 2 females, of which 37 were Caucasian, 3 American Indian, and 2 African American students.

Schoolwide Treatment Strategy

As a part of a schoolwide treatment strategy, all staff were expected to follow a "gated" schoolwide behavior intervention plan when dealing with a student's maladaptive behavior. This gated procedure requires staff to employ an array of interventions from the least restrictive form of intervention (inclusion time-out) to more restrictive procedures (seclusion time-out) where the latter can be used only when the former have been employed without success. According to this procedure, when a staff member first observes maladaptive behavior they initiate *simple intervention* techniques such as discussing the problem privately with the student or suggesting another activity (first gate or attempt at intervention).

If simple techniques fail, the next step or gate in behavioral intervention is *problem solving*. In this technique, the staff member(s) and student calmly discuss the inappropriate behavior, the consequence of the behavior, evaluate the situation, develop a plan and commitment to the plan, and design a follow-up plan. Staff use the opportunity to teach proper coping skills and develop plans for future behaviors (second gate).

An *inclusion time-out* is the next step (third gate) used if the student refuses to participate in the problem-solving step. At this point, the student is removed from the activity and required to stay quiet for three minutes before reengaging the problem-solving sequence. If the student continues the inappropriate behaviors, the student is placed in an *exclusion time-out* in a chair outside the classroom (fourth gate). The student is instructed to sit quietly for five minutes before attempting to reengage the problem-solving step.

If the student is unable to sit quietly for five consecutive minutes within a maximum duration of 15 minutes, the student is moved to a *seclusion time-out* (fifth gate). During this step the door to the seclusion room is left ajar, and a staff member monitors the student through the open doorway. The student may then begin the problem-solving step and rejoin the class after five minutes of quiet. After 60 minutes without successful completion of five quiet minutes the student is asked to rejoin his or her classroom again.

For safety reasons, students are required to remove shoes, belt, jewelry, pocket contents, and other materials prior to entering the time-out room. If a student: (a) attempts to leave the unlocked time-out room, (b) refuses to hand over objects that can be used to defaced property or inflict injury, (c) refuses to walk and must be physically escorted/restrained on the way to the time-out room, or (d) is physically aggressive, the door to the time-out room is locked (with an electromagnetic lock). After the student is able to remain calm and quiet for five minutes, a staff member will enter and try reengaging the problem-solving step. If the student refuses to leave the area, the door is relocked and the process begins again. Staff monitor the student through a window positioned next to the door. If an hour passes without the student successfully completing the problem-solving step, the student will be asked to rejoin the class. Each use of seclusion time-out is documented by the involved staff member(s), reviewed by the director, and filed in the student's folders.

This schoolwide treatment strategy is designed to insure that less restrictive or intrusive strategies are employed before the more intrusive strategies. Initial training on this overall treatment strategy is provided to new employees, and a discussion of this approach is regularly a part of staff meetings conducted every other week.

Staff Training

All staff underwent extensive training throughout the 2003–2004 academic school year in conflict de-escalation using *Therapeutic Intervention*, a curriculum developed by the Minnesota Department of Human Services. This training consisted of an initial training session of several hours, followed by ongoing discussion and follow-up training at semimonthly staff meetings on alternative strategies to de-escalate aggressive students.

In addition, all staff participated in the Crisis Prevention Institute (CPI)'s Nonviolent Crisis Intervention Training at the beginning of the 2003–2004 academic school year. The training program focuses on teaching staff how to successfully handle crisis and stressful situations with low anxiety and high security for all for involved individuals (Crisis Prevention Institute, 2002). The largest portion of the program training covers preventative techniques such as identifying maladaptive behaviors and choosing appropriate interventions, use of nonverbal techniques for de-escalating behaviors, and the ideology of personal well-being.

Another unit of the CPI program focuses on nonviolent physical crisis intervention and team interventions. For example, these techniques may be used in a situation where the student behavior escalated despite preventive techniques and safety is an issue. All staff practiced and rehearsed the procedures in training. The program concluded when staff applied the learned material in situational role-plays and discussion of postintervention techniques.

Procedure

Before data were gathered at the site, Institutional Review Board (IRB) approval was obtained for this study for gathering both existing archived incident data, as well as survey data at this site. IRB approval was obtained while the first author, J. Ryan, was a faculty member at James Madison University (IRB #05-001).

Incident Report Data. Data were collected from incident reports written during the school's 2002–2003 and 2003–2004 academic school years. School policy mandated that following the use of either a seclusion time-out or physical restraint, one of the participating staff were required to complete an incident report detailing the event and all staff involved. Variables coded by the school and verified by Ryan included:

1. age
2. gender
3. grade level
4. date and time
5. procedure used (seclusionary time-out or restraint)
6. duration of incident
7. staff involved
8. behavior necessitating intervention

Behaviors resulting in intervention included:

    a.   rule violation

    b.   property destruction

    c.   property misuse

    d.   physical aggression

    e.   leaving the area

    f.   disrespect

    g.   threatening

    h.   spitting

    i.   noncompliance

    j.   interfering with another student's education

    k.   harassment

    l.   violating another's personal space/privacy

    m. disruption

    n.   contraband

The incident report data for both years were gathered during the last half of the 2004–2005 school year and data gathering was completed at the end of the school term in May 2005.

Staff Survey. A staff questionnaire was administered to all of the 32 educational staff (i.e., teachers, educational assistants, administrators) assigned to the school. The 44 item questionnaire was designed to determine four factors: current school policies regarding restraint and time-out procedures, frequency with which these procedures are currently used, level of training staff receive regarding de-escalation strategies and restraint procedures, and level of agreement between administrative policy and actual implementation of restraint and time-out procedures with students.

Staff questionnaires were administered at the end of the school term of the second year and were implemented using a five-step process to ensure high response rates (Dillman, 2000). These elements included a respondent friendly questionnaire, multiple contacts, inclusion of stamped return envelopes, personalized correspondence, and a token financial incentive ($2 bill) included with the survey request.

Results

Incident Reports

Frequency of Time-Out and Restraint Procedures. Table 11-1 provides a detailed summary of all the seclusion and restraint procedures performed during both the 2002–2003 and 2003–2004 academic school years based on archived incident reports. During the 2002–2003 academic school year, 25 students were placed in seclusion time-out a total of 439 times. The number of time-outs per child ranged from a single event, to a maximum of 43 times. In comparison, the following school year staff administered 266 seclusion time-outs with 21 students, a 39.4% reduction. The number of time-outs experienced by each student ranged from once to a maximum of 66 times during the school year. During the first year, there were 15 students who were sent to seclusion time-out more than 10 times during the academic school year. The second year, the number of students placed in seclusion more than 10 times was reduced to 4 students.

During the 2002–2003 academic year, school staff performed 68 physical restraints on nine different students. Only one mechanical restraint was performed on a student who required this type of intervention based on his physical disability and behavioral intervention plan (BIP). The mechanical restraint consisted of a time-out chair. The following academic year, physical restraints were only implemented 56 times with five different students, a reduction of 17.6%. The use of mechanical restraints remained the same, with it being used only once during the academic school year.

Grade Level. The majority of students placed in seclusion during both school years came from elementary and middle school. High school students were rarely placed in time-out during either year (10.7% and 12.4% respectively). Restraints were also performed much more frequently among younger students during both years. During the 2002–2003 school year, the preponderance of all restraints (80.9%) were performed on elementary students. Students in middle school were much less likely to be restrained (14.7%), while high school students rarely (4.4%) experienced this procedure. During the second year, the elementary grades still represented the majority (67.9%) of all restraints performed, while no restraints were performed on high school students.

Escalation of Behaviors. When comparing the use of restraint procedures with students over both years, the number of physical restraints was effectively reduced by more than a third (39.4%), from 68 in 2002–2003 to 39 in 2003–2004. While the actual number of restraints decreased, the percentage

TABLE 11–1: Comparison of Seclusion/Restraint Use Pre- & Posttraining

| | SECLUSIONS | | RESTRAINTS | |
	PRE 2002/03	POST 03/04	PRE 2002/03	POST 03/04
Total Performed	439	266	68	39
Number of Students Involved	25	21	9	5
Duration of Seclusion	2–60 min $x = 13$	3–60 min $x = 15$	N/A	N/A
Age of Students	7–15 yrs $x = 12$	8–16 yrs $x = 13$	7–15 yrs $x = 8$	8–13 yrs $x = 8$
Elementary Students	30.5%	27.4%	80.9%	67.9%
Middle School Students	58.8%	60.2%	14.7%	32.1%
High School Students	10.7%	2.4%	4.4%	0%

of time-out incidents that necessitated the use of restraint procedures increased from 15.5% to 25.8% during the same period.

Behaviors Identified as Requiring Intervention. Table 11–2 shows the behaviors that were identified by staff via archived incident reports that required the use of either seclusion or restraint procedures. After reviewing the incident reports, the reasons cited by staff for implementing either a seclusion time-out or restraint procedure with students remained relatively consistent throughout the two-year time frame. The two most common reasons staff cited for using either intervention was for leaving an assigned area and noncompliance. Other less common reasons included disrupting the class and property misuse.

Staff Survey

The staff survey was completed by 93.75% (n = 30) of all staff. Findings are reported concerning the prevalence of seclusion and restraint procedures, application of procedures, and professional training.

Use of Time-Out and Restraint Procedures. The majority of all staff (90%) reported using inclusion time-out procedures with students, with three quarters (73.3%) of staff claiming they use it on at least a weekly basis. All staff reported using exclusion time-out, with the majority (90%) using it on at least a weekly basis. Almost all staff (96.7%) used seclusion, which is the most restrictive form of time-out, with nearly two-thirds using it on at least a weekly basis. Lastly, approximately three quarters of the staff (73.3%) used restraint procedures, with a quarter of staff (26.7%) reporting using restraints on a weekly basis. Staff who administered restraint procedures incorporated all of the

TABLE 11–2: Behaviors Identified on Incident Reports Requiring Seclusion / Restraint

REASON STATED FOR INTERVENTION	SECLUSION*	RESTRAINT*
Leaving Assigned Area	32.6%	19.4%
Noncompliance	31.9%	48.4%
Disrupting Class	11.2%	6.5%
Property Misuse	10.1%	7.3%
Disrespect	4.5%	7.3%
Physical Aggression	2.8%	3.2%
Harassment	2.4%	0.8%
Threats	2.0%	3.2%
Horseplay	0%	3.2%

* Columns do not add up to 100% due to several incomplete incident reports.

following types of restraints including: physical escorts, basket holds, prone restraints, and wall restraints. Only one staff member reported using a mechanical restraint that was specifically called for by the student's BIP.

Reasons for Use of Procedures. The most common reasons staff provided for having to implement restraint procedures in order of prevalence included: (a) displaying physical aggression towards staff (90%), physical aggression towards peers (86.7%), property destruction (63.3%), leaving assigned area (26.7%), physical threats (23.3%), and refusal to follow staff directions (13.3%). No staff member claimed they would use restraint procedures for refusing to perform an academic task.

Staff reported various responses in regard to when they would terminate a restraint procedure. The most common reason cited was when the student was placed in seclusion (93.3%). Other reasons staff provided for ceasing restraint procedures included: a student's verbal willingness to cooperate (30%), specific time elapses (20%), and when a student ceases struggling (13.3%).

Professional Training. All staff reported receiving training in de-escalation techniques during the past year, with nearly two-thirds (63.3%) receiving between 5 to 12 hours of this training. This extensive training resulted in nearly all staff (90%) reporting being satisfied with the level of training they had received. Staff reported learning de-escalation strategies from a variety of sources including staff development (100%), professional seminars (100%), teacher training in college (71.4%), and professional journals (50%).

Discussion

Efficacy of Staff Training

Overall, professional staff training in de-escalation techniques appears to have been effective in reducing the use of both seclusion and restraint (S/R) procedures by staff within the special day school. Staff performed 173 (39.4%) fewer seclusion time-outs and 12 (17.6%) less manual restraints following the staff training on de-escalation techniques. Unfortunately, this study was not able to control other possible explanations for the changes in use of restraint that were found. These could include differences in the population of students served from one year to the next (some students were included for both years), changes in staff (only a handful of staff changed during this period), changes in the internal climate of the school such as administration attitudes, or changes in the external climate such as awareness of the concerns about the use of these interventions, or combinations of these factors along with the training provided. While this pilot study does not provide conclusive evidence of the effectiveness of training in reducing the use of physical restraint and seclusion, it nevertheless seems to provide some support for this conclusion.

Several additional important findings are worthy of future research, including: (a) disproportionate use of S/R procedures among younger children, (b) reliance upon S/R procedures when they appear to be ineffective in modifying maladaptive behavior, and (c) discrepancy between staff beliefs regarding when S/R procedures should be used, and why they are actually performed.

Disproportionate Use of S/R Procedures Among Youth

When analyzing the school's incident reports it became readily apparent that the majority of all S/R procedures were performed on the school's younger population. The median age of students placed in seclusion was 13, while those restrained were even younger with a median of 8 years of age. The high use of these procedures among youth is consistent with research by Persi and Pasquali (1999) who reported an increased escalation of inappropriate student behavior with the onset of adolescence. It is posited the use of S/R procedures are more common among younger children, potentially due to either:

1. their possessing fewer mechanisms for coping with frustration,
2. staff may believe intrusive procedures may be more developmentally appropriate for younger children, or

3. that staff may be apprehensive to perform these procedures on larger and stronger individuals. (Miller, Walker, & Friedman, 1989; Persi & Pasquali, 1999)

To date, no research has been conducted to support either of the first two rationales (Day, 2002). If however, the latter explanation holds true, staff may be unknowingly more willing to violate a young child's individual rights under the Eighth Amendment, which prohibits administering cruel or unusual punishment, and the Fourteenth Amendment, which provides for an individual's liberty interests in freedom of movement and personal security (Kennedy & Mohr, 2001).

Over Reliance of S/R Procedures When Ineffective

Perhaps the most alarming finding from this study was the over use of S/R procedures with specific students. During the two years of data collection, 19 students had been placed in seclusion on more than 10 occasions. One of these students had been placed in seclusion 66 times during a single school year. Another student had been restrained 46 times during the first year, and 33 times during the second. Both the student and teacher being inadvertently reinforced through the use of these procedures may possibly explain the continued use of these aversive procedures despite their apparent ineffectiveness.

A student is often positively reinforced when removed from the classroom environment because he is escaping or avoiding an unpleasant task or environment (e.g., difficult academic assignment). In contrast, the teacher is frequently negatively reinforced when using seclusion. Once a paraeducator removes the misbehaving student from the classroom, the teacher's aggravation is also removed, providing the teacher with at least a brief reprieve from dealing with the student and the maladaptive behavior. Since both staff and student alike are being reinforced through the use of these procedures, its continued use as a behavior modification technique is frequently repeated, despite its ineffectiveness in modifying the student's maladaptive behavior.

Discrepancy Between Procedures and Practice

Another finding of interest is that there appears to be a large discrepancy between survey responses of why staff would implement S/R procedures according to the survey, and why staff actually performed them according to the actual incident reports. The survey, which was completed by almost all staff (93.75%), showed staff would primarily implement S/R procedures when students demonstrated aggressive behavior. The primary reasons given included physical aggression toward staff (90%) or peers (86.7%), followed by destruction of property (63.3%). This rationale followed the teachings of the crisis intervention training staff received throughout the year. However, the incident reports showed staff rarely utilized S/R procedures for such scenarios. Instead, nearly two-thirds of all restraints and seclusions were used in response to student noncompliance or leaving an assigned area. Physical aggression was stated as the precipitator of relatively few seclusion time-outs (2.8%) or restraints (3.2%). Theoretically, if S/R procedures had been limited to those reasons stated by staff in the survey, there would only have been a handful of seclusion and restraint procedures performed throughout the academic school year.

Limitations

There were several limitations to this study. A primary limitation of this study dealt with the use of a volunteer school and sample of staff. The leader of the school had expressed a desire to reduce their school's use of seclusion and restraint and that alone may explain part or all of the reductions in use of S/R. This makes it difficult to generalize the study's findings. As a pilot study, it was conducted in one medium-sized city located in Minnesota. This does not provide adequate representation of students with EBD placed across placement settings (e.g., public school, residential, psychiatric facilities) nationwide.

Implications

The use of S/R procedures continues to be an understudied but overused procedure among one of our nation's most vulnerable populations. While this pilot study demonstrated staff training in de-escalation techniques could have an apparent impact on reducing the use of S/R procedures, to achieve maximum efficacy staff not only need to be trained in crisis intervention, but also closely supervised. It is unclear what environmental factors may also be influencing the reduction in the use of these techniques. Further investigation about why staff did not apparently follow procedures outlined in school policy would also be helpful.

The use of both incident reports and a staff survey appeared feasible, and resulted in useful data. Future studies should incorporate a system of tracking and analyzing the use of seclusion and restraint procedures, that provides information about the outcomes (e.g., safety of students and staff; effect on symptoms; and academic or behavioral progress) related to using these procedures as well as the student's specific diagnoses, and a more detailed analysis of the behaviors which triggered the use of restraint or time-out.

References

American Academy of Pediatrics Committee on Pediatric Emergency Medicine. (1997). The use of physical restraint interventions for children and adolescents in the acute care setting. *Pediatrics, 99*(3), 497–498

Cribari, L. (1996). Facilities rethink policies on use of physical restraint. *Brown University Child & Adolescent Behavior Letter, 12*(8), 1–3.

Crisis Prevention Institute. (2002). *Participant workbook for the nonviolent crisis intervention training program.* Brookfield, WI: Compassion Publishing, Ltd.

Day, D. M. (2002). Examining the therapeutic utility of restraints and seclusion with children and youth: The role of theory and research in practice. *American Journal of Orthopsychiatry, 72*(2), 266–278.

Dillman, D. A. (2000*). Mail and internet surveys (2nd ed.).* New York, NY: John Wiley & Sons, Inc.

Gast, D. L., & Nelson, C. M. (1977). Legal and ethical considerations for the use of time-out in special education settings. *The Journal of Special Education, 11*, 457–467.

Kennedy, S. S., & Mohr, W. K. (2001). A prolegomenon on restraint of children: Implicating Constitutional rights. *American Journal of Orthopsychiatry, 71*(1), 26–37.

Long, N. J., Morse, W. C., & Newman, R. (1996). *Conflict in the classroom (5th ed.).* Austin, TX: Pro-Ed.

Miller, D., Walker, M. C., & Friedman, D. (1989). Use of a holding technique to control the violent behavior of seriously disturbed adolescents. *Hospital and Community Psychiatry, 40*, 520–524.

Moses, T. (2000). Why people choose to be residential childcare workers. *Child and Youth Care Forum, 29*(2), 113–126.

Persi, J., & Pasquali, B. (1999). The use of seclusion and physical restraints: Just how consistent are we? *Child and Youth Care Forum, 28*, 87–103.

Peterson, R. L. (2006). Suspension. In G. Sugai & R. Horner (Eds.), *The encyclopedia of behavior modification and cognitive behavior therapy* (pp.1552–1555). Thousand Oaks, CA: Sage Publications.

Redl, F., & Wineman, D. (1952). *Controls from within: Techniques for the aggressive child.* New York: The Free Press.

Romoff, V. (1985). Management and control of violent patients at the Western Psychiatric Institute and Clinic. In L. H. Roth (Ed.), *Clinical treatment of the violent person* (pp. 235–260). Rockville, MD: U. S. Dept of Health and Human Services, National Institute of Mental Health.

Rothschild, S. (2004, October 19). Committee considers special-ed guidelines. *Lawrence Journal-World.* Available online at www.tilrc.org/docs/wtp1104_05.htm.

Ryan, J. B., & Peterson, R. L. (2004). Physical restraint in school. *Behavioral Disorders, 29*, 154–168.

Weiss, E. M., Altimari, D., Blint, D. F., & Megan, K. (1998, October 11–15). Deadly restraint: A nationwide pattern of death. *Hartford Courant.*

CHAPTER 12

Lessons Learned From 30 Plus Years of No Physical Intervention

George Suess

Introduction

The Arc of Delaware County is a nonprofit community-based rehabilitation agency located in the Catskill Mountain Region of New York. Its mission is to enable people of all ages to meet the challenge of their disabilities with a growing sense of dignity, independence, and productivity. It primarily serves preschool age children and adults with a variety of delays or special needs. The children it serves through its early intervention and preschool programs may have delays of any type, but chief among these are behavior challenges, speech delays, and autism spectrum disorders. People with mental retardation and developmental disabilities constitute the largest segment of its adult population. Due to the rural nature and lack of other specialized providers in Delaware County, however, the Arc serves a smaller number of individuals with an array of physical and emotional disorders as well. Approximately 300 individuals are served daily and another 100 intermittently. Approximately 40 individuals are supported in various residential settings. Settings ranging from group homes to individual apartments. Many of the adults served have resided in state-run institutions such as developmental centers or psychiatric centers for extended periods of their lives. The Arc of Delaware County offers a variety of services and settings. The principles discussed in this chapter have been successfully applied to the full range of individuals, the full range of delays or disabilities, and in the full range of services it provides. The organization has a clear and successful history of serving even the most behaviorally challenging individuals from the community and from institutions.

In many ways and on the surface, the Arc of Delaware County appears to be quite similar to most other organizations of its type. The similarities end at the surface. The Arc of Delaware County's proactive philosophy and positive approach sets it apart, with progressive, values-based managerial practices distinguishing it further. Since 1973, it has been and continues to be the only such organization, in the state of New York, that has prohibited the use of restraints in any form. The agency's Board of Directors state in their policy on the Treatment of Participants, "The CEO shall not cause or allow physical restraint to be used as a general treatment method." The concluding phrase, "as a general treatment method" was developed to recognize their may be an occasion when someone might need to be pulled from the path of an on rushing vehicle or other similar emergency situation. But these are so rare as to be virtually absent. If such a situation were to occur, it would be reported, reviewed, and prevented (if possible) from happening again.

How has the organization been able to serve such individuals for such a long period of time without relying on techniques the rest of the field finds essential? This chapter presents several key components to consider.

Leadership

Leadership is about setting a vision and clarifying values. The decision to use or to not rely on restraints is all about leadership. What is the vision about how people should be treated? How does that vision fit an organization's values? Most rehabilitation agencies who have defined their values have something like, "the people we serve come first," as one of those values. If, in fact, the people served really do come first, one ponders why scores of professionals are so cavalier about using physical force upon the people they profess to be in such high priority? If we are committed to excellence, how can we tolerate using anything but the best techniques with people in our care? If we are as driven to achieve customer satisfaction, as the field's rhetoric would have us believe, why are allegations of abuse so common? These are all serious Leadership issues.

The Arc of Delaware County has trained thousands of individuals and scores of organizations over the last 15 years. When, during the course of such training it asks the question, "Why don't more organizations commit to a proactive philosophy and positive approach?" time and time again responses include:

"We would never receive the support we would need from our top administrators."

"It would be near impossible to change employee attitudes."

"We don't have sufficient training."

"Our team isn't ready."

Although typical and common, these responses all point to leadership as the source of the issue. It is our observation, leaders such as CEO's, superintendents, and executive directors are too often consumed with budgetary, regulatory, and hosts of operational matters. This, together with a lack of firsthand experience in the area of positive approaches to behavior management, results in the delegation of responsibility to others in the organization. These other individuals, also lacking in experience in progressive alternatives, find themselves in a situation where they have the responsibility to deal with behavioral issues but not the authority to address the fundamental cultural change needed to support a proactive philosophy.

Volunteer leaders, such as those on boards of directors, are for the most part unqualified in these matters. Consequently, they defer to professionals rather than setting clear policy. Government leaders also often lack specific firsthand experience and are further hampered by systems and political forces. To use or not use high-risk procedures is a policy decision too few leaders understand or seem willing to address. The lack of clear, progressive policies that prohibit the use of high-risk procedures seems to be a fundamental leadership shortcoming of organizations, their Boards, and the governments that fund and regulate them.

Published Values and Philosophy

The Total Quality Management movement of the 1990s had many, differing results. Leading among them was the fact that most organizations of today have written values statements. That is the good news. The troublesome news, in our opinion, is that too few organizations have found ways to fully actualize their values. Values statements are too often posters on a wall that few read and fewer follow.

Over the last 15 years, the Arc of Delaware County has painstakingly and meticulously built its values, or Unifying Principles, into all of its human resource practices including recruitment, orientation, training, supervision, time management, performance reviews, and career development. In doing so, it has become conscious of the need to further define or clarify them in order to inform its employees, consumers, and families with more detailed statements of philosophy that explain, "This is what we mean by our values and this is how we demonstrate them."

As the Arc of Delaware County has developed written statements of philosophy, its sensitivity to the fundamental importance of such has matured. This almost hypersensitivity has led it to look for the same in other organizations only to find them consistently lacking. The conclusion reached is that most organizations do not have a single, clear, well-defined philosophy about how people should be treated. They do not understand how vitally important it is to carefully and clearly communicate such a philosophy to their employees and customers.

Getting Started

Individuals and organizations who are interested in examining this matter often ask, "Where do we begin?" To assist them the following framework has been developed.

Introduction

Eliminating physical interventions, while dealing with challenging behaviors, often presents a paralyzing effect on organizations. Their hearts tell them there must be a better way. Their minds tell them the approaches they are using are not effective and often result in escalation, humiliation, and injury. Their eyes see the anger and panic that often results. Sometimes they fear the approach they are using is actually reinforcing the behavior they want to eliminate. Other times they fear they are teaching violence. Yet they often do not know what else to do. Their field has relied on traditional, reactive approaches for so long there is little belief and less conviction that positive, proactive philosophies and approaches do indeed work. So the status remains quo. Likewise a great deal of confusion often results when their system calls for a plan that includes both emergency and treatment methods. It is quite common for organizations to place formal emphasis on training for emergencies although training on effective treatment methods is woefully lacking. This results in treatment approaches that are often not effective causing emergencies to arise. Over time, too often, the emergency plan becomes the treatment plan.

The framework described below has been developed to provide organizations a multiyear, self-paced process to gradually improve their capacity to move away from, and to eliminate, physical interventions. The steps the framework identifies may need greater or lesser emphasis based on each organization's current capacity and expertise. Likewise the order of the steps can also be rearranged to better meet individual circumstances. It is important to understand this is only a framework. It is not intended to be a "how-to" manual. The steps involved are far too sophisticated and complex to fully address in such a brief space. It is intended to provide a basic framework for those who wish to move forward but are not certain as to how to proceed.

1. Gather Data

Gathering baseline data is important for several reasons. It is necessary in order to track progress, to encourage new thinking, and to demonstrate ultimate success. Organizations should determine what they wish to measure and how they will do so. Examples of data that can be identified include: number and types of physical interventions utilized by the organization and its various departments, numbers of injuries to consumers, number of injuries to staff, number of injuries to by-standers, number of tantrums (though further definition would be needed here), number of workers compensation claims due to injuries resulting from such interventions, the amount and the extent of property damage, etc. Each organization may determine what it will measure, but measurement is critically important.

2. Assess Internal Expertise

Instituting this type of change will go more or less easily depending on the expertise of current staff and their willingness to embrace whatever changes affect them individually. An early step in the process should be to objectively assess staff expertise as well as their willingness to change or improve. This will shed light on the types and amounts of training needed. It will also determine if staff currently have sufficient skills to move forward or if additional technical assistance will be needed.

3. Set a Goal, Develop a Plan, and Announce the Plan

Depending on their size and current expertise any given organization should be able to dramatically reduce their reliance on physical interventions within one to three years. A proper internal assessment will generate the information and analysis necessary to set a proper goal within a reasonable time frame. Example 1: "The XYZ Organization will reduce the number of physical interventions by 80% within 18 months." Example 2: "The ABC Organization will eliminate the use of physical interventions within 3 years." Once a measurable goal is determined, it should be announced loud and clear throughout the entire organization.

4. Increase Staff Training

The amount of training for direct service and especially supervisory and clinical staff must not be underestimated. Training should be lavish and competency based. Basic competencies should include: developing effective relationships, task analysis, the use of reinforcements, the ability to engage individuals meaningfully, and the role and proper use of Antecedents Behavior Consequence (ABC) Charts and Functional Assessments. Training should include hands-on practice under the skillful observation of highly qualified personnel.

5. Reorganize Existing Training

Many organizations using physical interventions follow a training curriculum that includes positive, proactive components. These are usually taught early on in a course. Stressing over-learning of this point of the curriculum can bring about significant improvement. This is best accomplished by adding structured field practice. Such courses often end with training on the use of certain physical intervention techniques. The message that is sent—sometimes directly, sometimes indirectly—is, "First, we will study positive practices. If these do not work we will then teach you how to properly use physical intervention." By simply changing the order by which the material is presented, a more effective message can be sent, "First, we are going to teach you how to properly use physical intervention techniques. Then we are going to teach you a number of other more positive techniques so you will never have to use more physical ones."

6. Develop a Campaign to Dramatically Increase Praise and Reinforcement

Dramatically increasing the effective use of praise and reinforcement is an essential element of a positive approach. Most people who work in this field have never worked in or experienced an environment where praise and reinforcement are used lavishly. This presents a dilemma whereby many staff feel they use praise and reinforcement effectively when, in fact, significant improvement is needed. To correct this an immediate step can be taken to collect baseline data. The types and rates of reinforcement should be counted for a particular time interval. Then goals can be established and an organized effort can be initiated to dramatically increase both the types and rates of praise and reinforcement. Consider challenging staff to praise or reinforce each person they are working with once per minute for one week.

7. Establish a New Paradigm for the Roles of Psychologists and Behavioral Specialists

The roles of these important specialists should evolve from doing to teaching. Job descriptions may need to be rewritten to reflect this change. They should adopt a view of themselves as behavioral mentors to direct service, supervisory, and clinical staff. The goal of this process is to put the tools of positive practice in the hands of the people who do the work. Rather than the traditional paradigm of having a very small percentage of "Behavioral Specialists" on staff, the emerging new paradigm will use existing specialists to train and develop the entire workforce so 100% of the workforce will become specialists in positive behavioral approaches.

8. Limit Intervention Training

In some organizations all employees are trained in the use of physical interventions. Simply adopting a policy whereby only an absolute minimum number of staff necessary in a given location are so trained sends a powerful message. As does adopting a policy stating, "Only our most *highly-skilled* or most *experienced* employees will be trained in the use of physical interventions, in an effort to assure they will only be used as a last resort."

9. Increase Scrutiny of Occurrences

Increasing management scrutiny when physical interventions are utilized also sends a powerful message throughout the organization stating they are serious about this goal. Scrutiny will be even more effective if it emphasizes a search for root causes rather than blame (Paterson et al., chapter 7).

10. Examine Hiring Practices

Are job candidates predisposed or open to positive practice? As organizations move forward in their attempts to reduce physical intervention by increasing their emphasis on such things as caring relationships, increasing praise and reinforcement, building self-esteem, and moving away from one size fits all rules to individualized services, they may very well find they need a different type of worker. If so, they will need to adjust their hiring practices.

11. Examine Supervisory Ratios and Schedules

An important ingredient of success will be the effectiveness of front-line supervisors. In addition to increasing the training they receive, organizations need to assess their supervisory loads. Ratios of one to five are ideal. Large ratios will jeopardize overall success. Likewise it is wise to examine the work schedules of supervisors. Schedules should be developed which provide supervisors the opportunity for direct observation, training, and quality control.

12. Facility Review

For the most part, this transition should be able to occur in any facility. However, nothing should be taken for granted and facilities should be reviewed to determine their disposition to a positive approach. Are hazards present that require a greater degree of control than desirable? Does the presence of a time-out room, even if it is not utilized, present a lingering threat?

Final Comments

The framework presented in this chapter can help organizations move forward in their efforts to reduce or eliminate high-risk interventions. Each element of the framework is complex and may require a significant investment of time, energy, and perhaps finances. The benefits, however, will make the investment well worthwhile.

Conclusion

Everyone wants to change, as long as they can keep on doing things the same old way. The results of training thousands of individuals and scores of organizations have led the Arc of Delaware County to several conclusions. Chief among these is that far too many rehabilitation agencies, schools, and nursing homes rely on practices and techniques that are out-dated, unnecessary, ineffective, shamefully disrespectful, and even harmful. Closely related is the lack of ownership volunteer and professional leaders display when it comes to the use of high-risk interventions within their organizations. At the core of the matter lies the battle between values-based rhetoric and values-based actions.

Asking questions at Board of Directors and School Board meetings like: how are our values demonstrated in our policies and procedures and in the behaviors of our employees; what type and how much training on progressive practices is provided to whom; how clear are the expectations regarding the personal interactions between employees and the children and adults they serve; how are those interactions monitored and improved; and how much of our organizational resources are devoted to positive, preventive strategies versus putting out fires, will direct volunteer leaders to demand more proactive, progressive practice from their professional leaders who in turn will need to take more personal ownership of same.

As stated, the framework can help leaders move forward in their efforts to eliminate high-risk intervention and introduce more progressive practice. Each element of the framework is complex and may require a significant investment of time, energy, and finances. If followed, the benefits will make the investment well worthwhile.

When someone, who has a long history of tantrums or assaults, learns they can get their needs met in other, much more socially acceptable ways, their life fundamentally changes. They develop more and better relationships, their self-esteem and confidence blossom, they apply themselves better to whatever skills they need to learn or duties they need to perform, and they are equipped to take charge of their lives. Using high-risk interventions is about control and convenience. Using positive techniques is about learning, growth, and rebirth. When it comes to organizations, using positive techniques is about change.

PART V

LEGAL
ISSUES

CHAPTER 13

Using Restraint
The Legal Context of
High-Risk Interventions

Sheila Suess
Kennedy

Introduction

As Kennedy and Mohr have noted (2001), the treatment of children by mental health professionals—particularly in an institutional setting—implicates three sets of important, and frequently competing, interests. The first of these is the parental interest in preserving family autonomy: minimizing state interference in decisions made about what constitutes the best interests of their child, and their right to transmit to that child their particular personal and cultural values. The second is the state's interest in protecting the child, preventing or controlling antisocial behavior, and, in furtherance of those goals, providing a system of mental-health care. Finally, there are the child's own interests in "being cared for, loved, and helped to become an autonomous individual with the rights and privileges of an adult" (Hopcroft, 1995, p. 545).

Navigating among those interests in a professional, ethical, and legal manner is a delicate process. Physicians and other health care providers relate to their patients—adults or children—from a position of trust, based upon the presumed expertise of the medical professional. Given this relationship asymmetry, such professionals have a special obligation to be strictly at the service of their patients, and to be particularly solicitous of their well-being. In the case of children, this obligation is more daunting, because children constitute a special class of vulnerable patient. Children generally do not initiate the professional relationship, and once they are party to it, they are disempowered by their presumed incompetent status under the law.

Although professional medical and psychiatric norms tend to supercede political and geographical boundaries, that is not the case with legal practices. Different constitutional contexts and disparate legal norms give rise to different legal approaches to these issues by different countries. In the United States, the central constitutional preoccupation has been to limit governmental power, and as a consequence, American law is not easily reconciled with that of systems in which fundamental rights are both affirmative and negative. (Certain portions of the United Nations Convention on the Rights of the Child, for example, are simply inapposite to the American legal system, which lacks a mechanism for constitutionalizing affirmative entitlements—a situation that leads to a great deal of confusion on both sides of what might be thought of as a cultural divide.) Even within the United States, laws governing the psychiatric hospitalization of minors vary considerably from state to state.

American courts have uniformly held that children do not enjoy the same degree of constitutional protection, as do adults. In *Parham v. J.R.* (1979), the U.S. Supreme Court explicitly held that the involuntary hospitalization of a minor without judicial review would not run afoul of the Constitution if the child's legal custodian consents, the treating clinicians concur, and the clinicians periodically review the need for continued inpatient treatment. Individual states are free to grant their own citizens rights additional to those ensured under the federal constitution, however, allowing this disenfranchisement of children to play itself out differently in different states. A substantial majority of states do apply a "least restrictive alternative" mandate to their civil commitments, requiring that any infringement on a patient's liberty be the minimum necessary to achieve the purpose for which the person was committed, but the scope of the protection offered—particularly to minors—is a matter of considerable dispute (Saks, 1986). In most states, the avenues for relief available to juveniles are considerably fewer than those available to adults. Without adequate provisions for judicial review, children can languish in psychiatric or residential treatment facilities for unspecified lengths of time and suffer the most basic deprivations of their rights as human beings.

Any discussion of the treatment of minors confined to psychiatric facilities must begin by recognizing that children are not voluntary patients in the commonly accepted meaning of the term. Forced hospitalization encroaches on their liberty by limiting their right to be free of unwanted bodily intrusion by way of physical restraint. To the extent that at least some of the more intrusive treatment techniques in psychiatric settings are experienced as painful and distressing, their recipients may see those treatments as "punishments."

(This is particularly true when the recipient is a child institutionalized for treatment of a mental illness whose capacity to understand what is happening in the moment might be impaired.) While the Supreme Court has declined to extend the Eighth Amendment's protection against "cruel and unusual punishment" to residents of hospitals and psychiatric facilities, it has ruled that even minors retain Fourteenth Amendment liberty interests[1] in freedom of movement and in personal security, interests that can only be outweighed by an "overriding, nonpunitive" state interest (*Youngberg v. Romeo,* 1982).

The use of restraints by psychiatric facilities is a common, albeit hotly contested, practice. The term "restraint" can refer to immobilization by force (for example, being held down by staff), or it can refer to mechanical devices (being tied to a chair; being strapped to a bed). It can be environmental (being locked in a seclusion room) or pharmacological (medication, whether delivered orally or by injection). As Day (2000) has noted, the use of the term "restraints" in the literature varies rather widely: "Brendtro and Ness (1991) used the term to describe a range of techniques including handcuffs and multiple point straps, interventions that are commonly referred to as mechanical restraints. Selekman and Snyder (1997) defined physical restraints as 'material and/or equipment that prevents the movement of one or more body parts'" (cited in Day, 2000, p. 8).

Restraints can be physical, mechanical, or chemical. Physical restraints have been defined as external controls that involve the use of physical force or holding techniques that restrain a child's movement. Mechanical restraints can include a variety of implements in addition to those described by Day—straps, belts, cuffs, body vests, and even geriatric chairs have been employed to restrict the patient's mobility. Chemical restraints are medications used to sedate or immobilize; those employed may include thioridazene, chlorpromazine, and haloperidol (Day, 2000; p. 9). Some of the literature defines restraint broadly enough to include seclusion—the practice of isolating or segregating the child—although most treat these as separate, albeit closely related, treatment issues.

---

1. The Fourteenth Amendment prohibited state governments from denying the "privileges and immunities" of citizenship to their own citizens; prior to passage of the Amendment, the limitations on state action imposed by the Bill of Rights did not apply to state and local governments. Subsequent cases have further defined the scope of the Amendment's equal protection and due process clauses, and have described the fundamental rights that are protected. The "liberty interest" encompasses much more than personal freedom from confinement; it includes those aspects of life deemed fundamental to happiness, like the right to travel, contract, practice a profession, and marry the person of ones own choosing.

Such control methods are not confined to psychiatric facilities or hospitals. Their use has been documented in a number of other settings: residential treatment centers, detention facilities, and special schools and classrooms. Whatever the arguments against their use in such environments, restraints are especially problematic when used to control children whose ability to understand and cope is by definition impaired.

The few research studies available indicate that approximately 30% of the children on some psychiatric units have been secluded or restrained in some manner (Garrison, Ecker, Friedman, Davidoff, Haeberle, & Wagner, 1990). More recent studies have suggested that the actual incidence of restraint use may be higher than previously estimated. A 2001 article puts the number at 47 incidents per month, per psychiatric facility, and estimates the number of restraint uses in the United States each year at 282,000 (Luna, 2001).

In 1998, a series of newspaper articles documented the deaths of 37 children during a 10-year period, attributable to the use of physical restraints in psychiatric facilities (Weiss, Altimari, Blint, & Megan, 1998). The articles reported deaths in all 50 states, and included only those that were reported and documented. The U.S. General Accounting Office (1999) issued a report entitled *Mental Health: Improper Restraint or Seclusion Use Places People at Risk*, confirming the problems, and raising a number of thorny questions: What are the medical and psychiatric indications for restraint use? What are the ethical issues involved? And what are the legal implications of these interventions?

Professional Indications

The reasons given for the use of restraints on children in a treatment facility are for the safety of the child or for the safety of other patients in the case of severe aggression (Kennedy & Mohr, 2001). Most often, health professionals justify their use of restraints as a matter of patient protection (Kapp, 1998). However, it has been asserted that the real reasons for the use of restraints were convenience (to control individual behavior with otherwise inadequate staffing, or without the need for other clinical interventions), coercion (to force the patient to comply with the staff member's wishes), or retaliation (to punish or penalize patients) (National Alliance for the Mentally Ill, 1999). Coercive interventions for reasons of staff convenience or punishment are expressly prohibited by applicable standards and regulations (U.S. Department of Health and Human Services, 1997, 1999).

Empirical literature addressing the use of coercive interventions with children is exceedingly sparse. There are no well-designed studies that compare interventions using equivalent groups of children, or studies that control for differences in staff knowledge. There are none comparing the use of less restrictive techniques with more restrictive ones, nor that explore the long-term effects of coercive interventions. Indeed, most studies available are anecdotal and non-generalizable (Mohr, Mahon, & Noone, 1998).

In 2000, Day reviewed the literature dealing with the use of restraints and seclusion on children, in an effort to determine how that literature might inform "the safe, appropriate, and proper use of restrictive interventions" (Day, 2000). He found a high degree of variability in that literature: different definitions of what constitute restraints; different estimates of the frequency with which such strategies are employed; different theoretical justifications for their use; and very different opinions with respect to their appropriateness. There was some agreement that younger children were at greater risk as a result of such strategies, and that a relatively small pool of children—estimated at between 7% and 15%—account for the majority of incidents in which such strategies are employed. Like others who have researched these issues, Day notes the need for a sounder theoretical grounding and the development of professional, evidence-based standards (see Day, chapter 2, this volume).

The lack of theoretical grounding for a potentially dangerous practice is one problem; the ambiguity of existing guidelines is another. In 1999, the Health Care Financing Administration (HCFA) (now the Centers for Medicare and Medicaid Services, or CMS), which finances and regulates Medicare and Medicaid, issued proposed rules for hospitals participating in these programs. These were known as "conditions of participation." HCFA declared that its "expectation is that a hospital would impose restraints or seclusion only when absolutely necessary to prevent immediate injury to the patient or others and when no alternative means are sufficient to accomplish the purpose" (*Hospital Condition of Participation in Medicare and Medicaid*, 1999). The rules contained no details, however, and HCFA has neither a monitoring plan nor clear enforcement provisions directly targeted to restraints and seclusion. HCFA asked for comments from a number of organizations and received a great many from members of the National Alliance for the Mentally Ill (NAMI), but in the final analysis gave no details related to physician authorization, procedures for issuing orders, time limits on the use of restraints, or requirements for checking on patients.

Similarly, the Joint Commission on Accreditation of Health Care Organizations (JCAHO) has issued standards with vague provisions related to restraints. JCAHO requires that "special treatment procedures" that include "restraint or seclusion" be documented in the medical record. A physician's verbal or written order is required, it must be time-limited, and there must be periodic observation. But none of these provisions is defined or explained. There are even more examples showcasing the ambiguity of guidelines than just these two (Kennedy & Mohr, 2001).

Braxton (1995) suggests that a major contributor to the problem of medically unnecessary use of restraints is the scarcity of appropriate staff. Due to funding constraints, limited resources, and lack of regulations or regulatory oversight, virtually anyone can get a job taking care of these vulnerable children. This has been the case for many years despite the fact that the profession and the federal courts have recognized the importance of adequately trained staff in the care of the mentally ill (*Wyatt v. King,* 1992). (Adequate training in this context would include specific knowledge of psychopharmacology, psychopathology, psychotherapeutic interventions, and interviewing and assessment of mental status [Kennedy & Mohr, 2001]).

All of these problems are exacerbated by the fact that children in these facilities are exceedingly difficult patients. They are wounded and mistrustful and their main mode of coping is to lash out in attack—behavior that can be frightening to inadequately prepared staff. From a theoretical standpoint, if not for purposes of constitutional analysis, the use of restraints and other coercive methods of controlling these children is punishment (Kennedy & Mohr, 2001). The most that can be said for punishment, or any other aversive intervention, is that it usually stops a child's misbehavior temporarily (Krumbolz & Krumbolz, 1972). Behavior theorists maintain that such interventions fail to teach children appropriate behaviors (Bandura, 1969; Skinner, 1953), and they clearly pose other risks to highly vulnerable children.

Ethical Considerations

Restraints pose a number of risks to young patients. There is the danger of further trauma to an already traumatized child who has, by definition, limited competence to understand what is happening to her, and few acceptable coping tools. (It bears emphasizing that these children are often being treated for problems stemming from previous traumatic experiences—physical or sexual abuse, a terrifying accident, etc.) There is the added danger that restraints will cause suffering—not just through the physical discomfort, but also by engendering feelings of isolation, anxiety, and humiliation. Of particular concern is the danger of significant physical injury, or even death or asphyxia, a danger that has been amply documented in the medical literature (Howard & Reay, 1997; Pollanen, Chiasson, Cairns, & Young, 1998).

If, as previously suggested, the use of restraints is an intervention that has little in the way of either theory or research to argue for its efficacy, its use raises serious ethical concerns. The fiduciary ethic, the principle of beneficence, and the obligation to do no harm require that professionals minimize any unintended adverse consequences of any intervention. Given the existence of substantial evidence of restraints' negative effects, their continued use in circumstances where less-restrictive alternatives are available arguably violates the principles of beneficence and nonmaleficence (Kennedy & Mohr, 2001). Given the risks, the dubious benefits, absence of clear guidelines, and lack of a research foundation validating their effectiveness, professionals must seriously question the ethics of continuing this practice.

This is not to say that there are no situations in which the use of restraints may be justified. When a child suffering from Lesch-Nyhan engages in auto-cannibalism, an autistic child persists in severe head banging, or an adolescent under the influence of PCP is in a homicidal rage, there may be no other choices. But as a routine intervention, as an assumed part of the repertoire of responses by staff members, restraints should be viewed as another nonvalidated therapy and be subject to the rules governing situations that require informed consent (Kennedy & Mohr, 2001).

Legal Considerations: The U.S. Context

There are two types of codified law that may constrain the use of restraints or other interventions. The first is sometimes referred to as "positive" law. Positive laws are statutes, like civil rights laws or the Americans with Disability Act. The second are rights guaranteed under the U.S. Constitution. Constitutional rights, as indicated previously, are negative in nature; these are our rights to be free of certain types of *government* interference. Because the Constitution restrains only government, in order to know whether a constitutional right has been violated, we must first ask whether the state—the government—has acted. And this is anything but a straightforward inquiry. In one such case, *Lebron v. National Railroad Passenger Corporation* (1995), Justice Scalia began his state action analysis by stating: "It is fair to say that our cases deciding when private action might be deemed that of the state have not been a model of consistency." To suggest that this was an understatement would itself be an understatement.

The Bill of Rights was initially designed to limit the reach of the federal government; the Fourteenth Amendment later extended those limitations to bar similar action by the states. Over the years, by the process known as "selective incorporation," most of the original eight amendments have been held to apply to state and local government units as well as to the federal government (*Twining v. New Jersey*, 1908; *Palko v. Connecticut*, 1937; *Adamson v. California*, 1947; Berger, 1977). But citizens are protected against public actions only. Discriminatory acts, or denials of liberty or due process by private parties are constitutional; indeed, they are entirely legal unless prohibited by virtue of legislation like the Civil Rights Act of 1964 or the Americans with Disabilities Act.

Blum v. Yaretsky (1983) is perhaps the best example of the inadequacies of current state action doctrine, and a case with obvious implications for the questions raised by the use of restraints. The case involved an alleged due process violation arising out of involuntary discharges and transfers of Medicaid patients in a nursing home. Rhenquist, writing for the Supreme Court, declined to find state action, saying "…a state normally can be held responsible for a private decision only when it has exercised coercive power or has provided such significant encouragement…that the choice must in law be deemed to be that of the State" (*Blum v. Yaretsky*, 1983, p. 992). Acknowledging that over 90% (and perhaps as many as 99%) of the patients in the facility were being paid for by the government, and that the nursing home actions being challenged were based upon government regulations, the Rhenquist majority nevertheless declined to find state action.

As Justice Brennan noted in an acerbic dissent,

> *The Court's analysis in this case [proceeds] upon a premise that is factually unfounded…A doctor who prescribes drugs for a patient on the basis of his independent medical judgment is not rendered a state actor merely because the State may reimburse the patient in different amounts depending upon which drug is prescribed. But the level of care decisions in this case, even when characterized as the 'independent' decision of the nursing home, have far less to do with the exercise of independent professional judgment than they do with the State's desire to save money…" (ibid., p. 1014–1019)*

Brennan and Marshall also dissented in *Rendell-Baker v. Kohn* (1982) a case involving the education by a private institution of "problem children" referred to the school by state officials. Nearly all of the school's funding came from the state, the facility was heavily supervised and regulated, and almost all its students were assigned to it by the state. Nevertheless, the Court once again declined to find state action, holding that "the school's fiscal relationship with the State is not different from that of many contractors performing services for the government" (*Rendell-Baker v. Kohn*, 1982).

Even constitutional lawyers have difficulty anticipating when, and whether, the actions of ostensibly private actors will be attributed to the state for purposes of applying constitutional constraints. Medical and psychiatric professionals can hardly be expected to know when they might be considered government actors, especially since results can be extremely counterintuitive: for example, in *Wade v. Byles* (1996), a private company providing security to a public housing project was held not to be a public actor despite the fact that the guards had authority to carry guns, arrest people, and use deadly force.

Complicating state action jurisprudence even further is the tendency of reviewing courts to apply different standards of analysis depending upon the nature of the Constitutional right involved, without, however, articulating the basis for those differences. Commentators have noted that, in cases involving racial discrimination or implicating First Amendment religious liberties, the Court has been much more willing to find—or assume—state action.

The point of this extremely cursory review of state action doctrine is that constitutional constraints will only apply against state actors, and in many situations, it is by no means clear who those actors are. Employees (but not necessarily doctors or nurses providing services under contract) of state-run facilities will be state actors. Private psychiatric institutions will probably not be bound by constitutional limitations, even if the government is paying for the patient's care. Prisons will be considered state actors for most purposes (although the law applicable to private prisons is still being sorted out), but it is simply not possible to predict in advance what a court may decide with respect to halfway houses, residential treatment facilities and other venues where restraints may be used. The constitutional discussion that follows must be understood in the context of that uncertainty.

Restraints as Eighth Amendment Cruel and Unusual Punishment

To the extent that therapy approaches are carefully designed to be serious attempts to extinguish maladaptive behavior patterns, they may legitimately be deemed treatment as opposed to punishment. On the other hand, logic suggests that inappropriately designed behavioral programs that constitute punishment disguised as treatment should be subject to analysis under Eighth Amendment standards. Some lower courts have so ruled (*Converse v. Nelson*, 1995). The Supreme Court, however, has expressly held that the Eighth Amendment standard can be applied only in a correctional context, and that the Eighth Amendment is inapplicable in a mental institution setting (*Youngberg*, 1982). The disparity occurs because the courts distinguish between prisons, as punitive institutions, and hospitals, where the object is to provide treatment (*Ingraham v. Wright*, 1977).

Persons who have not been convicted of a crime have a constitutionally recognized right to be free of state-imposed punishment (*Bell v. Wolfish*, 1979). Restraints have frequently been held to violate the prohibition against cruel and unusual punishment when used in a penal institution; prison officials have a duty under the Eighth Amendment to provide "humane conditions of confinement" and can be held liable for acting with "deliberate indifference" to the health or safety of an inmate (*Farmer v. Brennan*, 1994). In the noncriminal, nonpunitive context of a residential treatment facility, the Court has explicitly found Eighth Amendment analysis inappropriate (*Youngberg*, 1982). Innocent persons have a right to be free from punishment, and schools and hospitals are not penal institutions; therefore, Eighth Amendment standards governing the nature of punishment do not apply (*Ingraham v. Wright*, 1977). (Even if the Eighth Amendment does not offer protection, however, the Court has held that interventions that are not professionally indicated and are unnecessarily restrictive may violate a patient's Fourteenth Amendment liberty interest.)

Despite the legal distinction the courts have drawn between a "punitive" involuntary confinement triggering Eighth Amendment protections and a prophylactic one implicating Fourteenth Amendment interest, use of restraints seems factually to be little different from the corporal punishment that has been held to be cruel and unusual punishment in prison and juvenile cases (see, e.g., *Jackson v. Bishop*, 1968). It is difficult to defend the professional appropriateness of medical interventions that are considered too inhumane to be constitutionally applied to criminals in a penal facility.

The leading case on the issue of restraints is *Youngberg v. Romeo*, decided by the U. S. Supreme Court in 1982. The case involved a profoundly retarded youth who was involuntarily committed to a Pennsylvania state institution, where he suffered injuries due to the conditions of his confinement. His mother brought suit, alleging that he had the right to safe conditions of confinement, freedom from bodily restraint, and appropriate training or "habitation." The trial court had applied the Eighth Amendment standard, and had found the institution guilty of violating it. The Court of Appeals had reversed and remanded the case for a new trial, holding that a Fourteenth Amendment standard was the appropriate one. The Supreme Court agreed with the Appeals Court, but went further, holding that persons involuntarily committed to state institutions have a constitutionally protected liberty interest under the Due Process Clause of the Fourteenth Amendment to "reasonably safe conditions of confinement, freedom from unreasonable bodily restraints, and such minimally adequate training as reasonably may be required by these interests." The Court explicitly adopted that portion of the Appeals Court decision holding that persons involuntarily committed "retain liberty interests in freedom of movement and in personal security. These are 'fundamental liberties' that can be limited only by an 'overriding, nonpunitive' state interest."

In determining whether the State has protected a patient's right to freedom from "unreasonable restraint" a court must decide what is "reasonable." In its opinion in *Youngberg v. Romeo*, the Supreme Court highlighted its concern that courts not invade the province of those whose job it is to make medical and custodial decisions. The test to determine whether the use of restraints was reasonable under the circumstances of a particular case is whether professional judgment was in fact exercised. Such professional judgment, the Court ruled, was to be considered "presumptively valid." A presumption operates to shift the burden of proof to those alleging that the imposition of restraints was unreasonable.

The Court signaled its deference to the political realities of confinement, expressly noting that there are occasions in which it is necessary for the state to restrain institutional residents. This being the case, the proper inquiry for constitutional purposes will be not whether the patient's liberty interest has been infringed upon, but "whether the extent or nature of the restraint or lack of absolute safety is such as to violate due process." In short, the courts are to weigh an individual's interest in liberty against the state's asserted need to restrain. The standard to be used in making that determination is professional judgment. While the Court explicitly states that it is inappropriate for courts to specify which of several "professionally acceptable" choices should have been made, the emphasis on professional judgment highlights a central contention of critics of the use of restraints: the paucity of rigorous, clinically adequate research on restraints that can inform the necessary professional judgment, and the substantial existing evidence that restraints are rarely useful and frequently harmful. It is interesting to note that in Britain, psychiatrists have successfully done without the major forms of mechanical restraint for many years, and the British Mental Health Act Commission has even proposed forbidding their use (Saks, 1986). In 2005, the Welsh Assembly Government issued a Framework for Restrictive Physical Intervention Policy and Practice, disapproving certain types of restraints and restraint positions (Allen, Chapter 5, this volume). A variety of Canadian scholars and practitioners have called for restrictions on the practice (Day, 2000). The evolution of such international professional standards casts further doubt on the legal adequacy of American professionals' reliance on restraints, and will undoubtedly be cited in some future challenge to the professional basis of a decision to use restraints.

Non-Constitutional Considerations: Imposing Liability

Even when constitutional constraints do not apply, statutory, regulatory, and case law may provide guidance to providers, or offer remedies for litigants. In 1999, the U. S. Supreme Court applied the protections of Title II of the Americans with Disability Act (ADA) to mentally disabled people in government custody (*Olmstead v. L.C. by Zimring*, 1999), and held that keeping such patients in an overly isolated treatment environment amounted to discrimination under the terms of that Act. The implications of the *Olmstead* decision continue to be clarified as litigation citing the decision fleshes out the scope of the state's duty; however, it seems inevitable that the Court will eventually be asked to determine the propriety of specific psychiatric interventions in the context of the ADA.

Also in 1999, Congress passed the Children's Health Act (P.L. 106-310), setting out rules for the protection of young patients' rights. Section 3207 of that Act provided that patients be free from restraints used for discipline or convenience (Luna, 2001). While this was a relatively mild regulatory prohibition, the Act allows states to pass measures that are substantially more protective of children's rights, and some have done so.

In 2001, the Centers for Medicare and Medicaid Services promulgated a more protective version of the regulation applying to nonhospital psychiatric residential treatment facilities that are serving individuals under the age of 21 years. The regulation provided that restraints can only be used when necessary to ensure patient safety or the safety of others, and must end when the threat to that safety is over, and that only a physician or other licensed practitioner can give the order to employ the intervention. It also required a number of procedural safeguards, including prompt notification of the patient's parents or legal guardians, debriefing sessions, and a reporting requirement (Restraint Rules for Children's Psychiatric Residential Treatment Centers, 2001). It should be noted that the interim rule did not meet with uniform approval in the psychiatric community; the American Psychiatric Association (APA), for one, did not support it, citing—among other things—the costs of implementation, and the burden imposed in situations where repetitive use of restraints is necessary (Brown, Genel, Riggs, 2000).

In the early 1970s, most states enacted so-called "Patients' Bills of Rights," and those have been further amended and construed over time. While the provisions of such laws vary across the states, most began as efforts to codify the protections mandated by cases like *Wyatt v. Stickney* (1972). Depending upon the specific provisions of the laws of the state where the use of restraints occurred, patient bills of rights may provide yet another avenue for claims against either a public or private psychiatric institution arising out of the use of restraints.

In addition to these codified legal standards, of course, there is traditional tort law, including medical malpractice. It is important to note the intensely "fact-sensitive" nature of these cases; even more than the statutory and constitutional challenges, the resolution of such cases will ultimately depend upon the interpretation of a number of facts specific to the particular incident involved. In the majority of these cases, recovery has been denied—sometimes because the patient cannot prove damages, or prove that the damages involved were caused by the restraints. At other times, recovery is denied because the court defers to the professional judgment of the provider. Even when a challenge is successful, however, the deterrent value of the lawsuit may not be significant. In *Clark v. Ohio Department of Mental Health* (1989), for example, the court found that the use of restraints had indeed been punitive, rather than prophylactic, but since the patient could demonstrate no substantial harm, she was awarded only one dollar in damages.

Cases involving children are inevitably more complicated than lawsuits brought on behalf of adults, and any discussion of tort principles must acknowledge the special place children occupy in our society and jurisprudence. American laws concerning children have been informed by two very distinct approaches: a paternalistic, or progressive, approach that focuses upon nurturance and protection; and an individual-rights approach that emphasizes the child's age-appropriate right to personal autonomy (Kennedy, 2001). To the first approach we can attribute legislation making school attendance compulsory, establishing juvenile courts, and prohibiting child labor. These are measures that assume a large degree of dependence by children on adult society.

In the second category, we might list court cases such as *Brown v. Board of Education* (1954) which recognized children as rights-bearing individuals, or *In re Gault*, (1967), which entitled juveniles to court-appointed counsel, or *Tinker v. Des Moines* (1969) which protected the right of minors to express political opinions in a nondisruptive manner in a public-school setting.

Studies have shown that in the United States there is strong political support for the extension of the protective, "nurturant" rights, but far less support for rights of self-determination (Walker, Brooks, & Wrightsman, 1999).

The legal system has struggled with the balance between these two approaches, a struggle made more difficult because—as noted earlier—rights and duties of parents and (to a lesser but not inconsiderable extent) the interests of the state are also implicated. As one commentator has noted, the courts have tried to mediate the conflict between "democratic ideals of individual freedom and the sanctity of the family unit" (Rogers & Wrightsman, 1978). The result is a framework that rests on a sharp distinction between public and private responsibility for children's welfare, with the public assuming responsibility only when the private actors have defaulted. The primacy of the power given to parents and family rests on a belief that children need authority rather than autonomy.

Children—even healthy ones—have no political power, and the laws affecting them reflect that reality. Child labor laws went nowhere until labor unions decided that such laws would be economically beneficial to their members; similarly, court opinions affecting children typically arise in the context of other conflicts: child custody disputes, religious liberty cases, the criminal justice system, and conflicts around medical treatment and intervention. If parents have often been accorded unreasonably wide latitude over childrearing decisions, the Court has just as steadfastly refused to limit the scope of state interference with children's liberty interests. In 1979, in *Parham v. J.R.*, the Court declined to require that a hearing be held before a child could be institutionalized; and in 1984, in *Schall v. Martin*, it permitted the "preventive" detention of juveniles said to "pose a risk" of committing crime. The Court in *Schall* held that a minor's liberty interest was subordinate to his "best interests" as the state might define them. The trend since 1980 has been to diminish even such children's rights as the Court had previously established.

In the infamous *DeShaney v. Winnebago County Department of Social Services* (1989), the Court declined to find county social workers liable for severe brain damage suffered by a child at the hands of his father, despite the fact that the agency had been aware of the situation for months, had removed the child from the home at one point, had returned him to the father's custody and then allowed him to remain despite the father's noncompliance with required counseling and documented evidence of continued abuse. The case stands as a stark example of current legal principles sharply limiting the state's affirmative responsibility for the well-being of children. Litigation challenging the propriety of the use of restraints occurs in an environment that is heavily influenced by these conflicting approaches to the rights of children and the duties of the state.

Finally, it is important to note that tort and malpractice cases are also brought against facilities alleging neglect for *failure* to restrain. When patients do harm to themselves or others, and they were not restrained at the time, it is not uncommon for lawsuits to allege that the failure to restrain amounted to negligence, and was compensable. For providers, the decision to restrain or not can easily be experienced as a "lose-lose" situation—they are truly caught between "the devil and the deep blue sea."

Conclusion

The law governing the use of restraints is not unambiguous, but it is evolving, and certain trends are evident. The Fourteenth Amendment liberty interest test enunciated by the Supreme Court in *Youngberg* (1982) is a highly deferential one; nevertheless, deferential is not nonexistent. Providers will risk legal liability when a decision to employ restraints is so substantial a departure from accepted professional judgment, practice, or standards as to demonstrate that the person responsible actually did not base the decision on such a judgment. Given the limited evidence of efficacy, the self-referential nature of such research as is available, and the debate over guidelines for the use of such interventions, even that seemingly simple test, may be impossible to meet.

The Supreme Court's decision in *Olmstead* (1999) brought mental health facilities within the contemplation of the Americans with Disabilities Act, and a wide variety of associations working for the rights of the mentally ill have lobbied successfully for other state and federal standards—statutory and regulatory—that also restrict the use of these interventions, and apply to public and private facilities alike. The absence of any sound clinical basis for the use of restraints strengthens the case of plaintiffs bringing malpractice actions in wake of their use. All these developments evidence a clear trend against the employment of restraints.

It would thus seem to be high time to revisit the issue. The profession should produce standards governing the use of restraints that can be supported by sound theory and methodologically credible research, and justified under appropriate ethical and legal standards. Until such time as that research has been produced, restraints should be applied rarely and with extreme caution.

References

Bandura, A. (1969). *Principles of behavior modification.* New York, N.Y.: Holt, Rinehart & Winston.

Berger, R. (1977). *Government by judiciary: The transformation of the Fourteenth Amendment.* Indianapolis, IN: Liberty Fund.

Braxton, E. T. (1995). Angry children, frightened staff: Implications for training and staff development. *Residential Treatment for Children and Youth, 13*(1), 13–38.

Brown, R. L., Genel, M., & Riggs, J. (2000). Commentary: Use of seclusion and restraint in children and adolescents. *Archives of Pediatric and Adolescent Medicine, 154,* 653–656.

Day, D. M. (2000). *A review of the literature on restraints and seclusions with children and youth: Toward the development of a perspective in practice.* Report submitted to The Intersectorial/Interministerial Steering Committee on Behaviour Management Interventions for Children and Youth in Hospital Settings, Toronto, Ontario.

Garrison, W. T., Ecker, M. A., Friedman, M. D., Davidoff, M. D., Haeberle, K., & Wagner, M. (1990). Aggression and counter-aggression during child psychiatric hospitalization. *Journal of the American Academy of Child and Adolescent Psychiatry, 29*(2), 242–250.

Hospital Condition of Participation in Medicare and Medicaid, 64 Number Fed. Reg. 36089 (1999) (proposed July 2, 1999).

Hopcroft, T. E. (1995, Summer). Civil commitment of minors to mental institutions in the Commonwealth of Massachusetts. *New England Journal on Criminal and Civil Confinment, 21*(2), 543–574.

Howard, J. D., & Reay, D. T. (1997). Positional asphyxia. *Annals of Emergency Medicine, 32*(1), 116–118.

Kapp, M. B. (1998). *Our hands are tied: Legal tensions and medical ethics.* Westport, CT: Auburn House.

Kennedy, S. S. (2001). The muffled voice of the child: American health care and children's rights. *Journal of Medicine and Law, Michigan State University, 6*(1).

Kennedy, S. S., & Mohr, W. K., (2001) A prolegomenon on restraint of children: Implicating constitutional rights. *American Journal of Orthopsychiatry, 71*(1), 26–37.

Krumboltz, J. D., & Kurmboltz, H. B. (1972). *Changing children's behavior.* Englewood Cliffs, NJ: Prentice-Hall Inc.

Luna, J. (2001, August 29) Limiting the use of restraint and seclusion in psychiatric residential Treatment facilities for patients under 21. *Health Law Perspectives.* Available online at www.law.uh.edu/healthlaw/perspectives/Mental/010829Limiting.html.

Mohr, W. K., Mahon, M. M., & Noone, M. J. (1998). A restraint on restraints: The need to reconsider restrictive interventions. *Archives of Psychiatric Nursing, 12*(2), 95–106.

National Alliance for the Mentally Ill. (1999). *Cries of anguish: Reports of restraint and seclusion abuse received since October 1998 investigation by* Hartford Courant. Arlington, VA: Author.

Pollanen, M. S., Chiasson, D. A., Cairns, J. T., & Young, J. G. (1998). Unexpected death related to restraint for excited delirium: A retrospective study of deaths in police custody and in the community. *Canadian Medical Association Journal, 158*(12), 1611–1612.

Restraint Rules for Children's Psychiatric Residential Treatment Centers, 66 Fed. Reg. 28110–28117.

Rogers, C. M., & Wrightsman, L. (1978). Attitudes toward children's rights: Nurturance or self-determination. *Journal of Social Issues, 34,* 59–68.

Saks, E. R. (1986). The use of mechanical restraints in psychiatric hospitals. *Yale Law Journal, 95*(8), 1836–1856.

Skinner, B. F. (1953). *Science and human behavior.* New York, NY: Macmillan.

U.S. Department of Health and Human Services. (1997). *Health care financing administration conditions of participation.* Washington, DC: Author.

U.S. Department of Health and Human Services. (1999). *Health care financing administration conditions of participation.* Washington, DC: Author.

U.S. Government Accounting Office. (1999, September). *Mental health: Improper restraint or seclusion use places people at risk.* Washington, DC: U.S. Government Printing Office.

Weiss, E. M., Altimari, D., Blint, D.F., & Megan, K. (1998, October 11–15). Deadly restraint: A nationwide pattern of death. *Hartford Courant.*

Walker, N., Brooks, C., & Wrightsman, L. (1999). *Children's rights in the United States: In search of a national policy.* London: Sage Publications.

Case References

Adamson v. California, 322 U.S. 46 (1947).

Bell v. Wolfish, 441 U.S. 520 (1979).

Blum v. Yaretsky, 457 U.S. 991 (1983).

Brown v. Board of Education, 347 U.S. 483 (1954).

Clark v. Ohio Department of Mental Health, 573 NE2d 794 (1989).

Converse v. Nelson, No. 95-16776 (Mass. Superior Ct. July 1995).

DeShaney v. Winnebago County Department of Social Services, 489 U.S. 189 (1989).

Farmer v. Brennan, 511 U.S. 825 (1994).

Gault, In re, 387 U.S. 1 (1967).

Ingraham v. Wright, 430 U.S. 651 (1977).

Jackson v. Bishop, 404 F.2d 571, 579-80 (8th Circuit 1968) (Blackmun, J.).

Lebron v. National Railway Passenger Corporation, 513 U.S. 374 (1995).

Olmstead v. L.C. by Zimring, 119 S.Ct. 2176 (1999).

Palko v. Connecticut, 302 U.S. 319 (1937).

Parham v. J.R., 442 U.S. 584; (1979).

Rendell-Baker v. Kohn, 457 U.S. 830 (1982).

Schall v. Martin, 467 U.S. 253 (1984).

Tinker v. Des Moines, 393 U.S. 503 (1969).

Twining v. New Jersey, 211 U.S. 78 (1908).

Wade v. Byles, 83 F.3d 902 (7th Cir. 1996).

Wyatt v. King, 793 F.Supp. 1058 (1992).

Wyatt v. Stickney, 344 F.Supp. 373, 378-86 (1972).

Youngberg v. Romeo, 457 U.S. 307 (1982).

CHAPTER 14

The Reach of Liability for Physical Restraints

A Question of Professional Judgment

Andrea J. Mooney

On his first day as a resident at a juvenile detention facility, Lee Jackson made two errors. The first was going to the bathroom without being accompanied by a staff member. The second was attempting to throw away all of the contents of his breakfast tray, rather than retaining the plastic plates and utensils. For these two errors, Lee Jackson was restrained twice for a total of over an hour. As a result of these restraints, Lee Jackson spent the next months in a comatose state, and several more years in a nursing home. Lee Jackson eventually died from the injuries he sustained from being restrained. The Commissioner of the State of New York's Office of Children and Family Services, the facility director, five youth aides, a youth counselor and a nurse were required to pay Lee Jackson's estate a total of nine million seven hundred fifty thousand dollars. All because a fourteen-year-old child went to the bathroom alone and tried to discard used plastic plates and utensils. (Jackson v. Johnson, 2002)

Children in residential care are injured every day in physical restraints. Most injuries, such as rug burns, are not life threatening. Some injuries, however, as in Lee Jackson's case, are fatal. As has been noted elsewhere in this volume, the use of physical restraint, seclusion, and isolation has serious, sometimes deadly implications for both children and the adults charged with their care. This chapter will discuss some of the legal implications of restraint, particularly when the restraint results in injury or death.

Although restraints are conducted every day in schools, hospitals, and residential programs across this country and many other countries, restraint should not be viewed as a routine part of doing business. Just as police officers are issued guns, not as everyday tools but as tools to use in the most urgent of situations, child and youth care workers should view the use of restraint as an extraordinary tool, to be used only in extraordinary circumstances. Physical restraint is generally described as warranted when the child to be restrained is in danger of hurting herself or someone else. In some states or agencies, restraint is allowed so as to prevent the destruction of property. As in most human interactions, the intent of a child to hurt herself or someone else is frequently unclear.

Whether or not to physically restrain a child is always a judgment call but it is a judgment call within the professional parameters of overall child safety and risk, agency policy, and good practice based on individual crisis management planning. Even within the professional framework of specialized knowledge and skills that agency staff must possess and exercise, the professional decision to restrain a child can often result in injury or death. Depending on the severity of the injury, the incident of restraint may then result in administrative action (such as a firing or suspension for the youth care worker), a regulatory action (such as a sanctioning of the agency by its licensing body), or legal repercussions.

The question of professional judgment is particularly key, as residential care and physical restraint are areas largely unknown to the general public. Most people have little idea of the work involved in caring for traumatized, emotionally disturbed children in a residential setting. Most laypeople, the people who would serve as jurors in a legal proceeding, have no familiarity with physical restraint and would require an expert to explain what physical restraint is and when it is used.

In cases alleging inappropriate restraint, a plaintiff would need an expert witness to explain to a jury what the field expects in terms of the practices of restraint and seclusion. An expert would likely discuss the standards set by accrediting bodies such as the Joint Commission on Accreditation of Healthcare Organizations, the Council on Accreditation, the National Association of Psychiatric Treatment Centers for Children or the American Academy of Pediatrics. An expert would also be familiar with the various programs that teach physical restraint, and each of the various programs' requirements as to techniques, training, and certification. Many professional organizations, such as the American Medical Association, the American Academy of Child and Adolescent Psychiatry, the American Academy of Pediatrics, and the American Psychiatric Association, set guidelines regarding the use of restraint in their particular professions (Ryan & Peterson, 2004).

Additionally, an expert would be familiar with standard-setting agencies such as the Child Welfare League of America, which has published guidelines for those who would use restraint, isolation, or seclusion (Child Welfare League of America, 2004). A central question for the jury would be whether the techniques used are acceptable in the particular field, and whether the individuals using these techniques were properly trained and supervised.

Criminal Liability

A child who has been injured in a restraint may have several areas of legal recourse. The first is criminal. In the United States, state rather than federal law most often defines crimes. When a child is injured in a residential facility, the police may be notified especially if the injury is severe or life-threatening. The police investigate and determine whether it is likely that a crime has been committed. The prosecutor then determines whether to press charges against the alleged perpetrator. States vary as to the definitions and names of crimes. Depending on the actual act and on the level of injury of the child, alleged perpetrators may be charged with endangering the welfare of a child, assault, criminal negligence, manslaughter or murder, to name a few. In a criminal case, the prosecution (or the State) represents the people of the state rather than the individual who has suffered harm. A perpetrator convicted of violating a criminal law may face a variety of punishments ranging from probation and community service to long-term incarceration.

A prosecutor anticipating charging someone criminally faces several challenges. First, the prosecutor is faced with the highest burden of proof in the legal system: the prosecutor must prove each and every element of the alleged crime beyond a reasonable doubt. Second, many crimes require that the prosecutor prove that the alleged perpetrator either acted with intent to cause injury, or acted with such recklessness or criminal negligence as to cause the injury. Malicious intent is particularly difficult to prove in light of the presumed therapeutic nature of physical restraint. Third, prosecutors sometimes face reluctant witnesses and dubious juries. Children who have been placed in residential treatment are often traumatized, angry children whose methods of coping often include lashing out. Juries are unlikely to understand the dynamics of a child in crisis, and are more likely to sympathize with an adult who is trying to contend with the child's behavior, even if the adult's efforts are uninformed, inappropriate, or designed to injure.

Additionally, there is often little benefit to a child for participating in a criminal trial. Unlike a civil trial, a criminal trial has no possibility of any financial recompense for the child or the child's family. In fact, the child may actually be harmed if she must undergo the process of testifying, especially withstanding a difficult cross-examination. In addition, the victims of these crimes may be limited as to their language or their ability to provide credible testimony. Finally, a prosecutor anticipating charging a staff member of a residential facility may be prejudiced by thinking of the victim as a "bad" or "wild" child, and the perpetrator as a caring adult just trying to do the best they can. Prosecutors (and perhaps juries) may think of residential treatment facilities as "kiddie jails" and thus may be less enthusiastic about holding staff members accountable for inappropriate acts committed during the course of their employment.

Civil Liability

An injured child, or his family or guardian on his behalf, may also turn to civil law for recourse, either instead of or in addition to a criminal prosecution. Civil law has some advantages for a plaintiff. The level of evidence required in a civil matter is either a fair preponderance of the proof, or clear and convincing proof; both are less rigorous standards than beyond a reasonable doubt. A criminal trial is primarily about placing blame and according punishment. A civil trial may result in changes, not only for the injured child, but also for the entire system that is at issue. A civil trial may result in injunctions prohibiting certain practices, as in the civil rights cases that ended desegregation.

Civil law has a broader reach than does criminal law. Under civil law, the defendants may be not only the individual accused of a specific act, but also that individual's supervisors and employers. In practice, this may mean that a plaintiff may look to several sources who may be able to compensate them for their injuries or who may carry malpractice or other types of insurance.

Unlike criminal law, which is largely state-defined, civil law provides both state and federal statutes that an injured child may look to for relief. For example, in *Olmstead v. L.C. by Zimming* (1999), the child alleged that the facility's restraint practices violated the Americans with Disabilities Act. In *Winston v. Children and Youth Services of Delaware County* (1991), the allegation was that the facility's practices violated the federal Adoption Assistance and Child Welfare Act. Similarly, a child may charge an individual or a facility with violating a state's patients' bill of rights. A suit in civil law may result in injunctive relief (stopping the rights violations), compensatory relief (paying for the plaintiff's treatment), or even punitive damages. Thus, a civil trial may result in systemic changes, such as eliminating unfair or unreasonable practices, financial benefits to a victim, and punishment for the perpetrator. In addition, an attorney may negotiate to obtain a percentage of the victim's awards, thus making this kind of civil suit potentially more attractive to an attorney than a criminal trial, where the attorney is more likely to be paid by the hour. Finally, a criminal defense attorney may have a limited number of hours for which they may bill, as well as limited funds for resources such as expert witnesses, if the state is paying for the criminal defense.

Constitutional Violations

In addition to the statutory charges listed above, a child may allege that her constitutional rights were violated. Thus, even a child with no physical injury may still file a suit in civil court, alleging that the harm was to her rights rather than to her body. As Kennedy (Chapter 13, this volume) points out, most often, instances of inappropriate restraint or seclusion are claimed to violate a child's right to due process under the Fourteenth Amendment to the Constitution. The Fourteenth Amendment provides that "no state shall deprive any person of life, liberty or property, without due process of law."

Constitutional analysis requires that a person have a "liberty interest" before they can allege that their Fourteenth Amendment due process rights were violated. The two primary rights implicated in an inappropriate restraint are the right to be free from undue restraint, and the right to be treated by people who have been adequately trained. Persons in involuntary state custody, which includes residential care, mental health hospitals, and foster care, have a "liberty interest" in safe conditions (*Vogelsanger v. County of Cayuga*, 1998). Thus, under the Fourteenth Amendment, children have a right to be free from confinement and from unreasonable bodily restraint. In addition, the Fourteenth Amendment may provide a child with a right that those who are restraining or secluding them have minimally adequate training so as to protect their liberty interests. For example, *Wyatt v. King*, (1992), discusses class action suits and resulting settlements articulating proper conditions for those institutionalized in facilities for the mentally ill and mentally retarded.

Section 1983 Litigation

The statute most often used to challenge violations of the Fourteenth Amendment is Section 1983 of Title 42 of the United States Code, commonly known as "Section 1983." The statute, which had its origins in the Ku Klux Clan Act of 1871, is invoked as a means of obtaining relief to one who is deprived of federal constitutional rights (Williams, 2004).

State Actors Requirement

As Kennedy (Chapter 13, this volume) points out, the right to the protection of Fourteenth Amendment liberty interests extends only to alleged perpetrators who are state actors rather than private actors. Section 1983 may only be invoked against those who act as agents of the state, and may only be invoked against individuals, not institutions. The question of who is a state actor, and when a person acts for the state, is a thorny one. In *DeShaney v. Winnebago* (1989), the Supreme Court refused to hold a state child protective agency responsible for the brutal beating of a child by his father, even though the agency knew that the child was being beaten and had removed him and then returned him to the abusive father's home. According to the Court, the person responsible for the harm to the child was the father, rather than the state. Thus, the state did not violate the child's constitutional rights, even though the father was under state supervision at the time of the child's injury.

The cases seeking to sort whether a perpetrator is a state or private actor are quite convoluted, and the question is still quite unclear (Kennedy, Chapter 13, this volume). Generally, however, a plaintiff may prove that a defendant is a state actor by showing that the defendant is an agent of the state, that the state was a joint participant in a private enterprise, or by demonstrating that the private actor performed a function that was traditionally the province of the state (Williams, 2004, at 2a). For example, a mentally ill patient was transferred from a state hospital to a private one, and alleged that he had been physically mistreated at both hospitals. The private hospital sought to be dismissed from the suit on the grounds that they were not state agents. The court refused to dismiss them as defendants, stating, among other reasons, that the private hospital was performing a public function (*Ruffler v. Phelps Memorial Hospital*, 1978).

Exceptions to State Actors Requirements

Some courts have acknowledged exceptions to the rule that a plaintiff may not sue the state under Section 1983 for injuries sustained from a private actor. The "state-created danger exception" holds that a state actor can be held liable for the Fourteenth Amendment violation when the state actor takes an affirmative step so as to create or increase danger to a victim. (See *Dwares v. City of New York*, 1993.)

Another exception to the *DeShaney* (1989) rule that the state has no constitutional duty to protect a citizen from private acts of violence is the "special relationship" theory. This theory applies when the victim of the violence is somehow under the state's control, such as a child placed in a foster home or an institution (*Yvonne L. By and Through Lewis v. New Mexico Dept. of Human Services*, 1992). In *Yvonne*, the court refused to grant summary judgment to state defendants who had placed two children in a residential facility where they were then abused. Summary judgment is a pretrial motion, usually made after the parties have conducted significant discovery and learned a great deal about each other's case. The party moving for summary judgment is essentially saying to the court that there is no genuine issue as to any material fact, and, as a matter of law, the court must grant judgment to the moving party. In *Yvonne*, the court determined that there was an essential dispute as to whether the defendants had acted appropriately. The professional judgment standard was the appropriate standard for determining whether the defendants had violated the children's constitutional rights by placing the children in a facility where they were not appropriately supervised. Thus, the court returned the matter to the lower court for further proceedings (*Yvonne*, 1992, at 894).

Where State Actors Requirement Is Met

Where the actor is the state in some form, the reach of liability may extend beyond the individual. In *Doe v. New York City* (1981), the court determined that state officials or agency supervisory personnel might be held liable under Section 1983 for a child's injury. The test is whether the official or the supervisor exhibited "deliberate indifference" to a known injury, a known risk, or a specific duty, and if so, whether that deliberate indifference led to failure to ameliorate the risk, which was the proximate cause of the child's deprivation of rights (*Doe*, 1981, at 145). In other words, a supervisor who knows that a child is being restrained unnecessarily, or inappropriately, or a state official who knows that an agency has a practice of unsafe restraint or seclusion is possibly liable to a child under Section 1983. The standard of "deliberate indifference" is a more difficult standard to prove against a third party, than the standard used to evaluate an individual's conduct, which is "unreasonable restraint."

Application to Physical Restraints

The Supreme Court addressed the question of what constitutes unreasonable restraints in *Youngberg v. Romeo* (1982). In that case, the mother of a severely retarded child who was institutionalized complained that the injuries he was sustaining at the institution violated his constitutional rights. The Court said that the persons involuntarily committed to state institutions have a right to be free from unreasonable restraints, and that the defendant's conduct should be measured according to whether they exercised "professional judgment." The Court reasoned that because children had been removed from their homes and placed in a state-sanctioned facility, the facility has a special relationship with the child and owes them a duty of professional judgment (*Youngberg*, 1982, at 371).

The question of what is reasonable is thus left to the professionals. A professional's judgment is presumptively valid, that is, the person challenging that judgment has the burden of proving that it was in fact invalid. A court must decide only whether professional judgment was exercised; it need not specify which of several professionally acceptable choices should have been made (*Youngberg*, 1982, at 321). The Court stated,

> liability may be imposed only when the decision by the professional is such a substantial departure from accepted professional judgment, practice or standards as to demonstrate that the person responsible actually did not base the decision in such a judgment. (*Youngberg*, 1982, at 323)

Many of the cases challenging professional judgment have to do with a child protective agency's decisions regarding placing children in a foster home. One plaintiff was a young child who was placed in a foster care home with a brother who had previously sexually abused her (*Wendy H. v. City of Philadelphia*, 1994). In the foster home, both her brother and another child in the foster home further abused the child. Although the child's records indicated that her brother had previously sexually abused her, the placing caseworker had failed to read the child's records. The child sued the city, the child welfare agency, and the individual caseworker. In deciding a motion for summary judgment, the court dismissed the claims against the city and the child welfare agency but let stand the Section 1983 claim and some state claims against the caseworker. It would be a question for the jury to determine whether the caseworker's failure to read and evaluate the child's records was such a lapse in professional judgment so as to deprive the child of her Fourteenth Amendment rights.

On the other hand, the plaintiff children in *Hilbert S. v. County of Tioga* (2005) were unable to prevail on a claim that a child protective agency had violated their constitutional rights. The children had remained in an abusive home for several years while county child protective workers investigated and substantiated at least four reports for sexual abuse, without removing the children from the home. The children alleged that by ignoring their continued abuse and neglect, the caseworkers caused a "state-created danger." The court disagreed, finding that the parent's actions, rather than the state's, caused the harm to the children, and that the state's actions did not place the children in any worse position than they were already in (*Hilbert S.*, 2005).

Other cases address the question of the care a mentally ill or mentally retarded person has received in an institution. The parents of a man who committed suicide a week after being released from a mental hospital sued his doctors for failure to exercise professional judgment in releasing the man from the hospital after treating him for a month. The court dismissed the claim, determining that the parents did not allege a genuine issue of material fact on the question of whether the doctors had exercised professional judgment (*Scothorn v. Kansas*, 1991). But in a case with quite similar facts, another court refused to grant summary judgment to the defendants, and allowed the case to go to a jury to determine whether professional judgment was exercised (*Gann v. Schramm*, 1985). The difference between cases may simply reflect a more thorough set of complaints in one case than the other, or it may reflect different judicial philosophies of different jurisdictions (e.g., Kansas versus Delaware).

There are only a few examples of individuals suing under Section 1983 for injuries sustained during physical restraint, but they are noteworthy. Four mental hospital attendants placed a schizophrenic man into a stranglehold in an attempt to restrain him, ultimately killing him. The court dismissed the Fourteenth Amendment claims against the State of Rhode Island and against the attendants in their official capacity, but allowed the matter to go to trial against the attendants as individuals (*Jones v. Rhode Island*, 1989). A child who was totally disabled as a result of a physical restraint conducted at a juvenile detention facility settled a case in the amount of $9,750,000 with the various defendants he had sued under both Section 1983 and various state claims. Defendants included the facility's nurse, five youth detention aides, a youth division counselor, the facility's director, and the commissioner of the state agency that licensed and supervised the facility (*Jackson v. Johnson*, 2002). Although Section 1983 has not been used extensively in cases of inappropriate restraint and seclusion in residential facilities, increased interest in these types of injuries is surely going to lead to more extensive litigation in these matters.

Conclusion and Recommendations

So what does this mean for a residential child care agency? The first question will be whether a private agency will even be considered a state actor for the purposes of Section 1983. As Kennedy notes (chapter 13, this volume), this area of law is quite unclear. In the case of a state agency, alleged perpetrators are clearly "state actors." It is also possible that a plaintiff could persuade a court that an agency that is funded through contracts with state agencies and licensed by a state agency is, indeed, a "state actor." Once that is determined, the next question becomes the reach of liability. Who will the plaintiff sue? As in the case of Lee Jackson, it is likely that the plaintiff will sue everyone involved in the incident, from the direct perpetrators to the head of the state-licensing agency. The plaintiff is likely to challenge both the actual restraint incident and the training, supervisory, and administrative practices of the facility and the licensing agency.

Although the idea of criminal investigations and civil suits may cause distress and anxiety in an agency or among its employees, far more distressful is the idea of children being injured or killed due to a failure of professional judgment. Thus, it is important that every agency and individual employing any kind of restraint be absolutely certain that they are exercising the best possible professional judgment in every circumstance. An agency would do well to stay current in the area of restraint, including national and international efforts to reduce the use of restraint, as well as the most current recommendations for techniques, training, and supervision.

References

Child Welfare League of America. (2004). *Best practices in behavior support and intervention assessment.* Washington, DC: Author.

Ryan, J. B., & Peterson, R. L. (2004). *Physical restraint in schools.* Available online at www.bridges4kids.org/PBS/articles/RyanPeterson2004.htm. Michigan: Michigan Positive Behavior Support Network.

Williams, E. (2004). Annotation, *Action Under 42 U.S.C.A. § 1983 Against Mental Institution or Its Staff for Injuries to Institutionalized Person,* 118 A.L.R. Fed. 519 (2004).

Case References

DeShaney v. Winnebago, 489 U.S.189 (1989).

Doe v. New York City, 649 F.2d 134 (2d Cir. 1981).

Dwares v. City of New York, 985 F.2d 94 (2d Cir. 1993).

Gann v. Schramm, 606 F. Supp. 1442 (D. Del. 1985).

Hilbert S. v. County of Tioga, U.S. Dist. LEXIS 29423 (2005).

Jackson v. Johnson, U.S. Dist. LEXIS 20203 (2002).

Jones v. Rhode Island, 724 F. Supp. 25 (D.R.I. 1989).

Olmstead v. L.C. by Zimring, 527 U.S. 581 (1999).

Ruffler v. Phelps Memorial Hospital, 453 F. Supp. 1062 (SD NY 1978).

Scothorn v. Kansas, 772 F. Supp. 556 (D. Kan. 1991).

Wendy H. v. City of Philadelphia, 849 F. Supp. 367 (E.D. Pa. 1994).

Winston v. Children and Youth Services of Delaware County, 948 F.2d 1380 (3d Cir. 1991).

Wyatt v. King, 803 F. Supp 377 (M.D.Ala. 1992).

Vogelsanger v. County of Cayuga, U.S. Dist. LEXIS 3848, 12 (1998).

Youngberg v. Romeo, 457 U.S. 307 (1982).

Yvonne L. By and Through Lewis v. New Mexico Dept. of Human Services, 959 F.2d 883 (10th Cir. 1992).

PART VI

CONCLUSION

Conclusion

CHAPTER 15

Moving Forward

David M. Day,
Lloyd B. Bullard,
and Michael A.
Nunno

CONSIDERING THE LONGSTANDING AND CONTROVERSIAL HISTORY of physical restraints in psychiatry (Masters, Chapter 3, this volume), this book is long overdue. It seemed an opportune time, following from the 2005 international symposium, to take stock of the practice of physical restraints with children and youth and plumb its depths, as we have done in this volume. We think Pinel would be pleased.

So, what have we found? Deconstructing any human phenomenon invariably leads to one singular conclusion: human behavior is complex, and the consequences of any human behavior depend on the context in which the behavior is exhibited. Such is the conclusion we draw after examining the topic of physical restraints with children and youth: physical restraints are complex and their impact depends on the context of their use.

Where does that leave us? Perhaps the take-home message of this volume is that, as we articulated in the Introduction, it may be overly simplistic, inaccurate, or even unreasonable to view a physical restraint as merely an *event*. This is too mechanistic, reductionistic, and static a model to truly and fully account for the phenomenon. Rather, a physical restraint may be better conceptualized as part of a dynamic, transactional *process* that unfolds over time and space; a process that encapsulates a set of distal (distant to the episode in time and space) and proximal (close to the episode in time and space) antecedents, a present state, and its consequences. And that the consequences continue to unfold and cascade long after the restraint episode has transpired.

Once a child has been restrained, for example, the likelihood of a subsequent restraint is increased (Figure 15-1).

Making Sense of Complexity

How do we make sense of this complexity? It would be neither informative nor productive to simply generate a laundry list of all the factors that contribute to the complexity of physical restraints. Many of these were thoughtfully and thoroughly discussed in the preceding chapters. Rather, as an organizing framework, we could place the restraint process within the context of a theory such as the ecological systems theory described by developmental psychologist, Urie Bronfenbrenner (1979). Doing so not only aids our understanding of how variables fit together into a cohesive package, but, by separating information into the "what we know" from the "what we need to know," we can also advance a grounded, relevant, and contextualized body of research. This will serve to move the use of physical restraints forward towards an informed, evidence-based practice, a primary goal of this book. Of course, the ecological systems theory is not the only theory that can be applied to make sense of restraints. We may draw on many other current psychological, organizational, and sociological theories to guide thinking and research and we encourage writers on physical restraints to locate their observations within these contexts (see, e.g., Jones & Timbers, 2002; Paterson, Leadbetter, Miller, & Crichton, Chapter 14, this volume). As social psychologist Kurt Lewin (1951) said, "there is nothing so practical as a good theory" (p. 169) (Figure 15-2).

Working from the center of the model outward, through the increasingly larger systems in which physical restraints are imbedded, like concentric circles, is the child in care with his physical and personal attributes. Surrounding the child are the staff with whom the child interacts on a regular, daily basis. The staff are, themselves, contained within the agency's organizational structure, policies, values, mission statement, and treatment philosophy. In turn, these organizational dimensions are a reflection of various professional standards of practice as well as prevailing cultural and societal laws, values, attitudes, tolerances, and ideologies toward children, youth, family, aggression, violence, and myriad other factors that distally relate to our young clients.

Child Factors

Beginning at the center, the following is a brief review some of the key factors discussed in the preceding chapters that generate the complexity. First, children in care are vulnerable. Placement in a residential setting, for example,

FIGURE 15–1: A Process of Model of Restraints

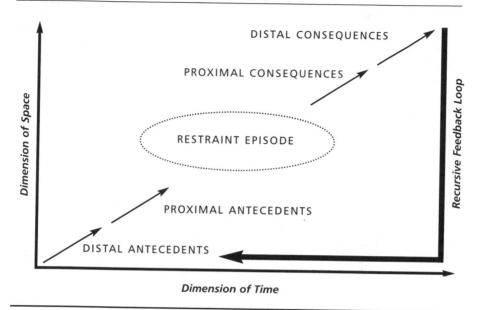

FIGURE 15–2: An Ecological Systems Model

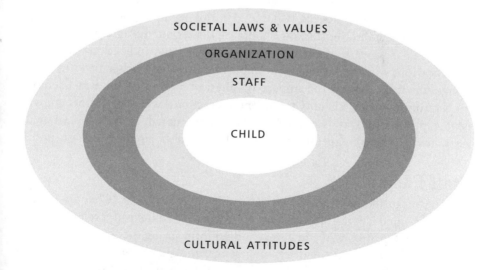

is regarded as the most intrusive level of intervention for children and youth and is associated with high levels of psychopathology, including both internalizing and externalizing problems (Baker & Purcell, 2005). Moreover, more than half of all children in residential facilities (Mohr & Anderson, 2001) and up to 93% of hospitalized adolescents (Lipshitz, Winegar, Hartnick, Foote, & Southwick, 1999) enter the mental health and child welfare systems with a history of physical, emotional, and sexual abuse, and neglect (Crenshaw & Mordock, 2004; Kerker & Morrison Dore, 2006) and many meet the criteria for posttraumatic stress disorder (PTSD) (Lipshitz et al., 1999).

Second, as Mohr, Allen, and Holden and Curry's chapters all clearly indicate, physical restraints are inherently dangerous, "high tariff" (Allen, chapter 5, p. 99) techniques. Third, child-related factors, such as obesity, substance use and abuse, agitation, and asthma, are known to increase the risk of harm. As well, there is now a growing awareness that psychological factors, such as those same features that bring children to our attention in the first place, can increase the risk. A history of physical, sexual, or emotional abuse, for example, may interact with certain restraint techniques to intensify a child's trauma or lead to retraumatization. Given the psychological vulnerability of young people in care and the invasive nature and force required of restraint procedures, it would not be difficult to see how these techniques could potentially be traumatizing.

Trauma-informed care is now seen as an important consideration in the use of intrusive measures (Child Welfare League of America [CWLA], 2004). As Carter, Jones, and Stevens (Chapter 10, this volume) noted, to minimize the risks, these contraindications should be documented in a child's file and staff should be aware of them. Indeed, clarifying the indications and contraindications of restraint use is an important area for further investigation. Longitudinal studies on the impact of physical restraints that can identify moderating variables (client X treatment interactions) will address this knowledge gap. Last, as Day (Chapter 2, this volume) noted, it is now clear that restraints have no therapeutic value and should not be used for this purpose.

Staff Factors

Moving on to the next system level, Steckley and Kendrick (Chapter 1, this volume) remind us "restraints take place within the context of a relationship" (Fisher, 2003, p. 73). While in care, children form strong therapeutic alliances with staff. Steckley and Kendrick suggest that the quality of this relationship may affect how a child responds to a physical restraint; in general, a positive therapeutic relationship with the worker implementing the restraint may militate against adverse child outcomes. These intriguing findings are noteworthy, particularly given the highly complex reactions children in their study had as a result of being restrained. The role of therapeutic alliance as both a moderator and outcome variable is an issue that needs to be investigated further. As well, their results reinforce the point made earlier that restraints are best viewed as a process. For example, a child's attachment style, which stems from early experiences with primary caregivers, may potentially affect the strength and nature of the therapeutic relationship (which becomes part of the restraint process), as well as the consequences and outcomes of the restraint episode. These outcomes, for the child, staff, bystanders, and so forth, in turn, affect the participants' experiences of a subsequent restraint episode. Research on restraints could develop such a process model into testable hypotheses.

Mohr (Chapter 4, this volume) raises important concerns about cognitive biases and errors in judgment that staff may experience that can impede effective decision-making processes to resolve high risk and potentially uncertain situations without the use of physical intervention. These biases, which are part of the human experience, could potentially leave staff open to misreading critical social and situational cues, resulting in mishandling the situation and increasing the risk of harm. As a result, Mohr concludes that the risks of physical restraints exceed the benefits and that strategies to reduce their use, such as developing alternate crisis interventions, are a worthy venture.

Further to the issue of safety, Holden and Curry (Chapter 6, this volume) suggest that competence in performing a physical restraint is essential to protecting both child and staff from injury. Various factors can undermine the effective execution of a restraint, however, and Holden and Curry offer ways to counter these in training sessions. One such strategy is for staff to over-learn the techniques. To be sure, further work needs to be done on monitoring the effective transfer of learning that is involved in training to use restraints. It is incumbent upon training vendors to ensure that staff acquire the necessary skills to safely and appropriately use these interventions and Holden and Curry's recommendations can serve as a useful model.

Organizational Factors

As important as it is for children and youth in care to feel safe in their residential environment, it is just as important for staff to feel supported by the agency in their work. Based on the findings reported in the preceding chapters on organizational change and development, there is a great deal an agency can do to ensure that children feel safe and staff feel supported. First, *investing in staff* is more than just a catchy slogan for the organizations described here. Strategic hiring and retention practices, adequate compensation and time off, responsive supervision, and opportunities for training—which, in the words of Suess (Chapter 12, p. 221, this volume), should be "lavish and competency based"—in relationship-building, active listening, and cultural diversity (CWLA, 2002; Thompson, Huefner, Vollmer, Davis, & Daly, Chapter 9, this volume), are just some of the ways in which an agency can support staff and, in turn, reduce their reliance on physical restraints.

Second, Colton (Chapter 8, this volume) and others identified effective leadership as one of the most important factors in organizational change and restraint-reduction efforts. An effective leader establishes a vision and guides an agency through a long-term change process that will likely last 3 to 5 years, setting a tone of optimism, open communication, and a determination that fundamental change is possible (though it will not be without its challenges!).

Third, monitoring restraint and seclusion data to identify emerging trends was cited as a critical factor in reducing physical restraint interventions and establishing a safe treatment environment. Such audits may take the form of reviews of serious occurrence reports, periodic interviews with residents and staff, and independent investigations of restraint practices. Involving committees at the board level can ensure that findings are given serious consideration and issues are resolved.

Societal and Cultural Factors

We live in a society that does not value children. If we did live in a society that valued children, 12.9 million children in the United States (U.S. Census Bureau News, n.d.) and more than 1 billion children worldwide (UNICEF, 2006) would not be living in poverty or exposed to abuse or denied such basic rights as access to food, shelter, health care, and education. Just as an agency needs to invest in staff, so, too, must society invest in children. The United Nations Convention on the Rights of the Child (U.N. General Assembly, 1989) formally recognized that children are entitled to political, educational, social, civic, and cultural rights. Protecting these rights, however, especially the rights of vulnerable children, is a challenge, according to Kennedy (Chapter 13, this volume) and Mooney (Chapter 14, this volume). A safe environment can be neither legislated nor guaranteed by policy. As Kennedy noted, the law concerning the use of restraints is not unambiguous, but it *is* hampered by various factors, not the least of which is "the paucity of rigorous, clinically adequate research on restraints" (p. 237). As we have heard repeatedly throughout this book, the clarion call for high-quality, theory-based research to inform practice is once again sounded.

Conclusion

This book raises more questions than it answers. We see this as a good thing. Ultimately, as practitioners and researchers, we can ask three questions: What is the goal of physical restraints? How well do they accomplish this goal? and How do they fit into the overall objective of residential care (and other types of treatment)? If the goal of restraints is safety and containment, which includes both *physical* safety and a sense of *psychological* safety, we must conclude that restraints fall far short in accomplishing this goal for all children. If other means of ensuring safety are available (and they are), they would be better put to use to optimally achieve the objectives of residential care for the largest number of children and youth in care. If they undermine the overall objective of residential care, their continued use should be seriously questioned. In the end, we feel that, through open communication, debate, discussion, research, and theory development, a comprehensive understanding of the behavioral, interpersonal, and environmental underpinnings of physical restraints will help harmonize the multiple dynamic and transactional systems in which they are imbedded. Only then can the goal of Paterson, Leadbetter, Miller, and Crichton (Chapter 7, this volume) to eradicate the conditions under which physical restraints are used be achieved.

References

Baker, A. J. L., & Purcell, J. F. (2005). New York State residential treatment center admissions: Differences in histories and maltreatment behavioral problems, and mental health. *Residential Treatment for Children and Youth, 22*, 39–53.

Bronfenbrenner, U. (1979). *Ecology of human development: Experiments by nature and design.* Cambridge, MA: Harvard University Press.

Child Welfare League of America. (2002). *CWLA best practice guidelines: Behavior management.* Washington, DC: Author.

Child Welfare League of America. (2004). *CWLA best practice guidelines: Behavior support and intervention training.* Washington, DC: Author.

Crenshaw, D. A., & Mordock, J. B. (2004). An ego-strength approach with multiply traumatized children: Special reference to the sexually abused. *Residential Treatment for Children and Youth, 21*, 1–18.

Fisher, J. A. (2003). Curtailing the use of restraint in psychiatric settings. *Journal of Humanistic Psychology, 43*(2), 69–95.

Jones, R. J., & Timbers, G. D. (2002). An analysis of the restraint event and its behavioral effects on clients and staff. *Reclaiming Children and Youth, 11*, 37–41.

Kerker, B. D., & Morrison Dore, M. (2006). Mental health needs and treatment of foster youth: Barriers and opportunities. *American Journal of Orthopsychiatry, 76*, 138–147.

Lewin, K. (1951). Problems in research in social psychology. In D. Cartwright (Ed.), *Field theory in social science: Selected theoretical papers by Kurt Lewin* (pp. 155–169). New York: Harper & Row.

Lipshitz, D. S., Winegar, R. K., Hartnick, E., Foote, B., & Southwick, S. M. (1999). Posttraumatic stress disorder in hospitalized adolescents: Psychiatric comorbidity and clinical correlates. *Journal of the American Academy of Child and Adolescent Psychiatry, 28*, 385–392.

Mohr, W. K., & Anderson, J. A. (2001). Faulty assumptions associated with the use of restraints with children. *Journal of Child and Adolescent Psychiatric Nursing, 14*, 141–151.

UNICEF. (2006). *The state of the world's children 2006: Excluded and invisible.* Available from www.unicef.org/sowc06/profiles/poverty.php.

United Nations General Assembly. (1989, November 20) *Adoption of a convention on the rights of the child.* New York: Author.

U.S. Census Bureau News. (no date). Available from www.census.gov/Press-Release/www/releases/archives/income_wealth/002484.html. Washington, DC: U.S. Department of Commerce.

About the Editors and Authors

Editors

Lloyd B. Bullard

Lloyd B. Bullard, MEd, is Vice President of Program Services for Youth for Tomorrow, Inc., Bristow, Virginia. He was on staff at CWLA from June 1998 to June 2007. While at CWLA, he served as the Director of Residential Care and later as Senior Consultant and Behavior Support & Intervention Specialist. He led the CWLA initiatives to develop the Coordinating Center on Best Practices in Behavior Support & Intervention: Preventing and Reducing the Use of Restraint & Seclusion and the Cultural Competence and Racial Disproportionality & Disparity of Outcomes. He has served as an Adjunct Professor for Concordia University, St. Paul, Minnesota. Mr. Bullard serves as an Independent Consultant for CWLA and has over 25 years experience in child welfare programs serving children, youth, and their families.

David M. Day

David M. Day, PhD, C. Psych., is an Associate Professor in the Department of Psychology at Ryerson University, Toronto. He has published over 30 book chapters, articles, and research reports and has given about 40 conference presentations and workshops on a variety of topics including the development and treatment of antisocial behavior in children and youth. His current research interests are in the areas of physical restraint use with children in residential care, developmental criminology, and children's rights.

Michael A. Nunno

Michael Nunno, DSW, is a Senior Extension Associate with the Family Life Development Center, the College of Human Ecology, Cornell University, and the principal investigator of the Residential Child Care Project. His research has examined how children die in restraints, the dynamics of adolescent female restraints episodes, and the impact of training on organizational climates. Dr. Nunno is a member of the faculty of the International Society for the Prevention of Child Abuse and Neglect.

Contributors

David Allen

David Allen, PhD, is a consultant clinical psychologist with Bro Morgannwg NHS Trust and Head of Specialist Services for the Learning Disability Directorate. He is also a professor at the Unit for Development in Intellectual Disability at the University of Glamorgan, and a Fellow of the British Psychological Society and of the International Association for the Scientific Study of Intellectual Disabilities.

Jeffery R. Carter

Dr. Jeff Carter, C. Psych., started working in children's mental health as a Child and Youth Worker in 1988. He is a psychologist and the Coordinator of Research and Education at Vanier Children's Services. He is also an Adjunct Clinical Professor in the Department of Psychology and Assistant Professor in the Department of Psychiatry at the University of Western Ontario. He has a small private practice. Jeff and his wife, Dayna, live in London, Ontario, Canada.

David Colton

David Colton, PhD, MPA, MEd, is employed at the Commonwealth Center in Staunton, Virginia, a treatment center for children and adolescents operated by the Virginia Department of Mental Health. David is an Adjunct Professor of Health Care Administration at Mary Baldwin College, Staunton, VA, and he teaches a graduate course in questionnaire design at the Curry School of Education, University of Virginia. He is a member of the American Evaluation Association.

John Crichton

Dr. John Crichton is consultant forensic psychiatrist at the Orchard Clinic, Royal Edinburgh Hospital. He studied at Nottingham University and completed training in Psychiatry at Cambridge. At University of Cambridge Institute of Criminology, he completed a PhD. He has published over 40 peer review papers and book chapters and edited *Psychiatric Patient Violence: Risk and Response* in 1995. He held academic posts in Cambridge and Edinburgh and was Medical Director of Scotland's Forensic Network and State Hospitals' Board.

Dale Curry

Dale Curry, PhD, LSW, Associate Professor of Human Development and Family Studies at Kent State University, has over 30 years of experience in direct service, supervision, administration, education and training in child and family services. He is the editor of the journal *Training and Development in Human Services* and the Principal Investigator of the North American Certification Project. He has published on topical areas such as staff retention, transfer of learning, trainer development, and ethics.

Daniel L. Daly

Daniel L. Daly, PhD, is Vice President and Director of Youth Care at Girls and Boys Town. Dr. Daly received his Doctorate in Clinical Psychology from West Virginia University. He has held a number of clinical and administrative positions at Girls and Boys Town. Dr. Daly is also Adjunct Associate Professor in the Department of Human Development and Family Life at the University of Kansas. He has authored numerous articles and book chapters and presented papers at psychological and child care conferences.

Jerry L. Davis

Jerry L. Davis, PhD, is Associate Executive Director of Girls and Boys Town USA, which includes programs across America outside of the Home Campus. Thousands of children and families are served each year from its 19 sites in 14 states. Dr. Davis holds a Doctorate in Psychology from the University of Arkansas. His areas of specialty were child development and human learning. He has been a consultant, trainer, researcher, professor, and author and co-author of numerous articles and publications.

Martha J. Holden

Martha J. Holden, MS, Senior Extension Associate, Director of the Residential Child Care Project, assists agencies in implementing the Therapeutic Crisis Intervention System; conducts violence prevention training, and the Investigation of Institutional Maltreatment throughout the United States, Canada, United Kingdom, Ireland, Australia, Bermuda, Israel, and Russia. Ms. Holden has published in *the Children and Youth Services Review, Journal of Emotional and Behavioral Problems, Residential Treatment for Children & Youth*, the *Journal of Child and Youth Care Work*, and coauthored a chapter in the book *Understanding Abusive Families*.

Jonathan C. Huefner

Jonathan C. Huefner, PhD, is a Research Scientist in the Girls and Boys Town National Research Institute for Child and Family Studies. Dr. Huefner has a PhD in Organizational Social Psychology from Brigham Young University and has 20 years of experience conducting research. Experience includes four years at Girls and Boys Town, five years in the managed behavioral healthcare industry, and 10 years in university lecturing. Dr. Huefner has published a number of scientific journal articles and presented at many professional and scientific conferences.

Judy Jones

Judy Jones is an Intensive Services Supervisor at Vanier Children's Services. In her over 20 years at Vanier, Judy has worked in residential and day treatment milieus, provided individual play therapy, and led groups such as anger management, early years assessment, adolescent girls groups, violence prevention, and social skills. Judy chairs Vanier's Reducing Physical Restraint Working Group. Judy lives with her family in London, Ontario, where she is highly involved in her church and community.

Andrew Kendrick

Andrew Kendrick is Professor of Residential Child Care in the Glasgow School of Social Work (Universities of Strathclyde and Glasgow) and the Scottish Institute of Residential Child Care. He gained his PhD in Social Anthropology at the London School of Economics in 1984. He has carried out a wide range of research on child welfare issues, with a particular focus on children in state care. He is coeditor of the *Scottish Journal of Residential Child Care*.

Shelia Suess Kennedy

Shelia Suess Kennedy, JD, is Associate Professor of Law and Public Policy in the School of Public and Environmental Affairs at Indiana University Purdue University at Indianapolis. Her scholarly publications include five books and numerous law review and journal articles. Professor Kennedy is an Associate Editor of *Policy Sciences,* a columnist for the *Indianapolis Star,* and a frequent lecturer, public speaker, and contributor to popular periodicals.

David Leadbetter

David Leadbetter, MSc, BA (Hons), Dip SW, CQSW, Cert. SW Ed., Cert. MTD, is currently the Director of the CALM (UK) system of aggression management training which achieved the lowest injury rates in the recent Child Welfare League of America restraint reduction project (Site E). He combines a recreational martial arts experience and a professional background in Social Work. He has written extensively on violence related issues and is a regular contributor to national and international conferences and policy development at agency and national levels.

Kim J. Masters

Kim J. Masters, MD, FACP, is a board certified adult, child, and adolescent psychiatrist and is currently Medical Director of Alternative Behavioral Services Columbia and Charleston South Carolina Campuses. He is Assistant Clinical Professor of Health and Behavior at the Medical College of Georgia, and the College of Health Professions at the University of South Carolina. He was the lead author of the Academy of Child and Adolescent Psychiatry's Practice parameter on restraint and seclusion. He also represents the Academy on the Professional and Technical Advisory committee of the Joint Commission on the Accreditation of Health Care Organizations.

Gail Miller

Gail Miller is a registered mental health nurse with a degree in Cognitive Behavioral Therapy. She has over 20 years experience working in a variety of services as a clinician, manager, and tutor in the safe and therapeutic prevention and management of aggression and violence. In May 2005 she was seconded to NHS Security Management Service as Mental Health Manager. She is presently Associate Director for violence reduction at West London Mental Health Trust.

Wanda K. Mohr

Wanda K. Mohr, PhD, RN, FAAN, is an Associate Professor of Psychiatric Nursing at the University of Medicine and Dentistry NJ and an Associate Clinical Professor of Child Psychiatry at the Robert Wood Johnson Medical School. She is a leader in the movement of reform conditions in mental health settings, with special evidence on seclusion and restraint. Dr. Mohr has testified before the U.S. Congress and other legislative bodies on behalf of numerous advocacy agencies on the danger of restraints.

Andrea J. Mooney

Andrea J. Mooney, JD, is an Associate Clinical Professor at Cornell Law School, where she specializes in legal writing and child advocacy. She returned to law school after an extensive career as a special education teacher and child welfare trainer. As a Program Manager at Cornell's Residential Child Care Project (RCCP), she was an original author of the Therapeutic Crisis Intervention curriculum. She continues as a consultant to RCCP, and to represent children in Family Court.

Brodie Paterson

Brodie Paterson, MEd, BA (Hons), RN (MH), (LD), (NT), Dip Nursing, is presently a lecturer at the Department of Nursing and Midwifery at the University of Stirling in Scotland where his interests include both research and teaching. His research and publication record is extensive and he has participated in a number of national and international projects involving policy development, research and training. He is a regular contributor to national and international conferences.

Reece L. Peterson

Reece L. Peterson is Professor of Special Education at the University of Nebraska-Lincoln. He has worked with schools to develop and improve effective behavior management and school discipline policies, and to address school violence and student aggression. His research has focused on policy issues related to these topics. He is affiliated with the UNL Center on Children, Families, and the Law and has served as President of the International Council for Children with Behavioral Disorders.

Joseph B. Ryan

Dr. Joe Ryan is an assistant professor of Special Education at Clemson University. Professional interests include: classroom management, special education law, and psychotropic treatments for students with behavioral disorders. He currently serves as the Associate Editor for the *Journal of At-Risk Issues*, Treasurer for the International Council for Children with Behavioral Disorders (CCBD), and is the founder and Director of Clemson's Challenger Baseball League for youth with special needs.

Laura Steckley

Laura Steckley, MSc, is a lecturer at Glasgow School of Social Work and has 11 years of practice experience in residential child care (in Scotland) and residential treatment (in the United States). She jointly directs the MSc in Advanced Residential Child Care. Her research interests include the benefits and challenges of sport as a therapeutic vehicle for young people, and young people as active researchers.

Kim Stevens

Kim Stevens has been a Child and Youth Counselor of CYC Training and Development for Vanier. Kim is an instructor in the Prevention and Management of Aggressive Behavior (PMBA). She has had a long-standing commitment to the promotion of safety in managing crisis situations through her involvement in the training of crisis management programs since 1988, to a variety of audiences and disciplines.

George Suess

Mr. Suess has over 35 years of experience in human services and education. He has been employed by The Arc of Delaware County for 27 years and has served as the Chief Executive Officer for the past 20 years. In addition to his duties as CEO, he also serves as the organization's lead consultant and trainer.

George Tetreault

George Tetreault is a Licensed Psychologist and Director of the Minnesota Learning Center, a school for severely emotionally disturbed students, in the Brainerd School District.

Ronald W. Thompson

Ronald W. Thompson, PhD, is the Director of the Girls and Boys Town National Research Institute for Child and Family Studies. Dr. Thompson has held faculty positions at Creighton University School of Medicine in Omaha and the Department of Human Development and Family Life at the University of Kansas. He has a PhD in Educational Psychology from the University of Nebraska. He has been a clinician, program administrator, researcher, and research administrator. He has also published over 30 articles and scientific papers and presented at numerous professional conferences.

Emily van der Hagen

Emily van der Hagen is a recent graduate of College of Saint Benedict/Saint John's University with a Bachelor's degree in Psychology. She spent a summer working as a psychology intern at the Minnesota Learning Center.

Dennis G. Vollmer

Dennis G. Vollmer received his Bachelor's degree in Counseling from Wayne State College and his Masters Degree in Human Development from the University of Kansas. Mr. Vollmer has been employed at Girls and Boys Town for nearly 20 years. He has held a number of clinical and administrative positions and currently is the Director of the Intensive Residential Treatment Center.

INDEX

on motor skills for restraint,
110
and ongoing supervision, 160
on parallel processing, 115
on physical restraints, 120
preservice, 170, 176
refresher, 120
of school staff, 207
using proprietary programs, 58
using Therapeutic Crisis
Intervention, 107
on vicarious trauma, 198
tranquilization of youth, 96
transitional phase of change, 162
transport carriers, 60
transport techniques, 174, 191
trauma
during and after restraint
episodes, 87
and attachment disorders, 187
direct, 3
neglect, 193
retraumatization, 13, 232
at seeing others restrained,
14–15, 98
sexual, 98, 193
vicarious, 73
trauma-informed care, 159, 260
treatment model evaluation,
169, 171
Treatment Progress Checklist (TPC)
system, 174, 181
treatment teams, 170
trials, civil and criminal, 247
tricyclic antidepressants, 75
turnover, staff, 154–156, 162,
168, 181
Two-Minute Restraint, 199

U.N. Convention on the Rights of
the Child, 5, 41, 228, 262
United Kingdom
physical restraint in, 3–5
deaths in, 89, 94
history of restraint use, 27
mechanical and chemical
restraint use, 6, 237
United States
deaths in, 90
history of restraint use,
27–28, 48
unjustified restraint, 21
"unreasonable restraint" standard,
251
U.S. Supreme Court, see Supreme
Court

values, organizational, 80, 162, 218
ventricular fibrillation, 75
verbal abuse, 7
vicarious trauma, 3, 73, 198
violence
assault, 4
and contagion effects, 186, 190
definition of, 71
denial of, 130
primary prevention of, 129–130
restraint causing injuries, 16
societal frame for, 127
toward self, 13
toward staff, 7, 13
between youth, 7
virtual reality, 61, 63
vision statements, 131, 262
vital signs, monitoring during
restraint, 101
volunteer leaders, 219